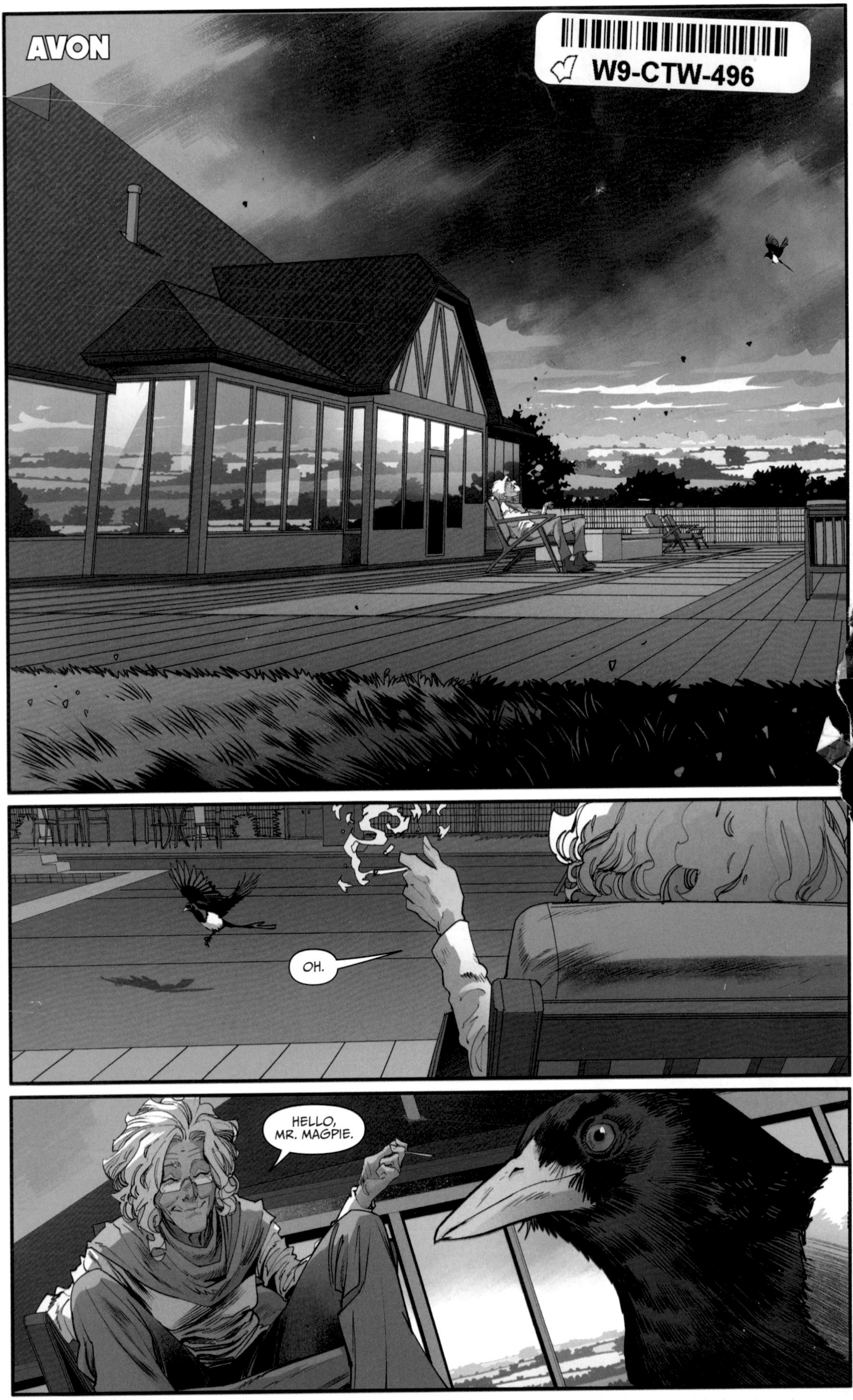
OH.
HELLO, MR. MAGPIE.

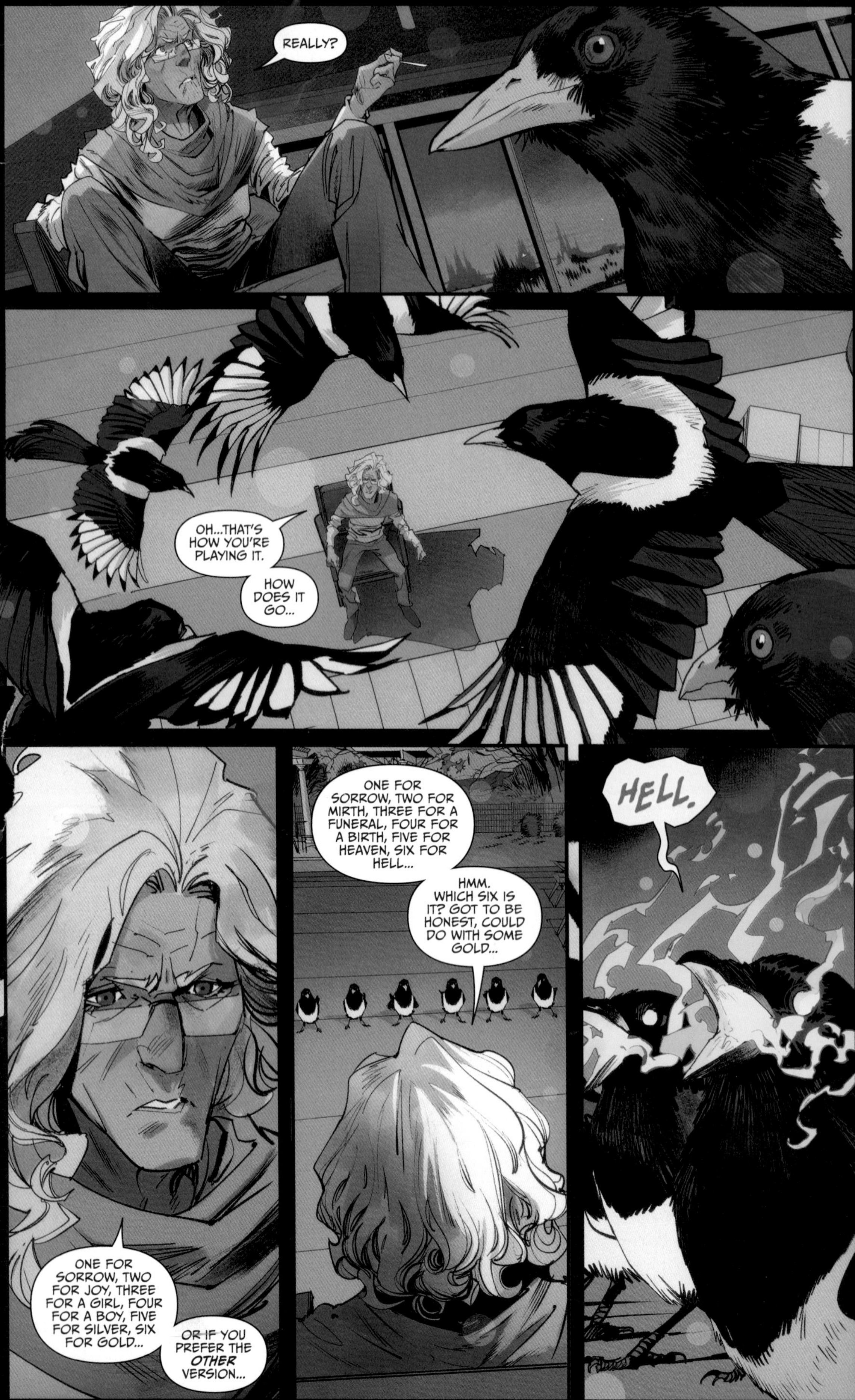
REALLY?
OH...THAT'S HOW YOU'RE PLAYING IT.
HOW DOES IT GO...
ONE FOR SORROW, TWO FOR JOY, THREE FOR A GIRL, FOUR FOR A BOY, FIVE FOR SILVER, SIX FOR GOLD...
OR IF YOU PREFER THE *OTHER* VERSION...
ONE FOR SORROW, TWO FOR MIRTH, THREE FOR A FUNERAL, FOUR FOR A BIRTH, FIVE FOR HEAVEN, SIX FOR HELL...
HMM. WHICH SIX IS IT? GOT TO BE HONEST, COULD DO WITH SOME GOLD...
HELL.

KIERON GILLEN   DAN MORA

TAMRA BONVILLAIN

ONCE & FUTURE

VOLUME THREE
THE PARLIAMENT OF MAGPIES

Published by

BOOM!
STUDIOS

CO
YAGN
741.5942
GIL
V.3

DESIGNER
SCOTT NEWMAN

ASSOCIATE EDITOR
AMANDA LaFRANCO

EDITOR
MATT GAGNON

BOOM! STUDIOS™

ONCE & FUTURE Volume Three, July 2021. Published by BOOM! Studios, a division of Boom Entertainment, Inc. Once & Future is ™ & © 2021 Kieron Gillen, Ltd. Originally published in single magazine form as ONCE & FUTURE No. 13-18. ™ & © 2020, 2021 Kieron Gillen, Ltd. All rights reserved. BOOM! Studios™ and the BOOM! Studios logo are trademarks of Boom Entertainment, Inc., registered in various countries and categories. All characters, events, and institutions depicted herein are fictional. Any similarity between any of the names, characters, persons, events, and/or institutions in this publication to actual names, characters, and persons, whether living or dead, events, and/or institutions is unintended and purely coincidental. BOOM! Studios does not read or accept unsolicited submissions of ideas, stories, or artwork.

BOOM! Studios, 5670 Wilshire Boulevard, Suite 400, Los Angeles, CA, 90036-5679. Printed in Canada. First Printing.

ISBN: 978-1-68415-703-7, eISBN: 978-1-64668-247-8

APRIL 2022

WRITTEN BY
KIERON GILLEN

ILLUSTRATED BY
DAN MORA

COLORED BY
TAMRA BONVILLAIN

LETTERED BY
ED DUKESHIRE

COVER BY
DAN MORA

SPECIAL THANKS CHAPTERS FIFTEEN & SIXTEEN
MARIE-PAULE NOËL

ONCE & FUTURE ™

CREATED BY **KIERON GILLEN** AND **DAN MORA**

CHAPTER THIRTEEN

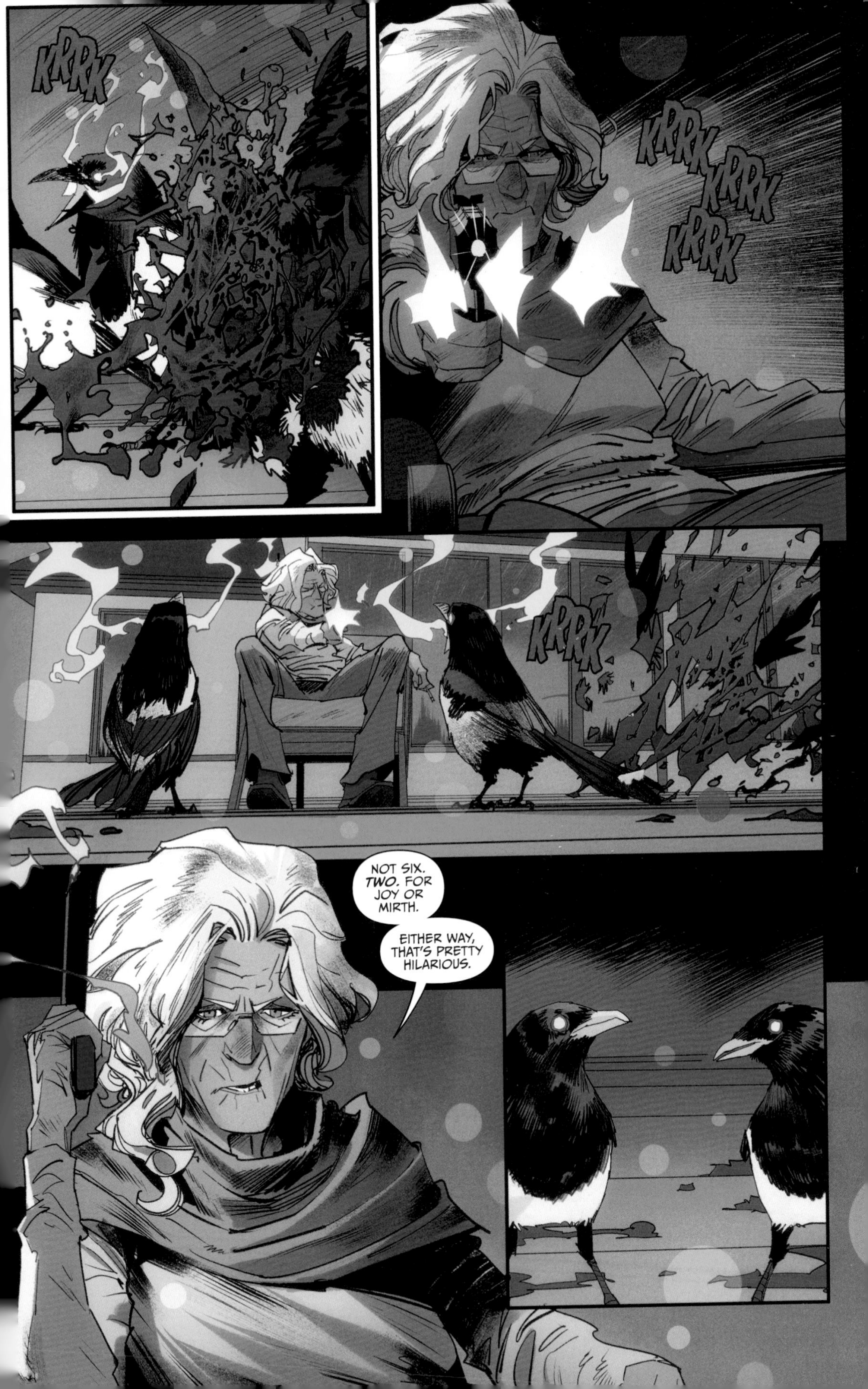
KRRK
KRRK KRRK KRRK
KRRK
NOT SIX. *TWO.* FOR JOY OR MIRTH.
EITHER WAY, THAT'S PRETTY HILARIOUS.

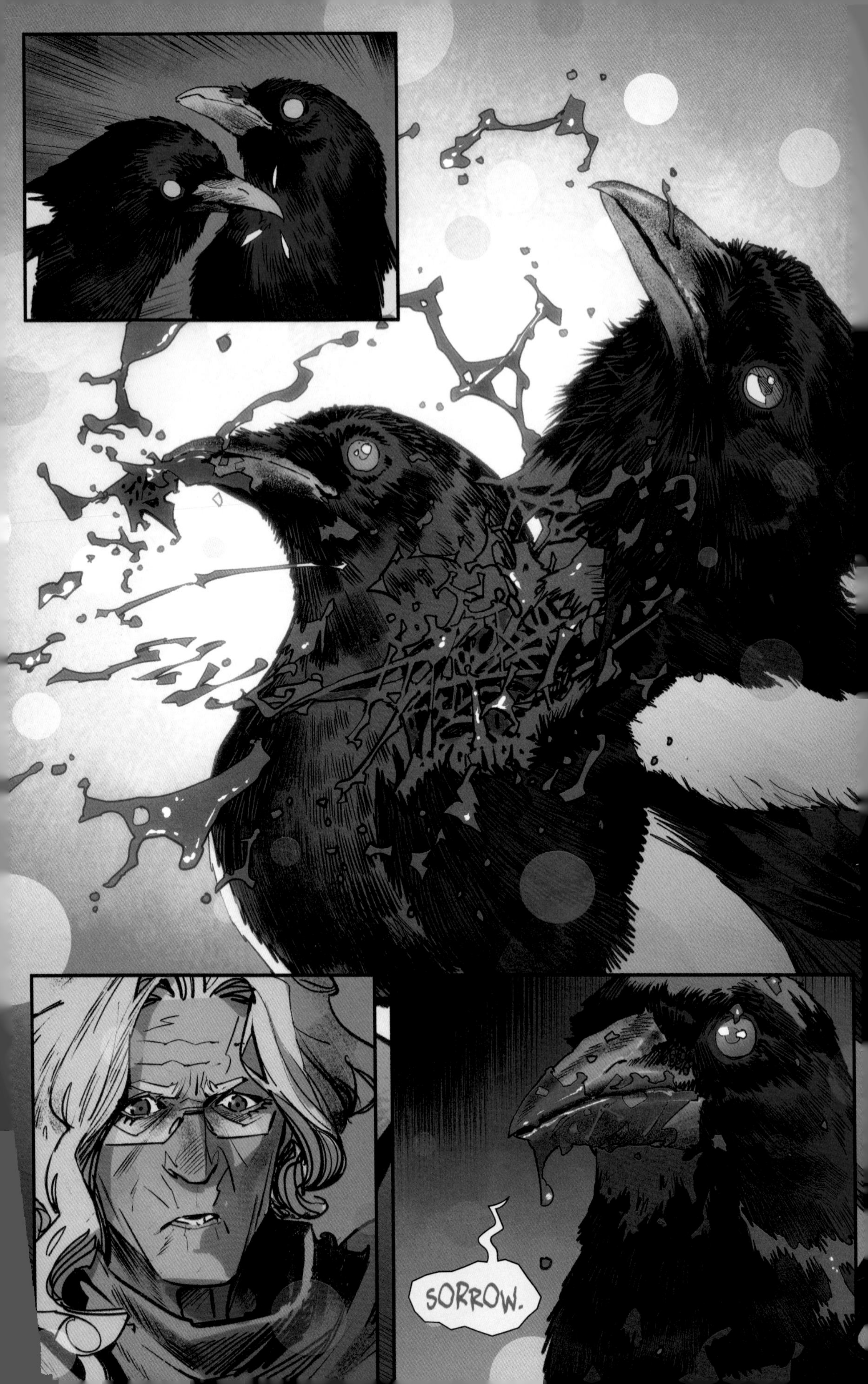
SORROW.

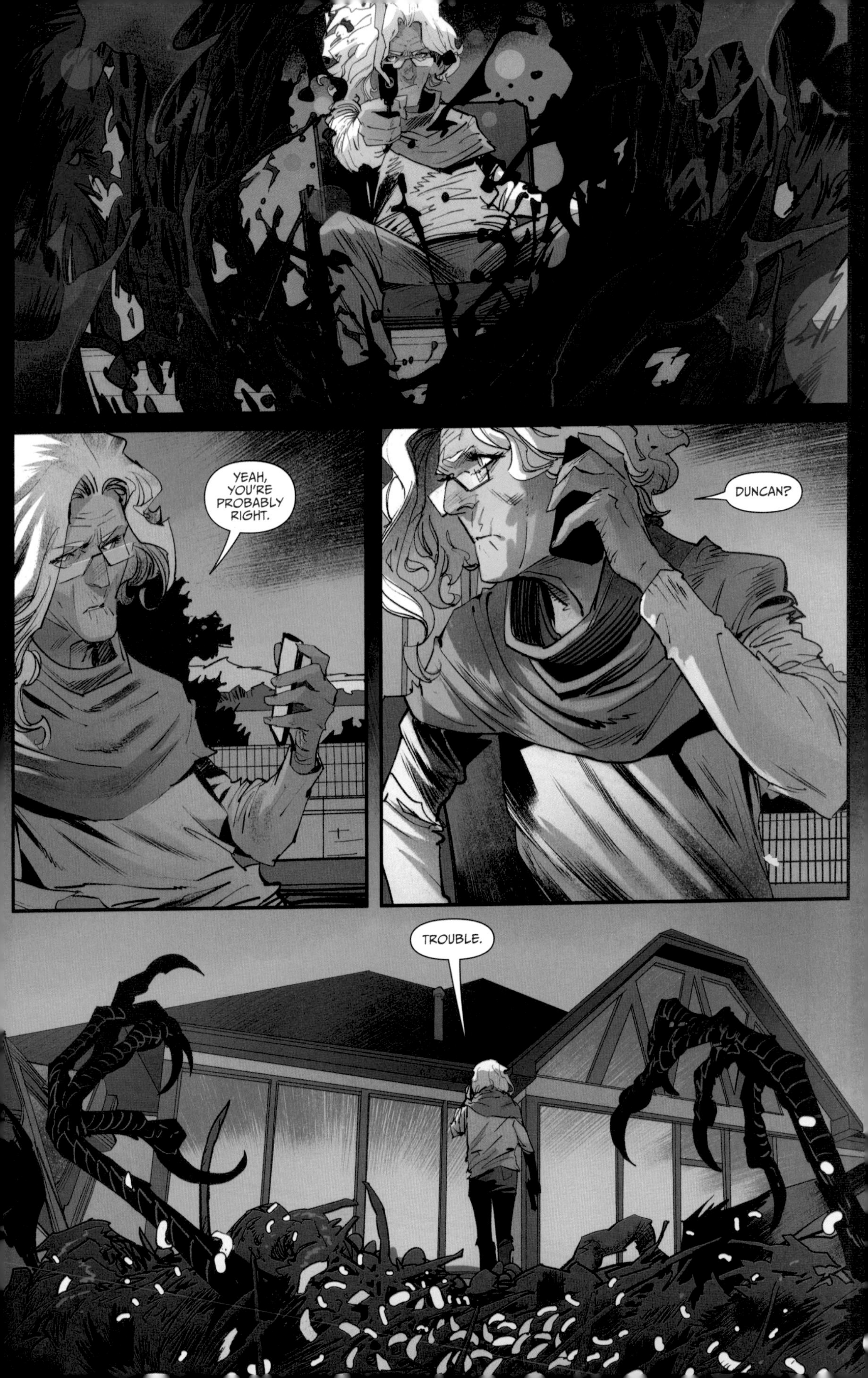
YEAH, YOU'RE PROBABLY RIGHT.
DUNCAN?
TROUBLE.

ONCE & FUTURE™

THE PARLIAMENT OF MAGPIES

GILLEN

MORA

BONVILLAIN

DUKESHIRE

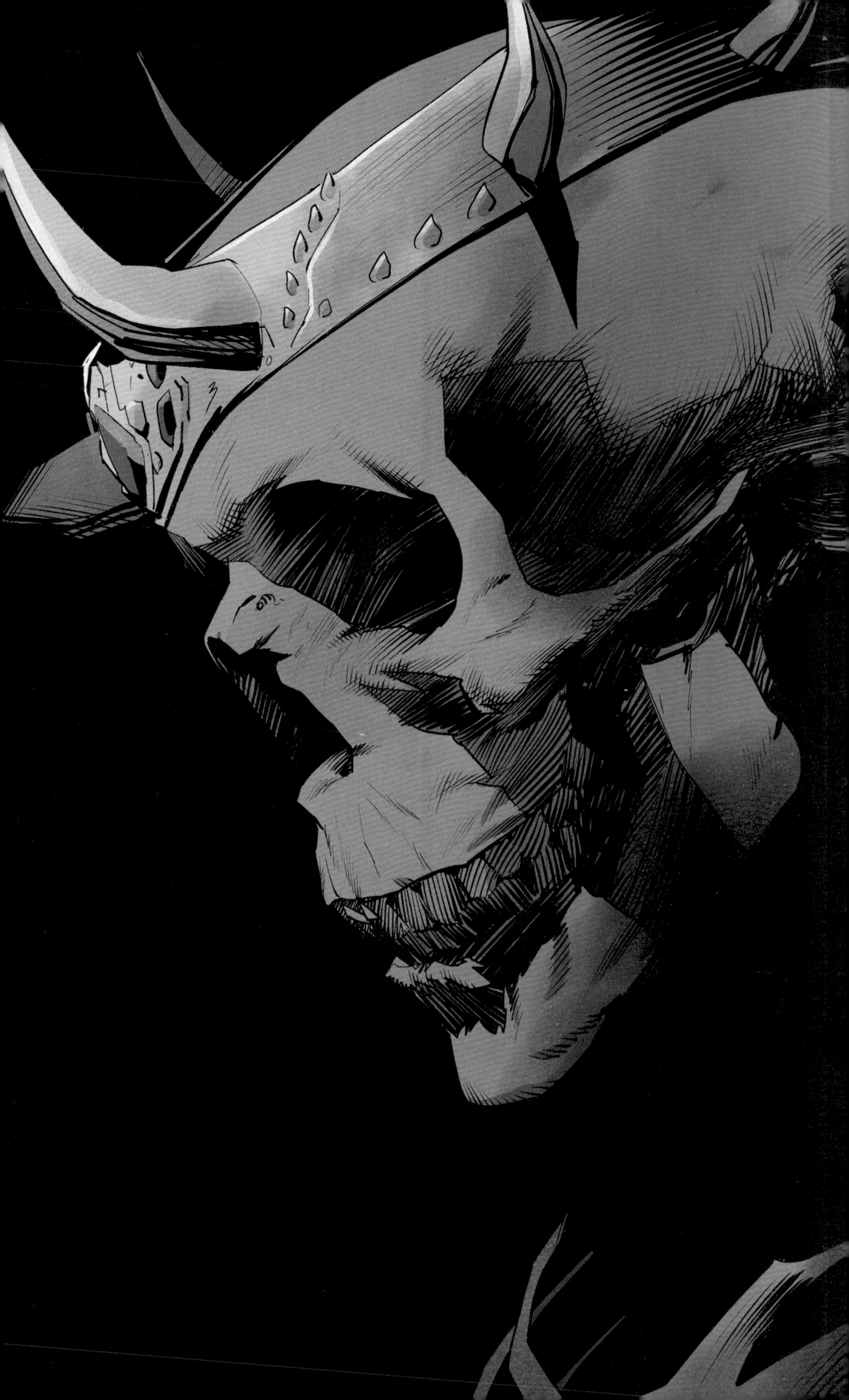

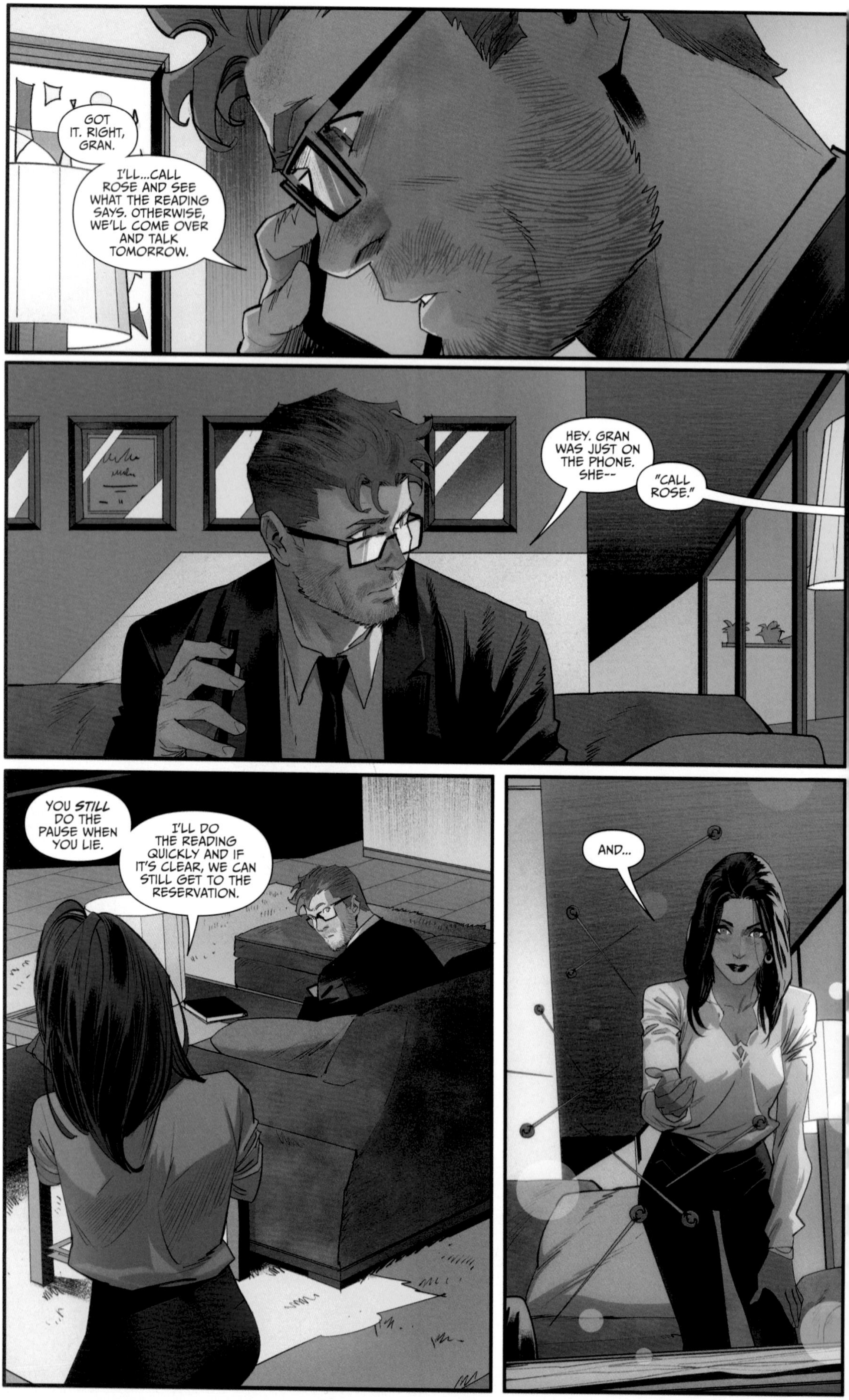
GOT IT. RIGHT, GRAN.
I'LL...CALL ROSE AND SEE WHAT THE READING SAYS. OTHERWISE, WE'LL COME OVER AND TALK TOMORROW.
HEY. GRAN WAS JUST ON THE PHONE. SHE--
"CALL ROSE."
YOU *STILL* DO THE PAUSE WHEN YOU LIE.
I'LL DO THE READING QUICKLY AND IF IT'S CLEAR, WE CAN STILL GET TO THE RESERVATION.
AND...

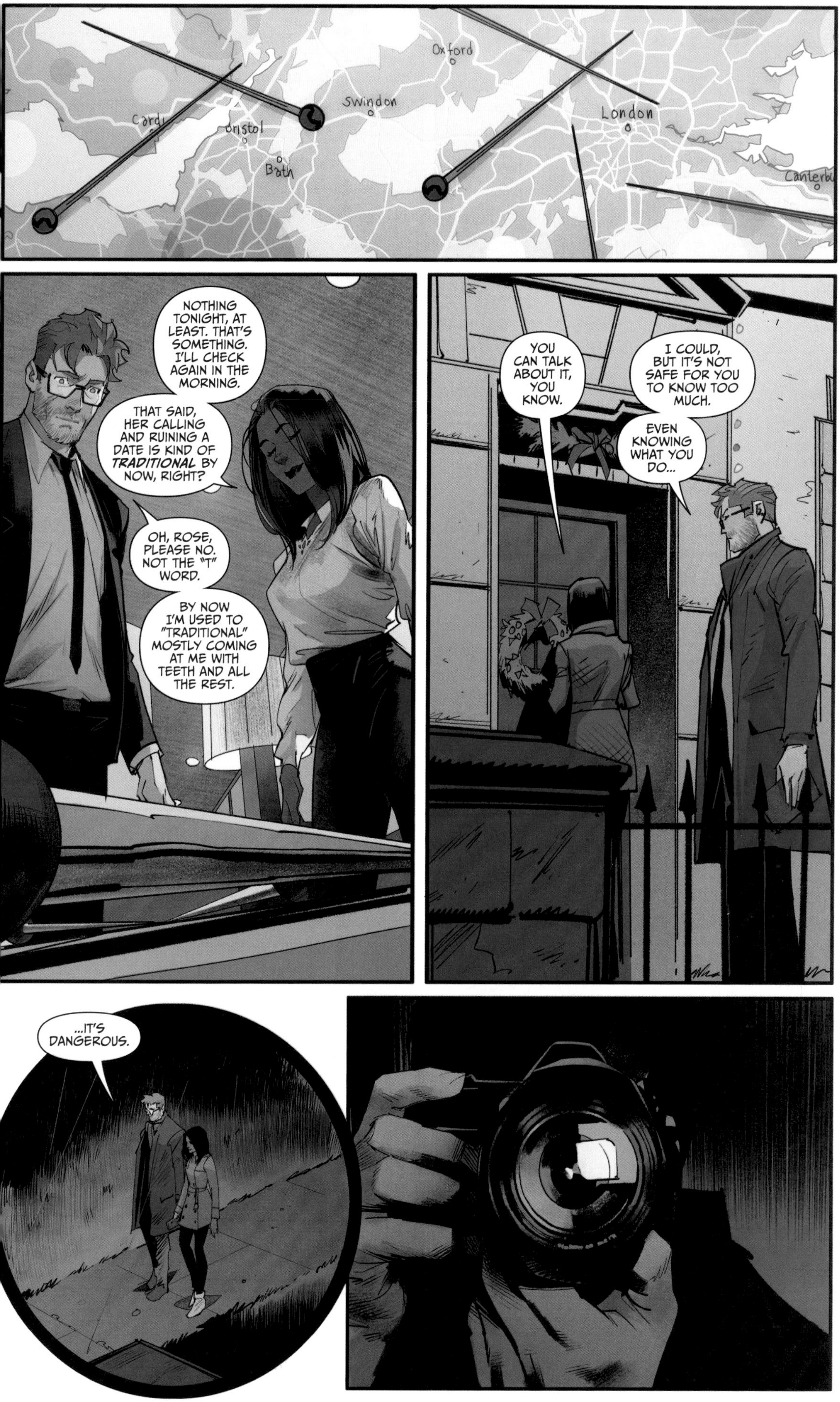
Oxford
Swindon
Cardi
Bristol
Bath
London
Canterbu
NOTHING TONIGHT, AT LEAST. THAT'S SOMETHING. I'LL CHECK AGAIN IN THE MORNING.
THAT SAID, HER CALLING AND RUINING A DATE IS KIND OF TRADITIONAL BY NOW, RIGHT?
OH, ROSE, PLEASE NO. NOT THE "T" WORD.
BY NOW I'M USED TO "TRADITIONAL" MOSTLY COMING AT ME WITH TEETH AND ALL THE REST.
YOU CAN TALK ABOUT IT, YOU KNOW.
I COULD, BUT IT'S NOT SAFE FOR YOU TO KNOW TOO MUCH.
EVEN KNOWING WHAT YOU DO...
...IT'S DANGEROUS.

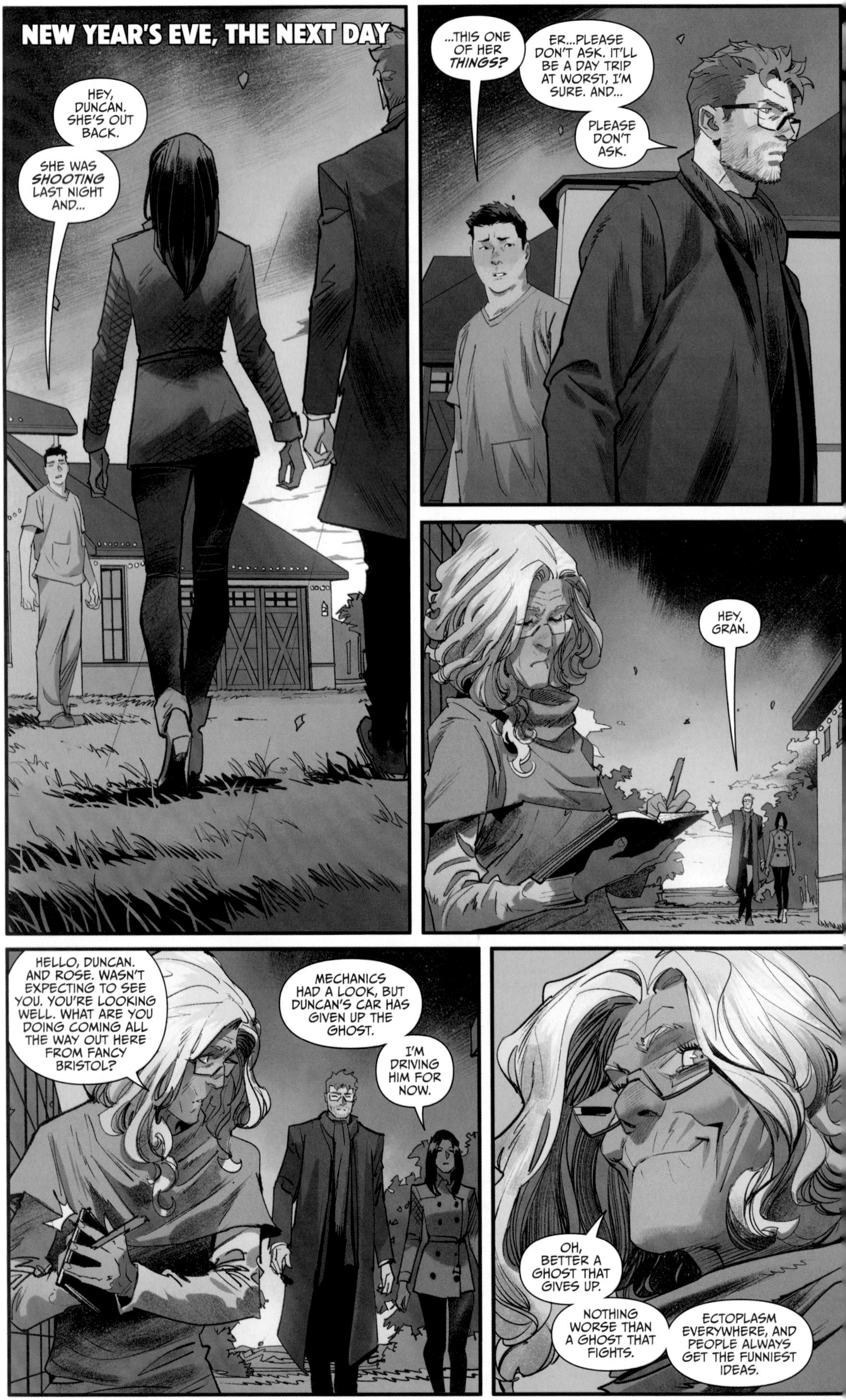
NEW YEAR'S EVE, THE NEXT DAY
HEY, DUNCAN. SHE'S OUT BACK.
SHE WAS *SHOOTING* LAST NIGHT AND...
...THIS ONE OF HER *THINGS?*
ER...PLEASE DON'T ASK. IT'LL BE A DAY TRIP AT WORST, I'M SURE. AND...
PLEASE DON'T ASK.
HEY, GRAN.
HELLO, DUNCAN. AND ROSE. WASN'T EXPECTING TO SEE YOU. YOU'RE LOOKING WELL. WHAT ARE YOU DOING COMING ALL THE WAY OUT HERE FROM FANCY BRISTOL?
MECHANICS HAD A LOOK, BUT DUNCAN'S CAR HAS GIVEN UP THE GHOST.
I'M DRIVING HIM FOR NOW.
OH, BETTER A GHOST THAT GIVES UP.
NOTHING WORSE THAN A GHOST THAT FIGHTS.
ECTOPLASM EVERYWHERE, AND PEOPLE ALWAYS GET THE FUNNIEST IDEAS.

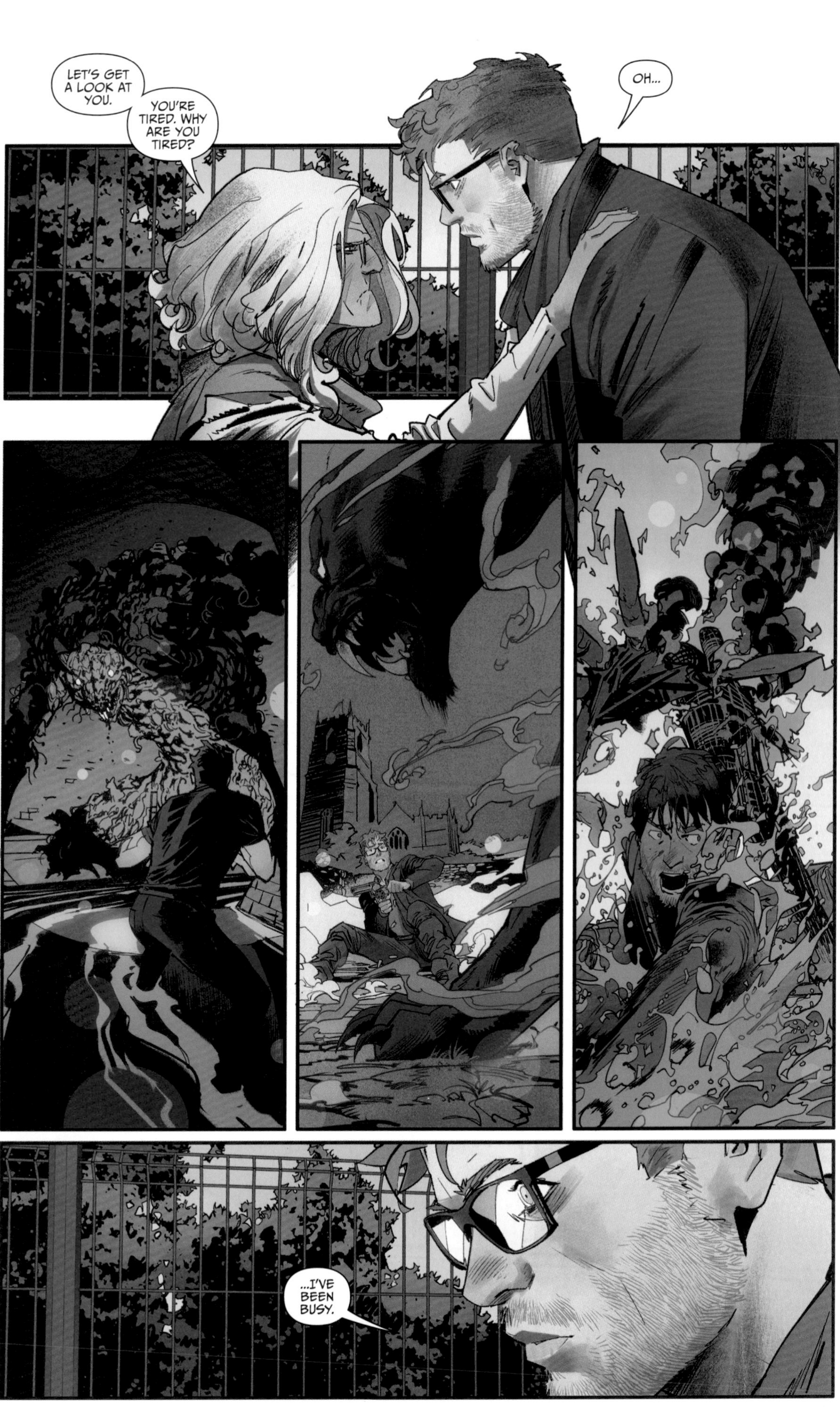
LET'S GET A LOOK AT YOU.
YOU'RE TIRED. WHY ARE YOU TIRED?
OH...
...I'VE BEEN BUSY.

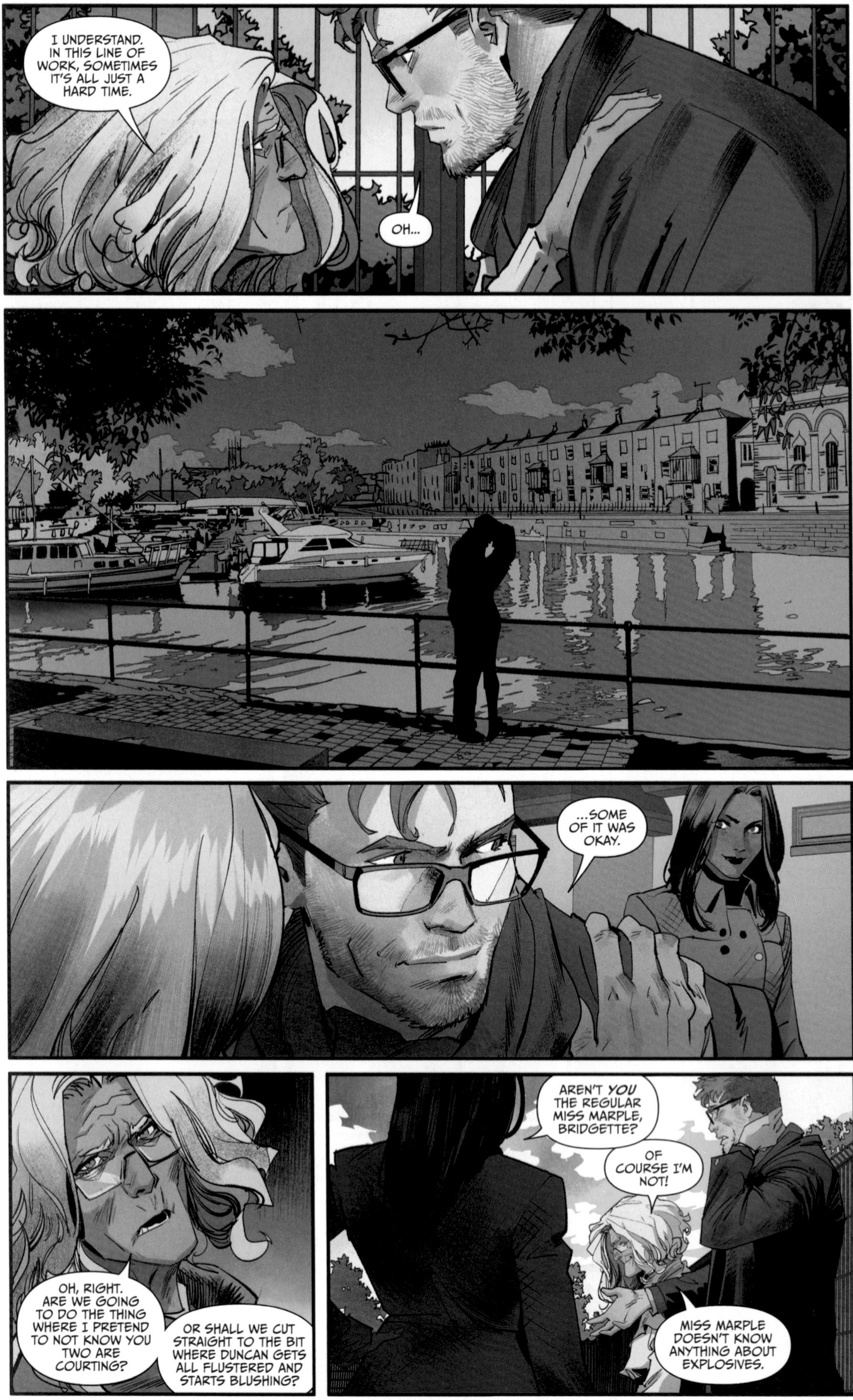
I UNDERSTAND. IN THIS LINE OF WORK, SOMETIMES IT'S ALL JUST A HARD TIME.
OH...
...SOME OF IT WAS OKAY.
OH, RIGHT. ARE WE GOING TO DO THE THING WHERE I PRETEND TO NOT KNOW YOU TWO ARE COURTING?
OR SHALL WE CUT STRAIGHT TO THE BIT WHERE DUNCAN GETS ALL FLUSTERED AND STARTS BLUSHING?
AREN'T *YOU* THE REGULAR MISS MARPLE, BRIDGETTE?
OF COURSE I'M NOT!
MISS MARPLE DOESN'T KNOW ANYTHING ABOUT EXPLOSIVES.

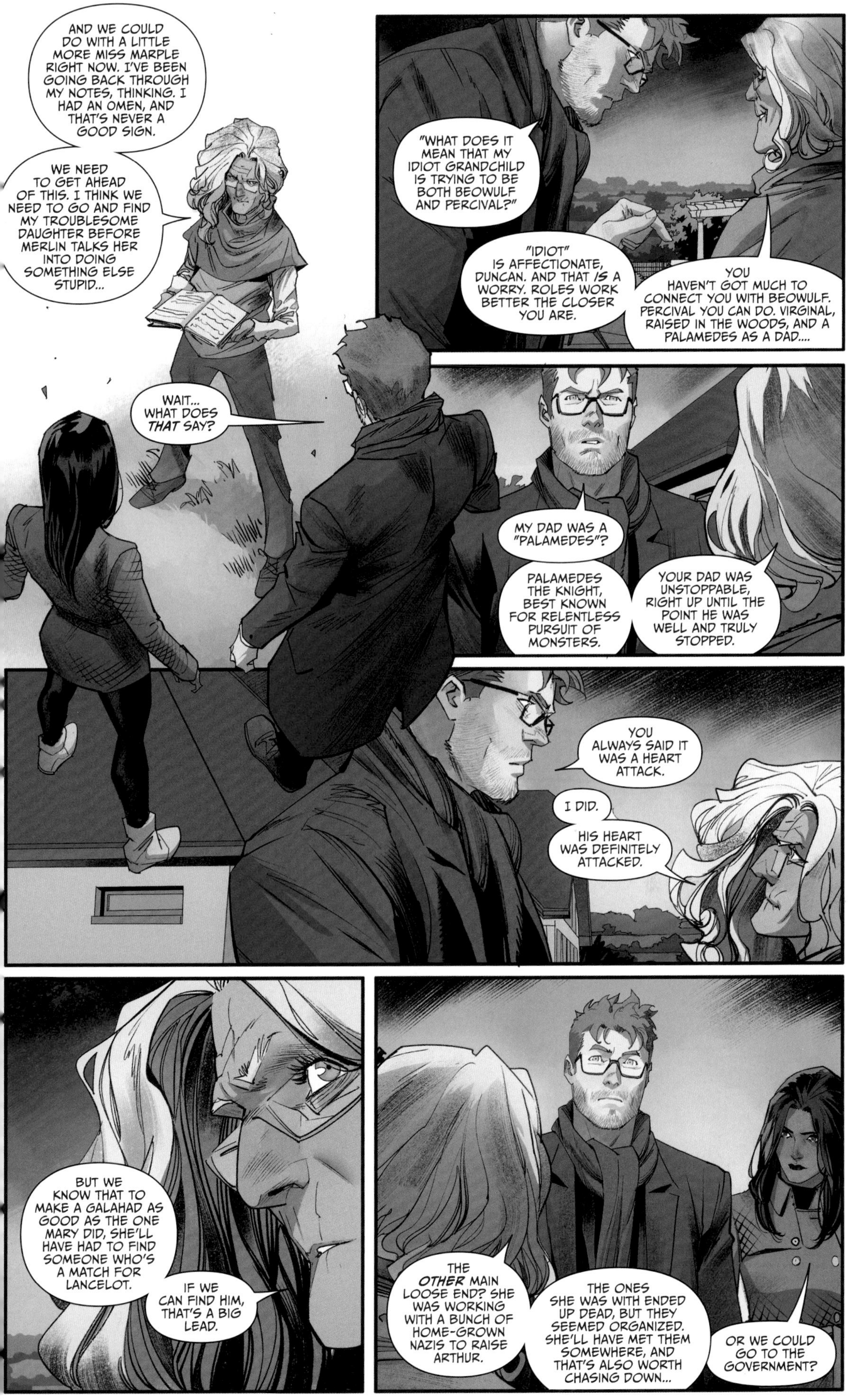
AND WE COULD DO WITH A LITTLE MORE MISS MARPLE RIGHT NOW. I'VE BEEN GOING BACK THROUGH MY NOTES, THINKING. I HAD AN OMEN, AND THAT'S NEVER A GOOD SIGN.
WE NEED TO GET AHEAD OF THIS. I THINK WE NEED TO GO AND FIND MY TROUBLESOME DAUGHTER BEFORE MERLIN TALKS HER INTO DOING SOMETHING ELSE STUPID...
"WHAT DOES IT MEAN THAT MY IDIOT GRANDCHILD IS TRYING TO BE BOTH BEOWULF AND PERCIVAL?"
"IDIOT" IS AFFECTIONATE, DUNCAN. AND THAT *IS* A WORRY. ROLES WORK BETTER THE CLOSER YOU ARE.
YOU HAVEN'T GOT MUCH TO CONNECT YOU WITH BEOWULF. PERCIVAL YOU CAN DO. VIRGINAL, RAISED IN THE WOODS, AND A PALAMEDES AS A DAD....
WAIT... WHAT DOES *THAT* SAY?
MY DAD WAS A "PALAMEDES"?
PALAMEDES THE KNIGHT, BEST KNOWN FOR RELENTLESS PURSUIT OF MONSTERS.
YOUR DAD WAS UNSTOPPABLE, RIGHT UP UNTIL THE POINT HE WAS WELL AND TRULY STOPPED.
YOU ALWAYS SAID IT WAS A HEART ATTACK.
I DID.
HIS HEART WAS DEFINITELY ATTACKED.
BUT WE KNOW THAT TO MAKE A GALAHAD AS GOOD AS THE ONE MARY DID, SHE'LL HAVE HAD TO FIND SOMEONE WHO'S A MATCH FOR LANCELOT.
IF WE CAN FIND HIM, THAT'S A BIG LEAD.
THE *OTHER* MAIN LOOSE END? SHE WAS WORKING WITH A BUNCH OF HOME-GROWN NAZIS TO RAISE ARTHUR.
THE ONES SHE WAS WITH ENDED UP DEAD, BUT THEY SEEMED ORGANIZED. SHE'LL HAVE MET THEM SOMEWHERE, AND THAT'S ALSO WORTH CHASING DOWN...
OR WE COULD GO TO THE GOVERNMENT?

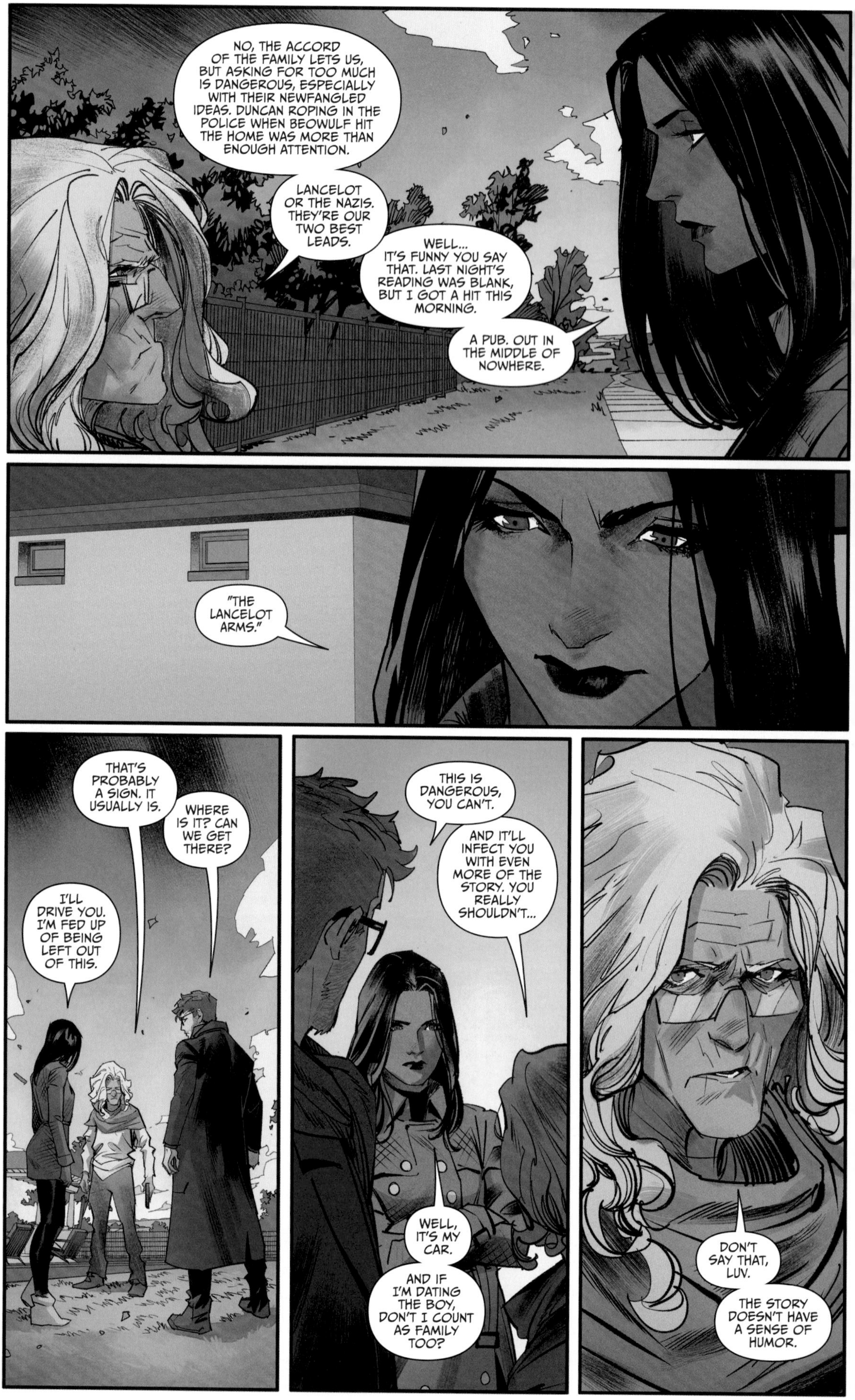
NO, THE ACCORD OF THE FAMILY LETS US, BUT ASKING FOR TOO MUCH IS DANGEROUS, ESPECIALLY WITH THEIR NEWFANGLED IDEAS. DUNCAN ROPING IN THE POLICE WHEN BEOWULF HIT THE HOME WAS MORE THAN ENOUGH ATTENTION.
LANCELOT OR THE NAZIS. THEY'RE OUR TWO BEST LEADS.
WELL... IT'S FUNNY YOU SAY THAT. LAST NIGHT'S READING WAS BLANK, BUT I GOT A HIT THIS MORNING.
A PUB. OUT IN THE MIDDLE OF NOWHERE.
"THE LANCELOT ARMS."
THAT'S PROBABLY A SIGN. IT USUALLY IS.
WHERE IS IT? CAN WE GET THERE?
I'LL DRIVE YOU. I'M FED UP OF BEING LEFT OUT OF THIS.
THIS IS DANGEROUS, YOU CAN'T.
AND IT'LL INFECT YOU WITH EVEN MORE OF THE STORY. YOU REALLY SHOULDN'T...
WELL, IT'S MY CAR.
AND IF I'M DATING THE BOY, DON'T I COUNT AS FAMILY TOO?
DON'T SAY THAT, LUV.
THE STORY DOESN'T HAVE A SENSE OF HUMOR.

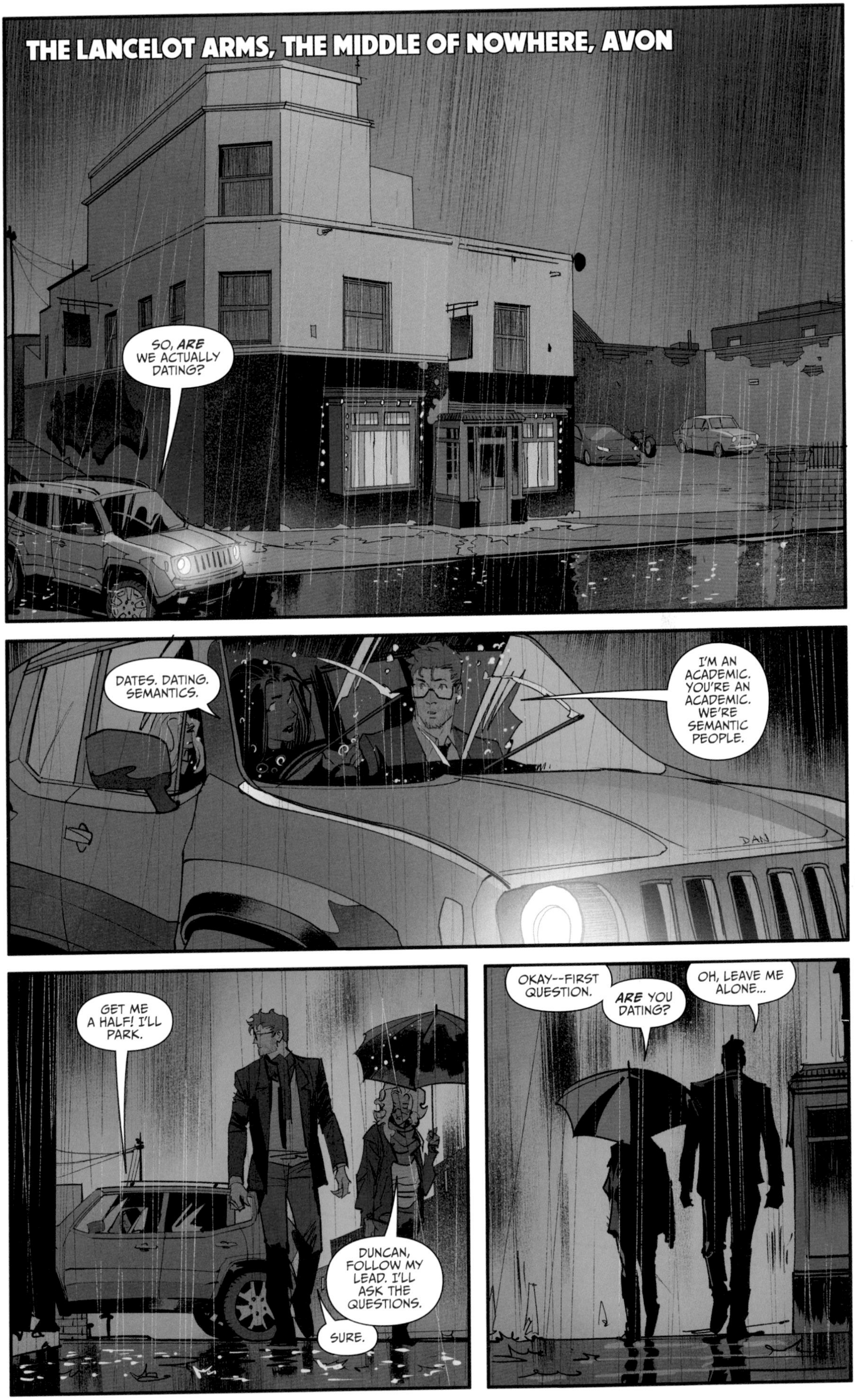
THE LANCELOT ARMS, THE MIDDLE OF NOWHERE, AVON
SO, ARE WE ACTUALLY DATING?
DATES. DATING. SEMANTICS.
I'M AN ACADEMIC. YOU'RE AN ACADEMIC. WE'RE SEMANTIC PEOPLE.
GET ME A HALF! I'LL PARK.
DUNCAN, FOLLOW MY LEAD. I'LL ASK THE QUESTIONS.
SURE.
OKAY--FIRST QUESTION.
ARE YOU DATING?
OH, LEAVE ME ALONE...

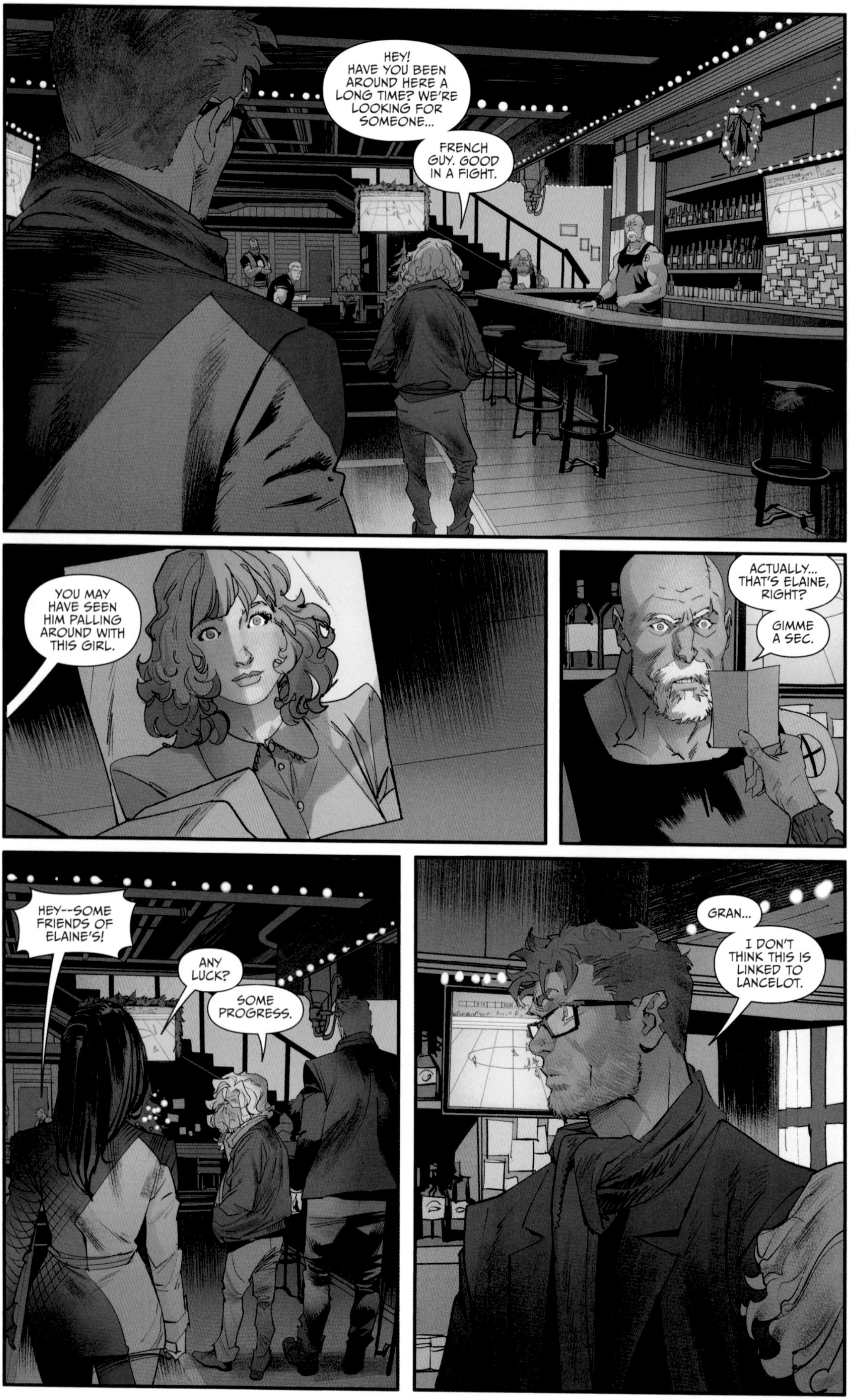
HEY! HAVE YOU BEEN AROUND HERE A LONG TIME? WE'RE LOOKING FOR SOMEONE...
FRENCH GUY. GOOD IN A FIGHT.
YOU MAY HAVE SEEN HIM PALLING AROUND WITH THIS GIRL.
ACTUALLY... THAT'S ELAINE, RIGHT?
GIMME A SEC.
HEY--SOME FRIENDS OF ELAINE'S!
ANY LUCK?
SOME PROGRESS.
GRAN...
I DON'T THINK THIS IS LINKED TO LANCELOT.

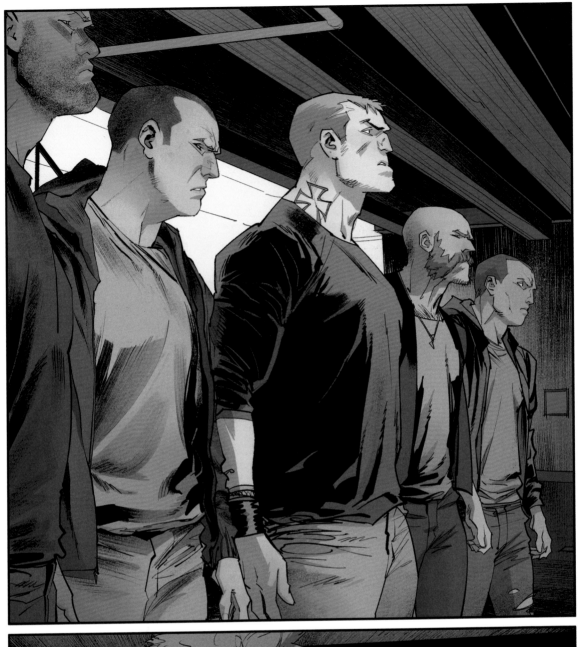

IT'S ABOUT THE OTHER LEAD.

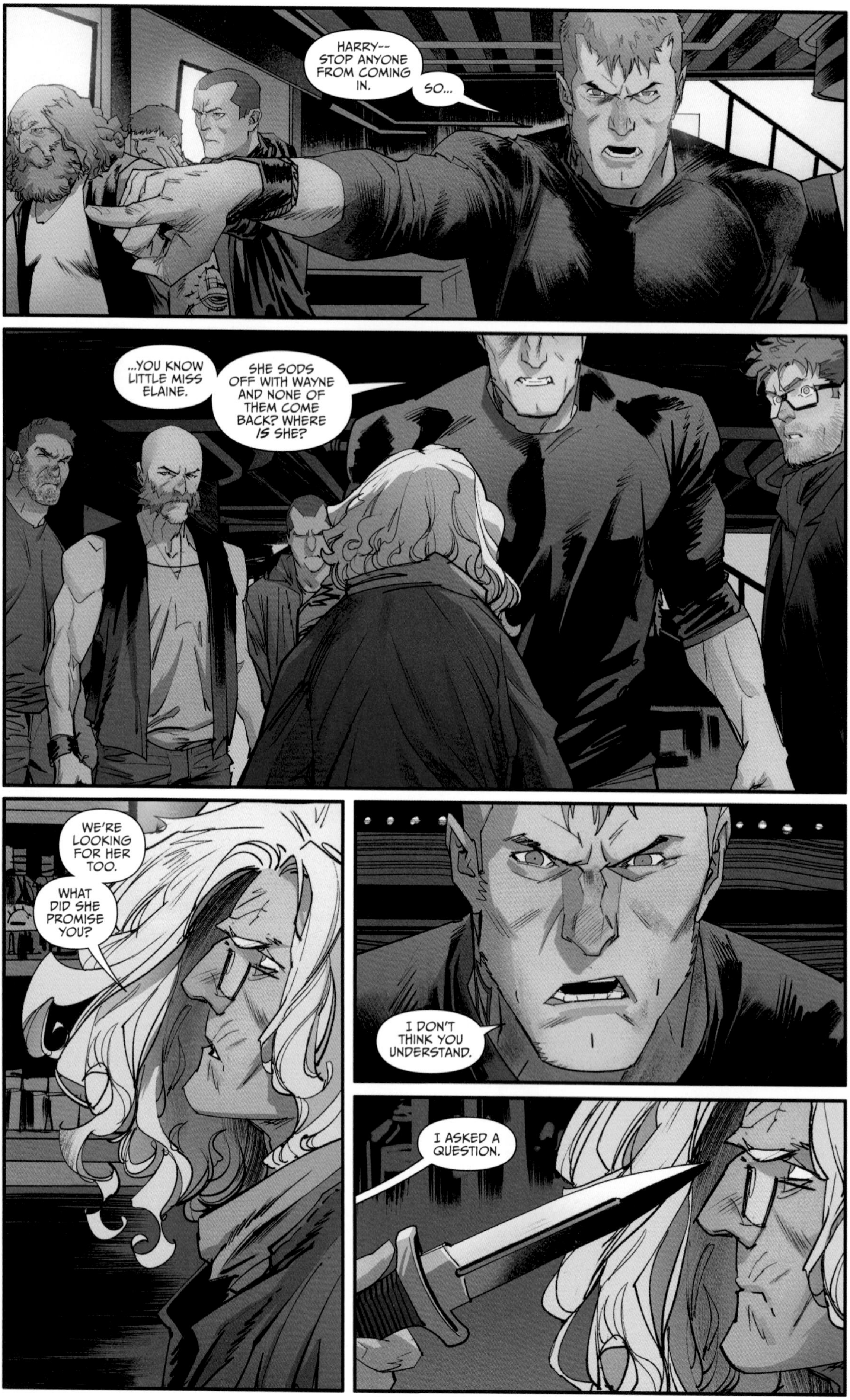
HARRY-- STOP ANYONE FROM COMING IN.
SO...
...YOU KNOW LITTLE MISS ELAINE.
SHE SODS OFF WITH WAYNE AND NONE OF THEM COME BACK? WHERE *IS* SHE?
WE'RE LOOKING FOR HER TOO.
WHAT DID SHE PROMISE YOU?
I DON'T THINK YOU UNDERSTAND.
I ASKED A QUESTION.

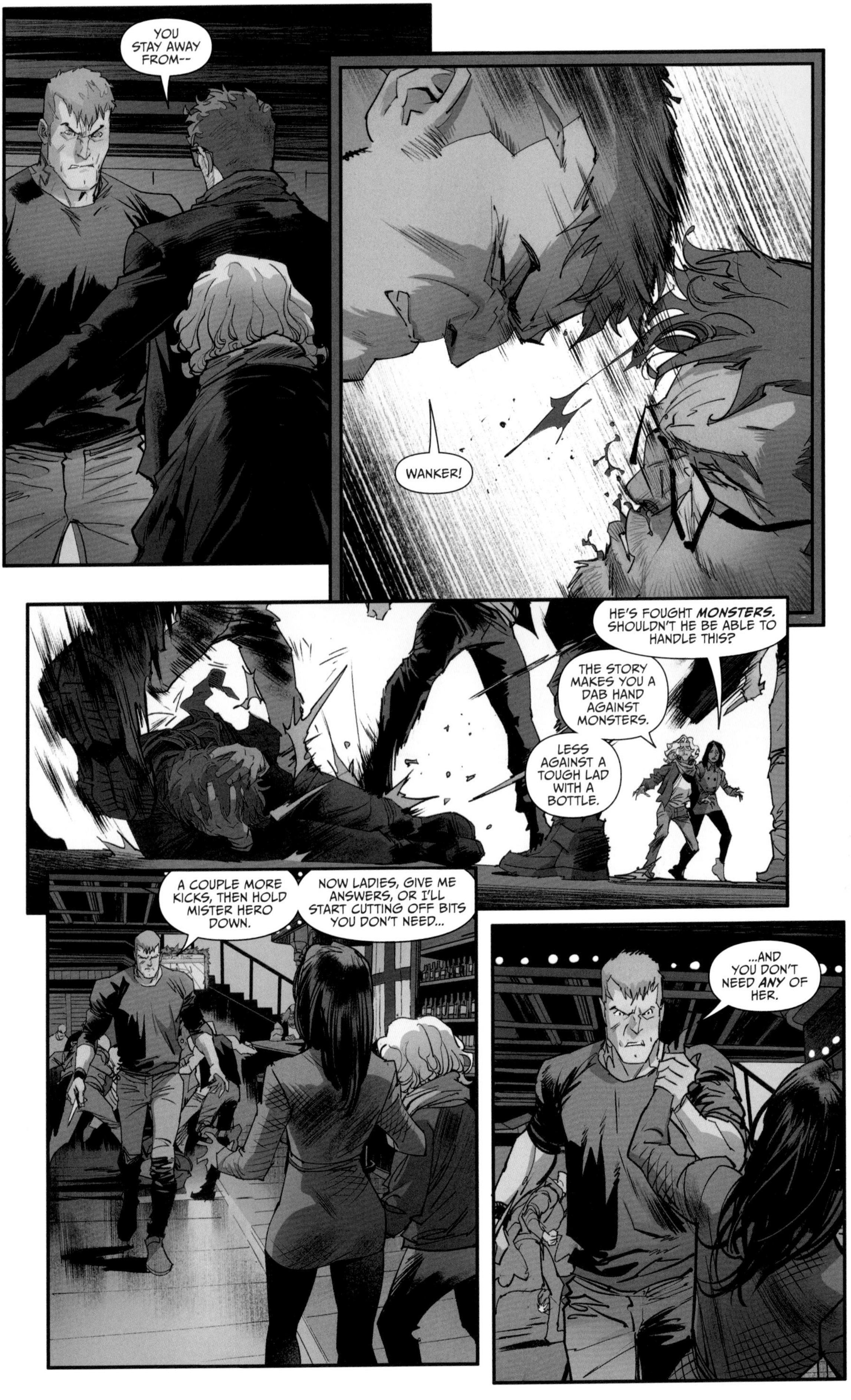
YOU STAY AWAY FROM--
WANKER!
HE'S FOUGHT MONSTERS. SHOULDN'T HE BE ABLE TO HANDLE THIS?
THE STORY MAKES YOU A DAB HAND AGAINST MONSTERS.
LESS AGAINST A TOUGH LAD WITH A BOTTLE.
A COUPLE MORE KICKS, THEN HOLD MISTER HERO DOWN.
NOW LADIES, GIVE ME ANSWERS, OR I'LL START CUTTING OFF BITS YOU DON'T NEED...
...AND YOU DON'T NEED ANY OF HER.

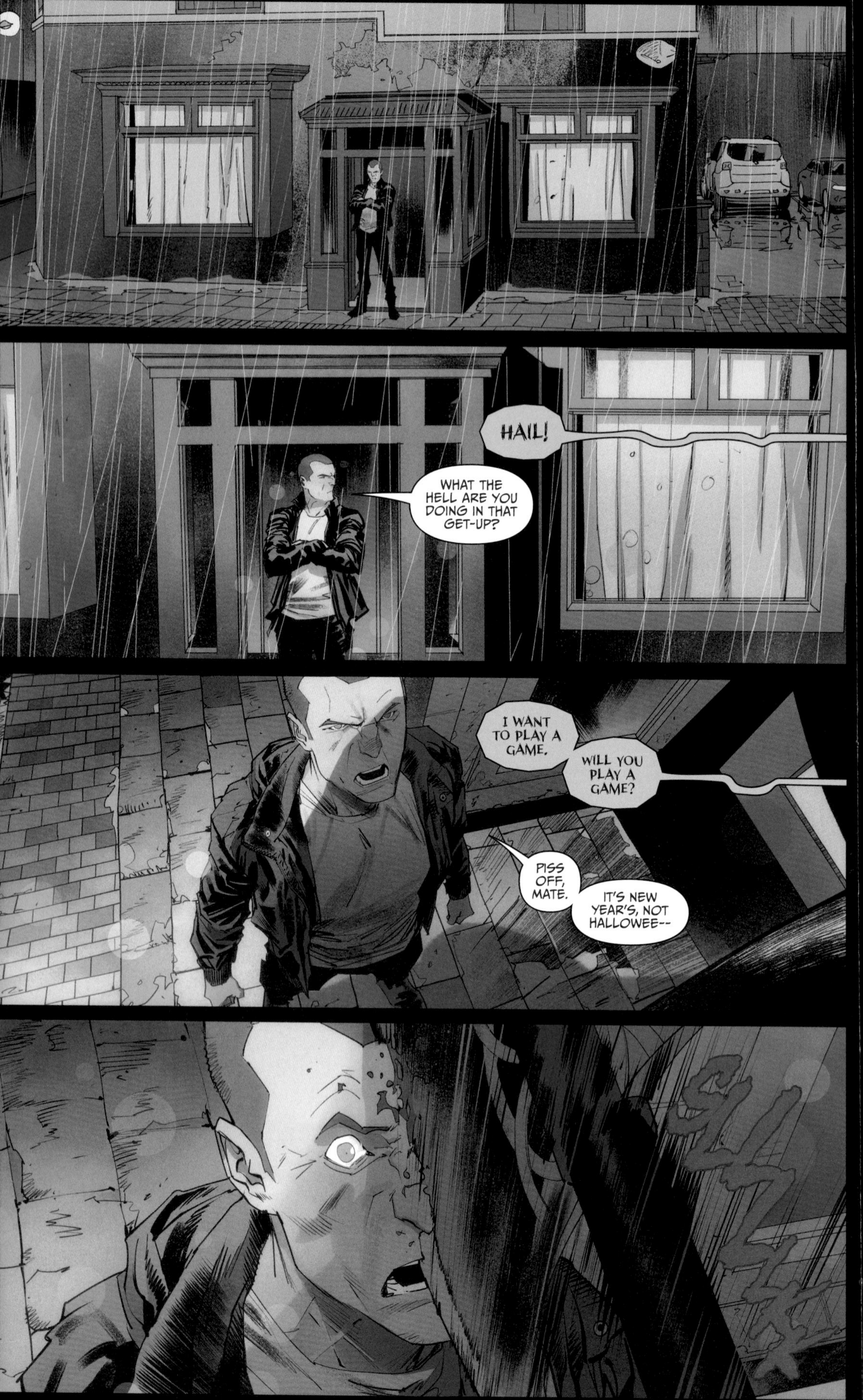
HAIL!
WHAT THE HELL ARE YOU DOING IN THAT GET-UP?
I WANT TO PLAY A GAME.
WILL YOU PLAY A GAME?
PISS OFF, MATE.
IT'S NEW YEAR'S, NOT HALLOWEE--

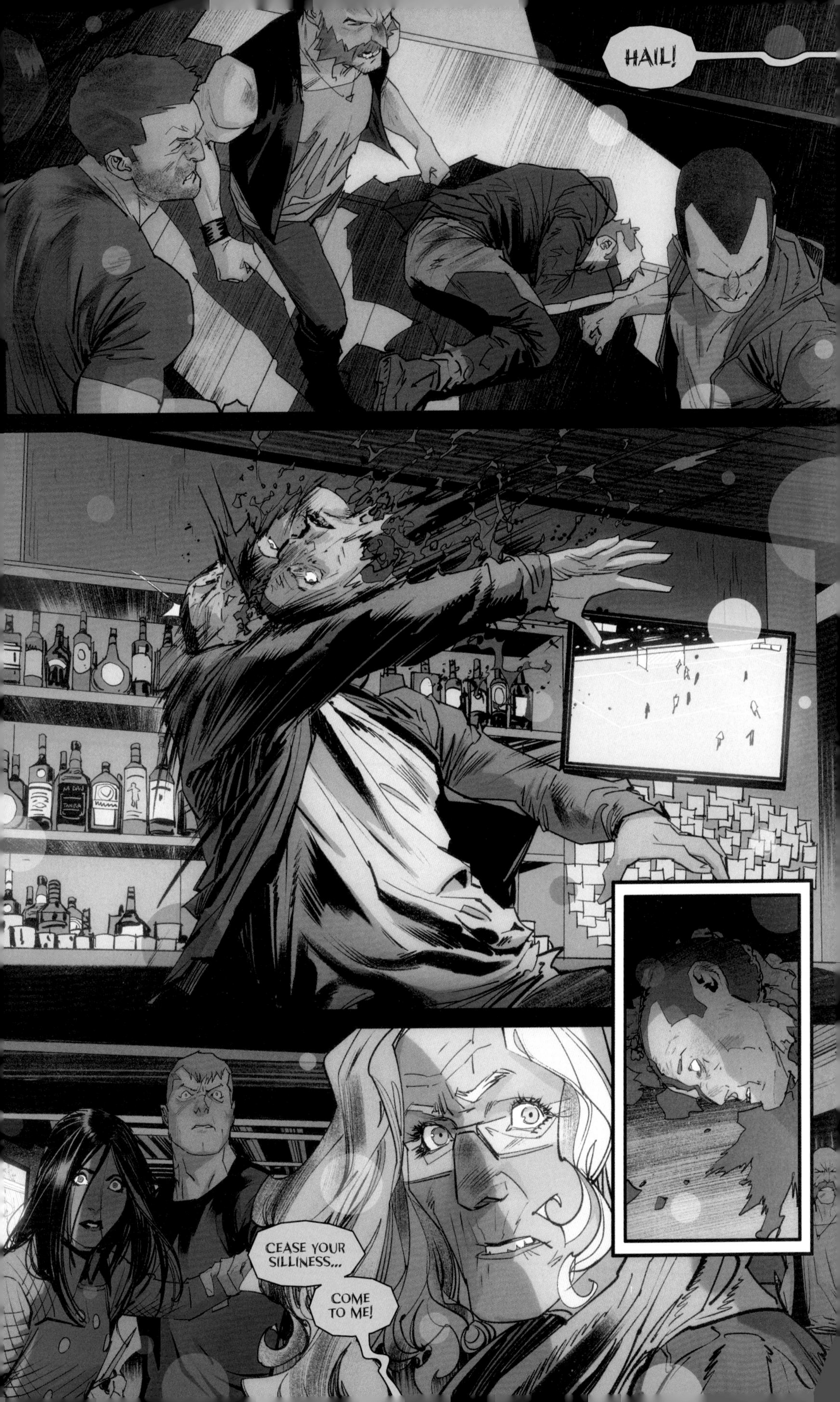
HAIL!
CEASE YOUR SILLINESS...
COME TO ME!

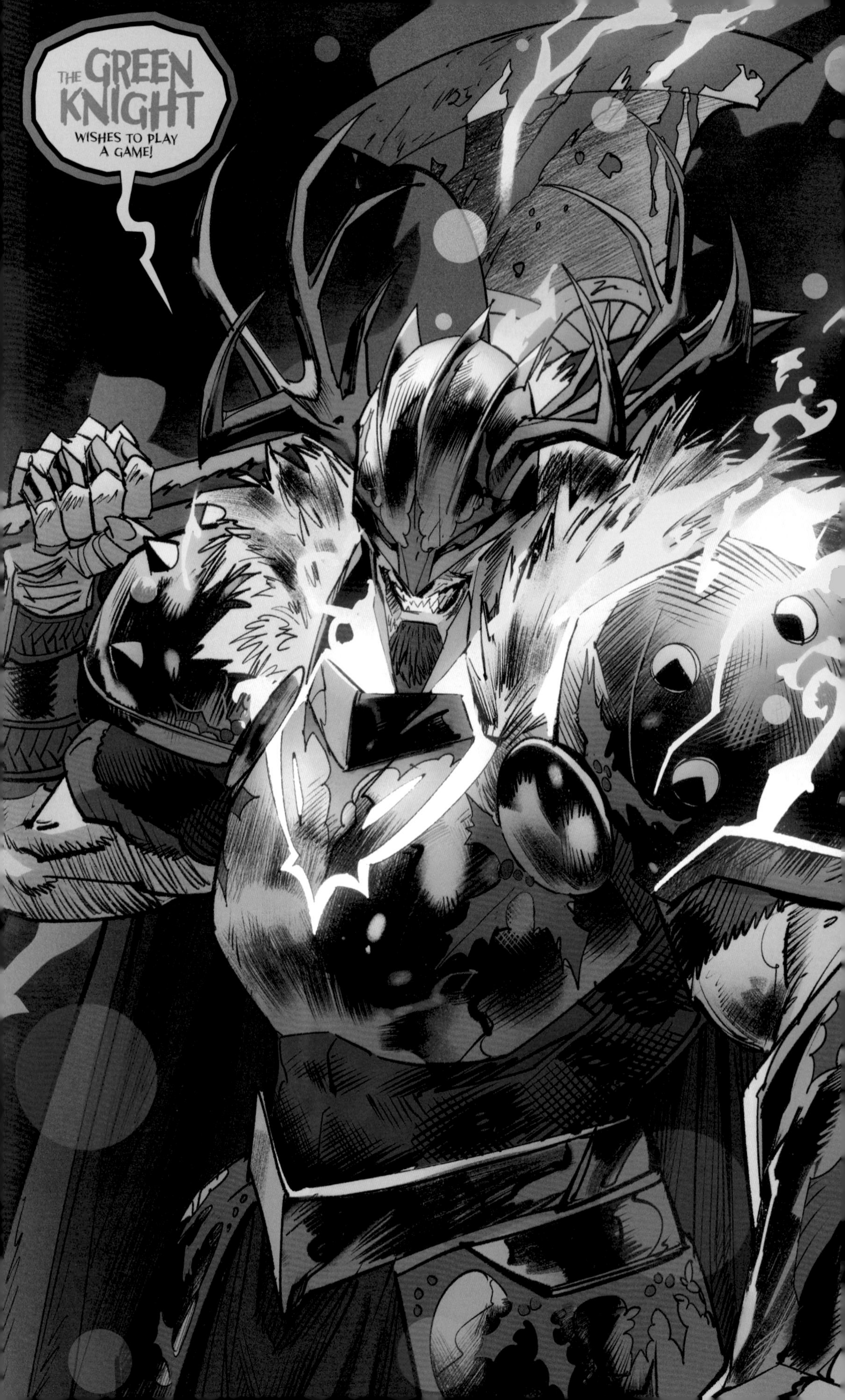
THE GREEN KNIGHT WISHES TO PLAY A GAME!

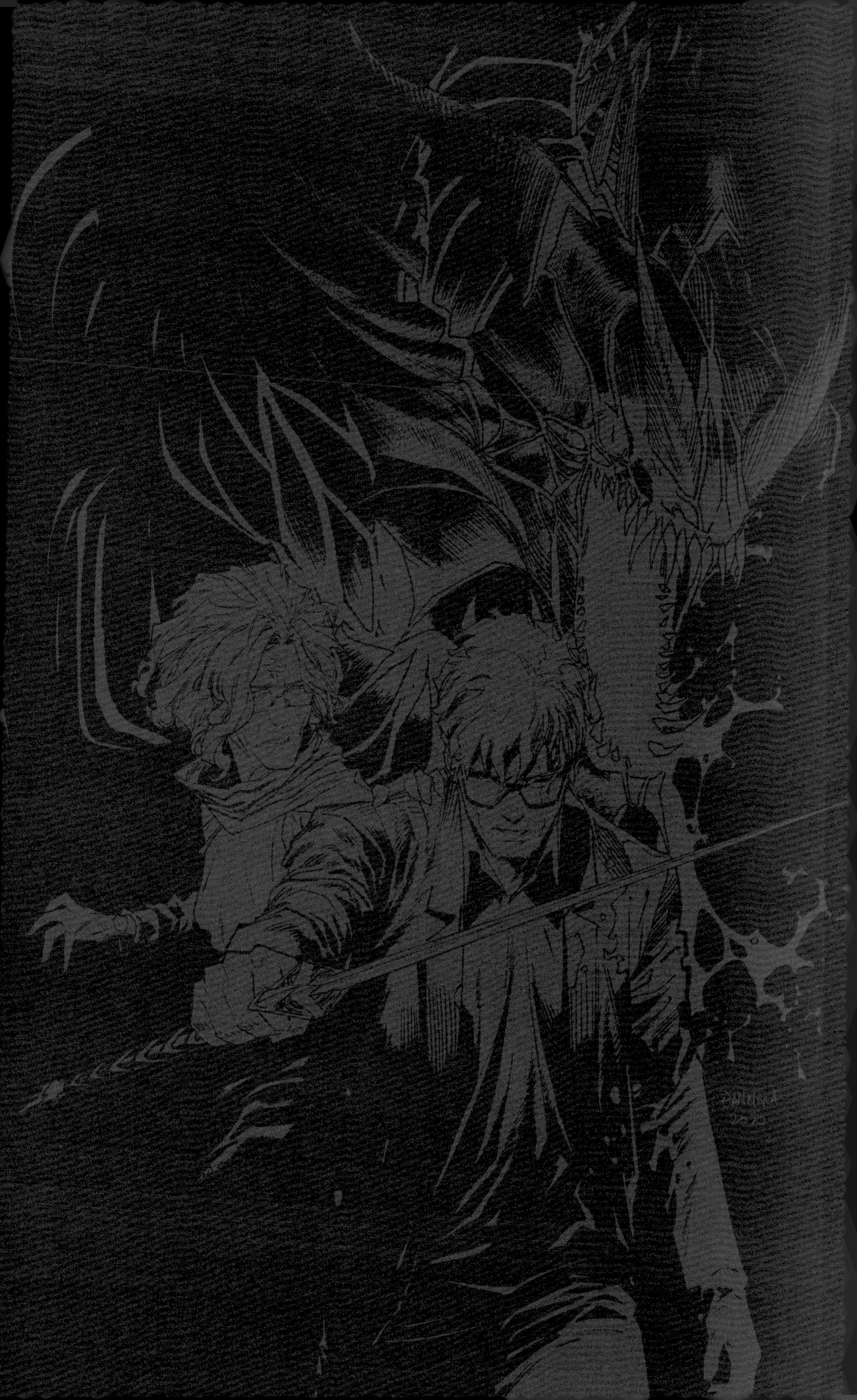

CHAPTER FOURTEEN

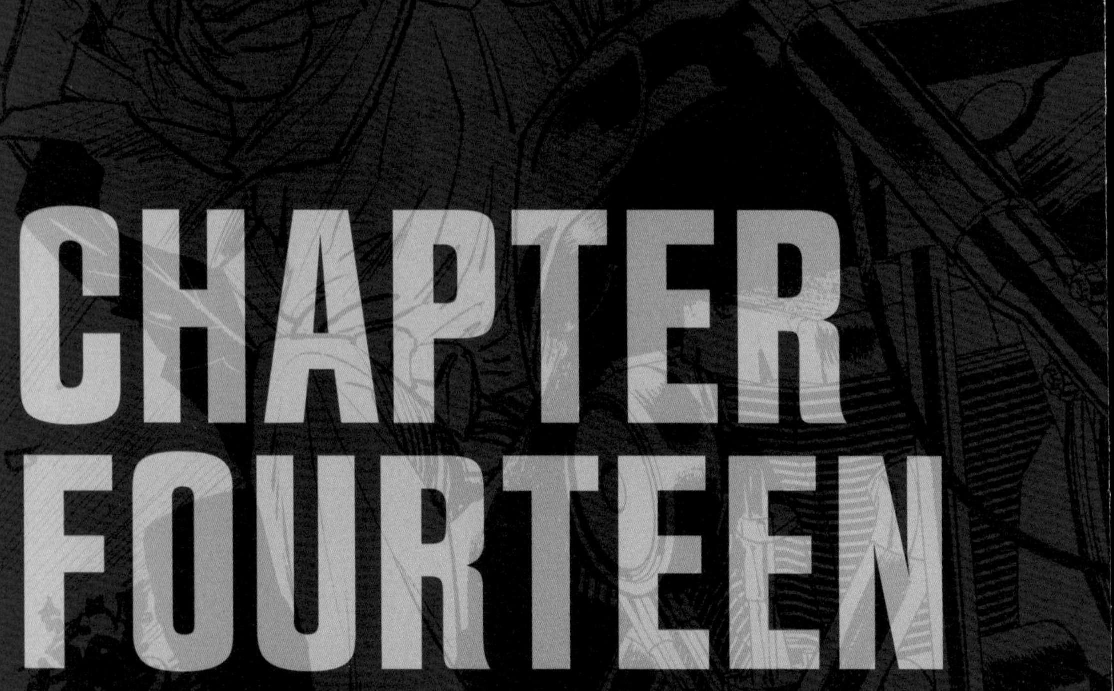

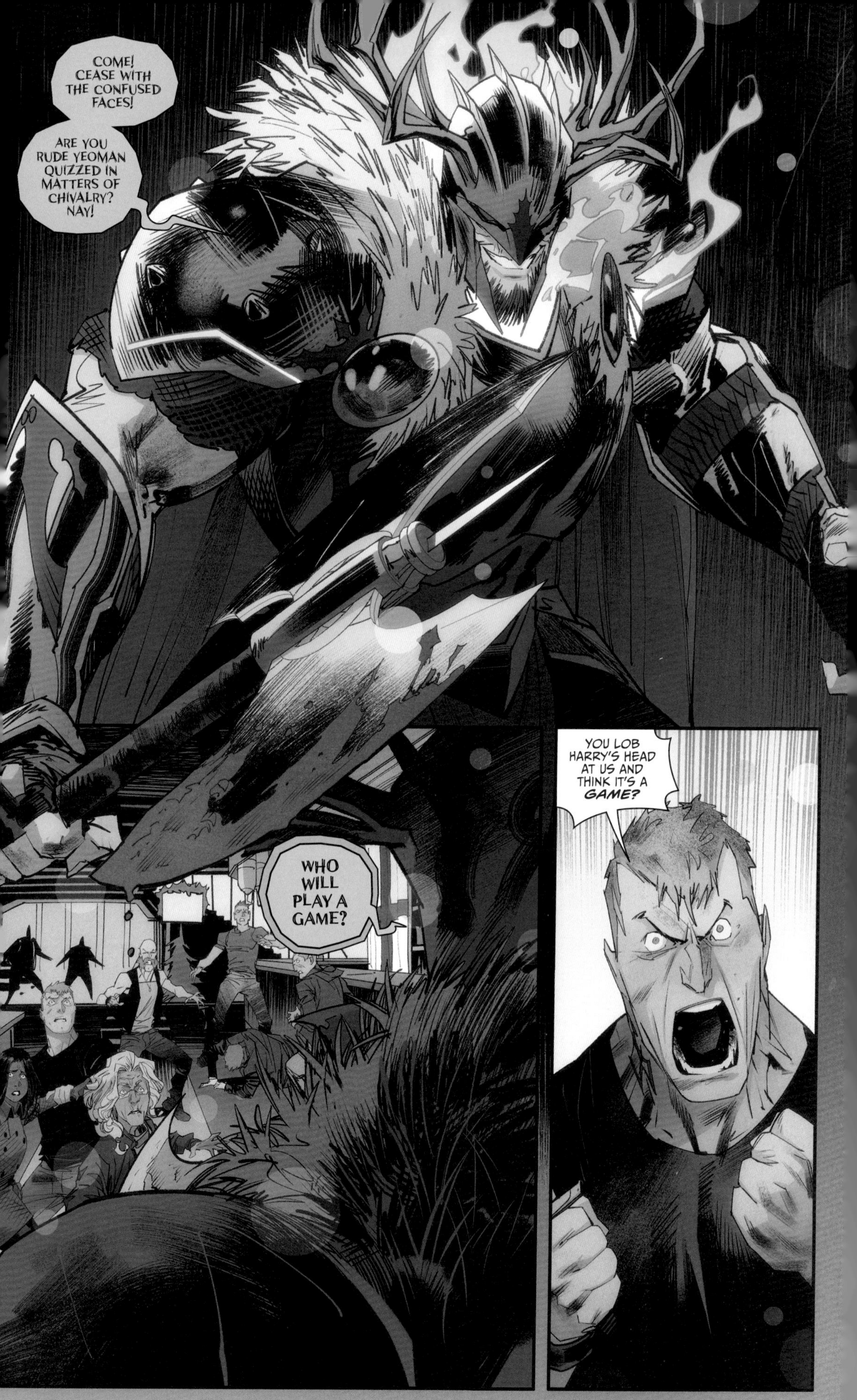
COME! CEASE WITH THE CONFUSED FACES!
ARE YOU RUDE YEOMAN QUIZZED IN MATTERS OF CHIVALRY? NAY!
WHO WILL PLAY A GAME?
YOU LOB HARRY'S HEAD AT US AND THINK IT'S A GAME?

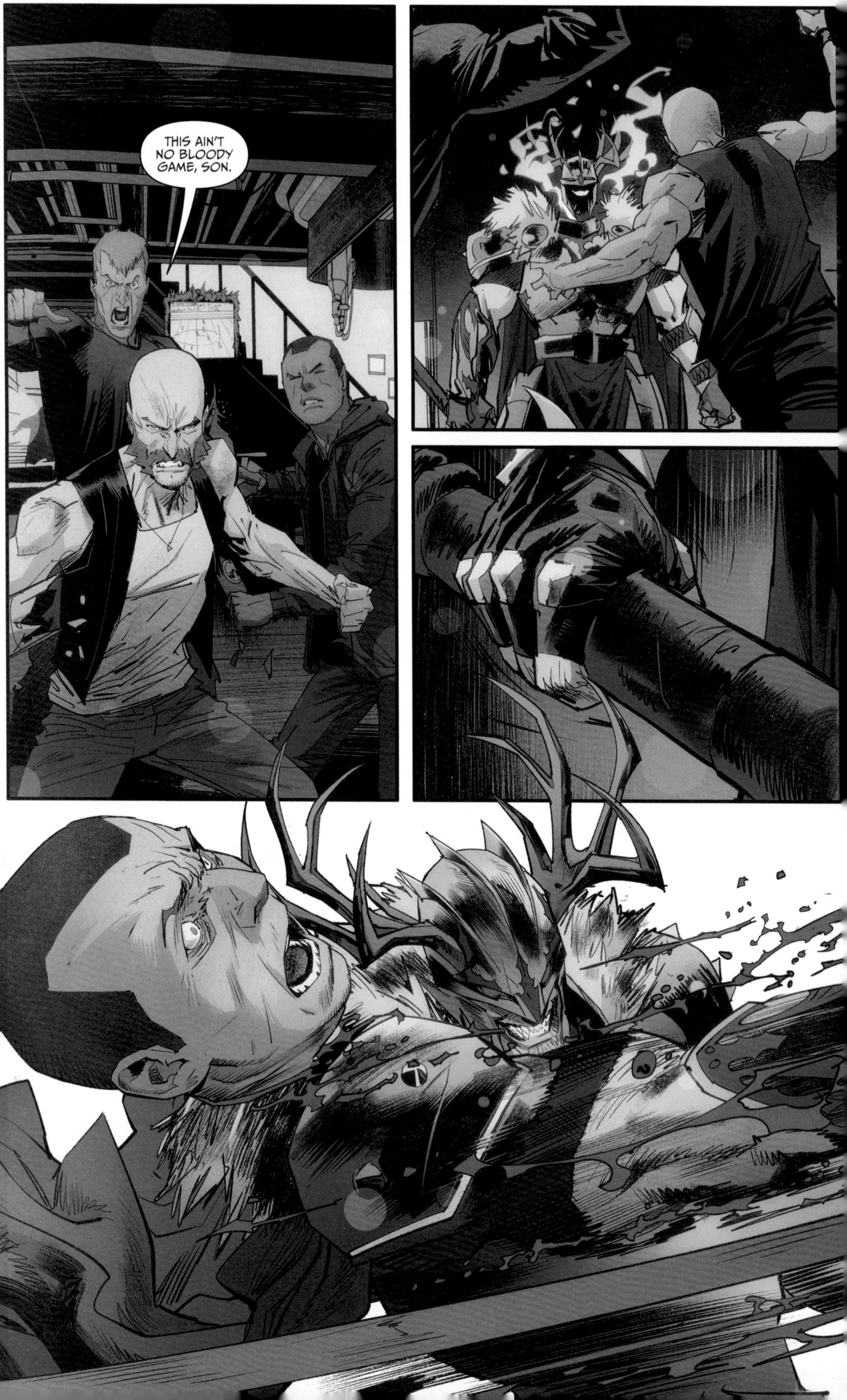
THIS AIN'T NO BLOODY GAME, SON.

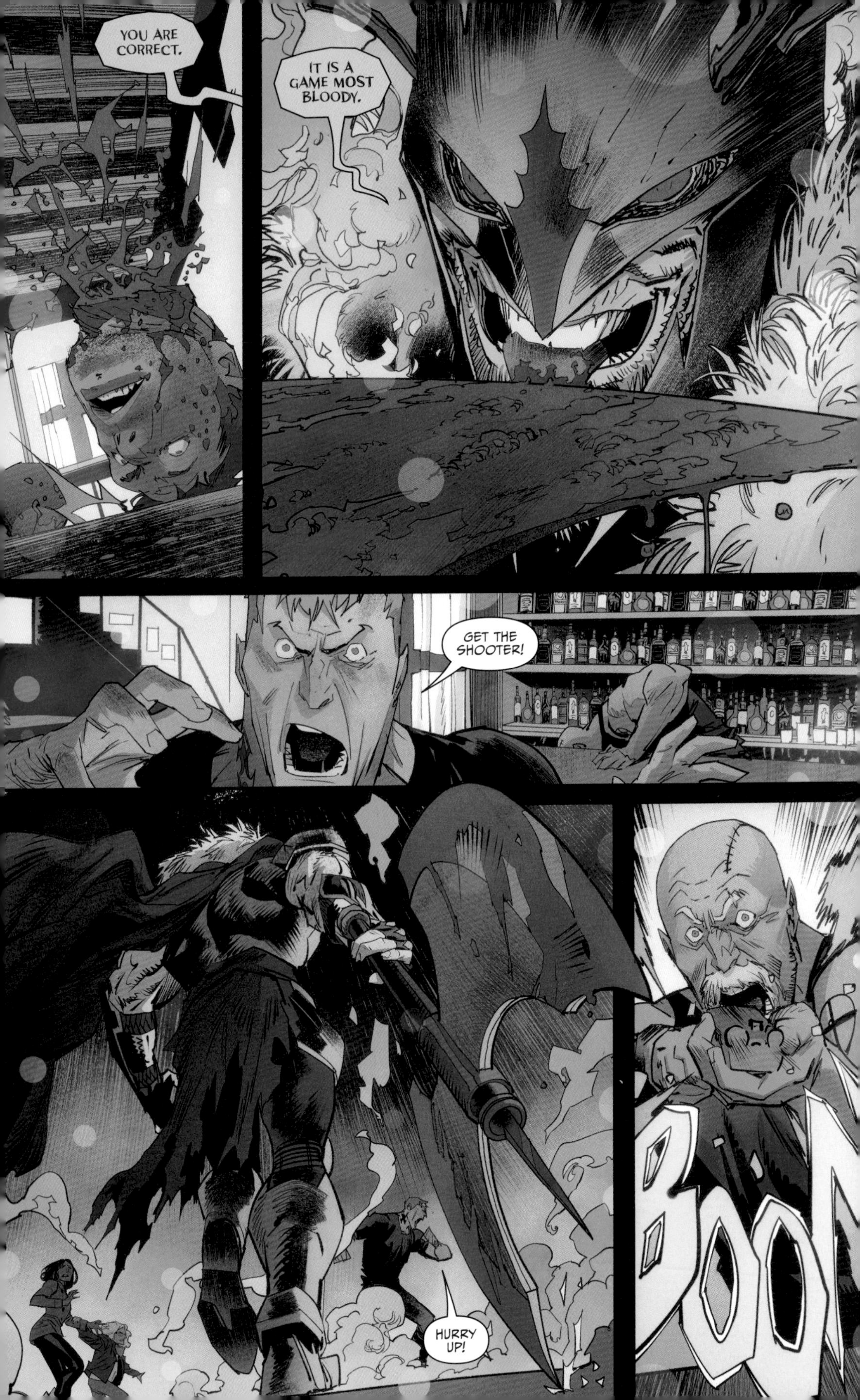
YOU ARE CORRECT.
IT IS A GAME MOST BLOODY.
GET THE SHOOTER!
HURRY UP!
BOO

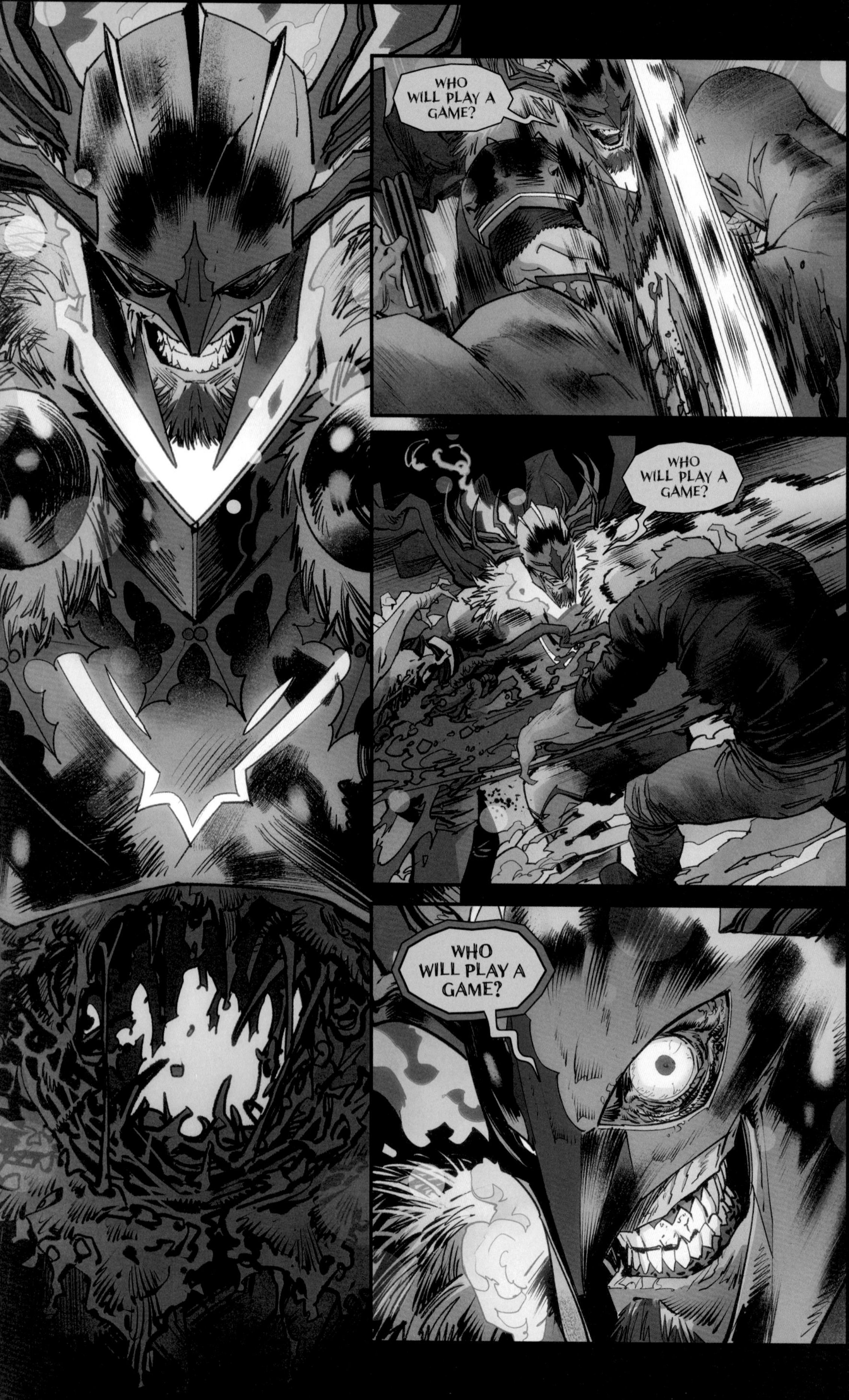
WHO WILL PLAY A GAME?
WHO WILL PLAY A GAME?
WHO WILL PLAY A GAME?

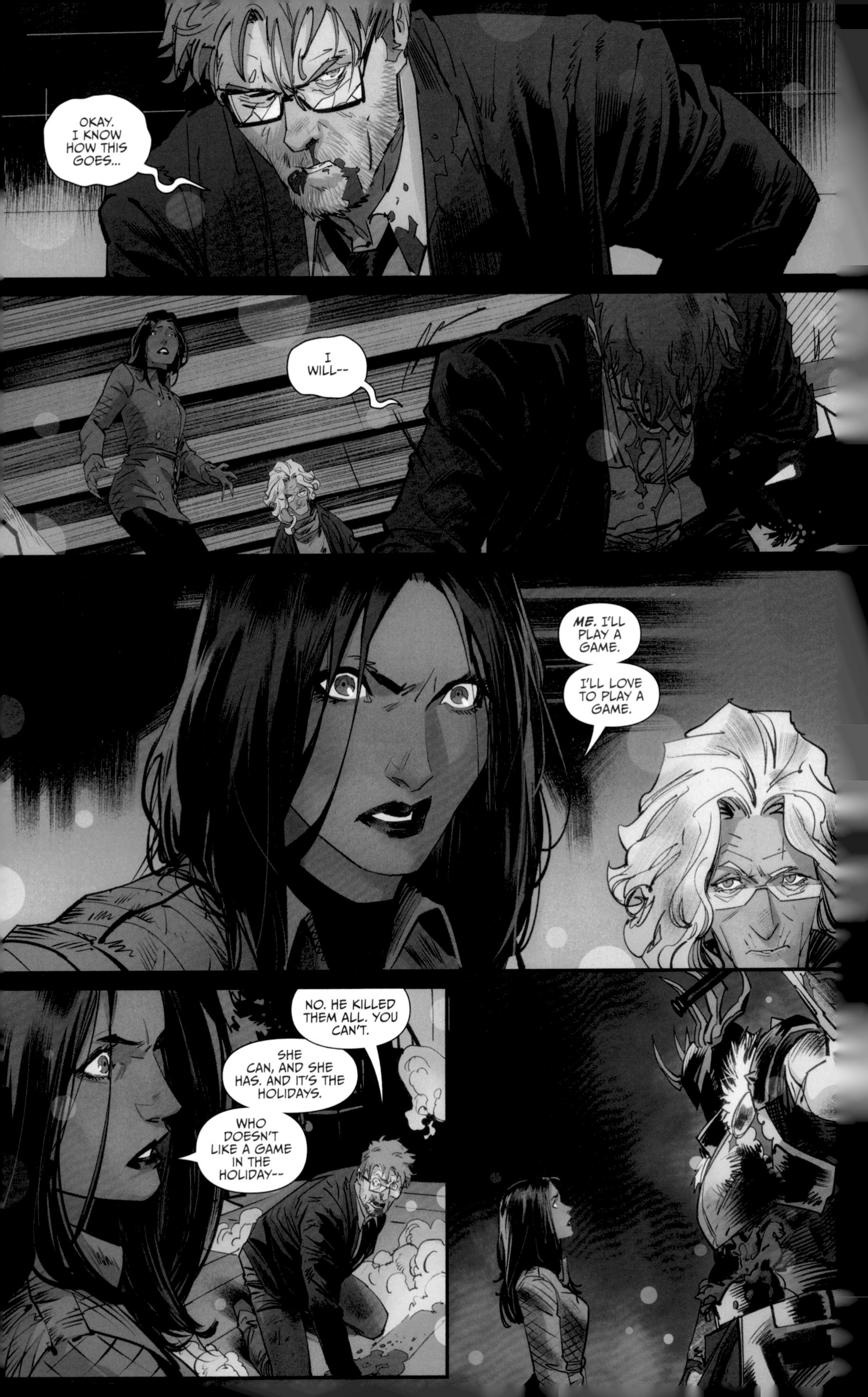
OKAY. I KNOW HOW THIS GOES...
I WILL--
ME. I'LL PLAY A GAME.
I'LL LOVE TO PLAY A GAME.
NO. HE KILLED THEM ALL. YOU CAN'T.
SHE CAN, AND SHE HAS. AND IT'S THE HOLIDAYS.
WHO DOESN'T LIKE A GAME IN THE HOLIDAY--

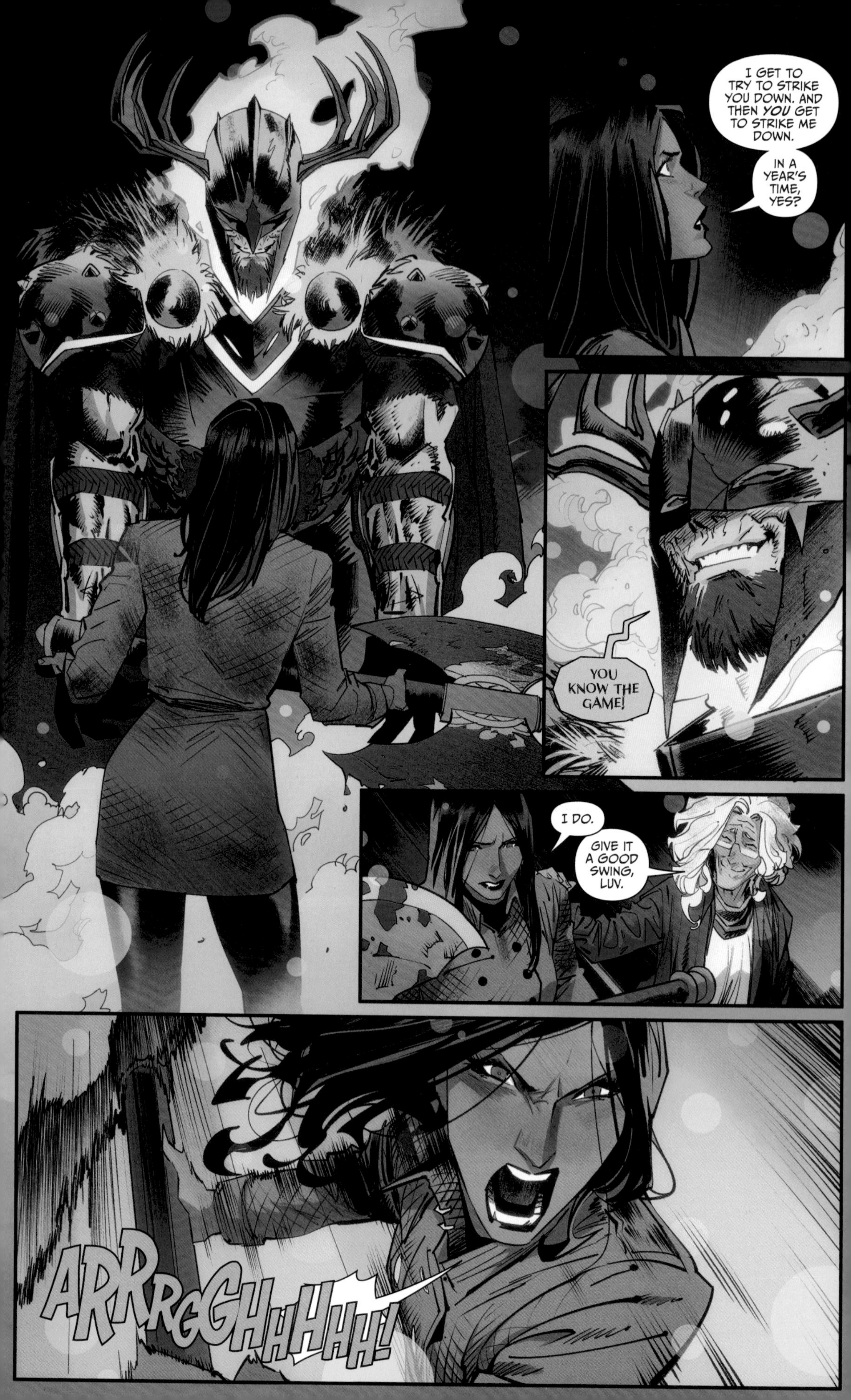
I GET TO TRY TO STRIKE YOU DOWN. AND THEN YOU GET TO STRIKE ME DOWN.
IN A YEAR'S TIME, YES?
YOU KNOW THE GAME!
I DO.
GIVE IT A GOOD SWING, LUV.
ARRRGGHHHHH!

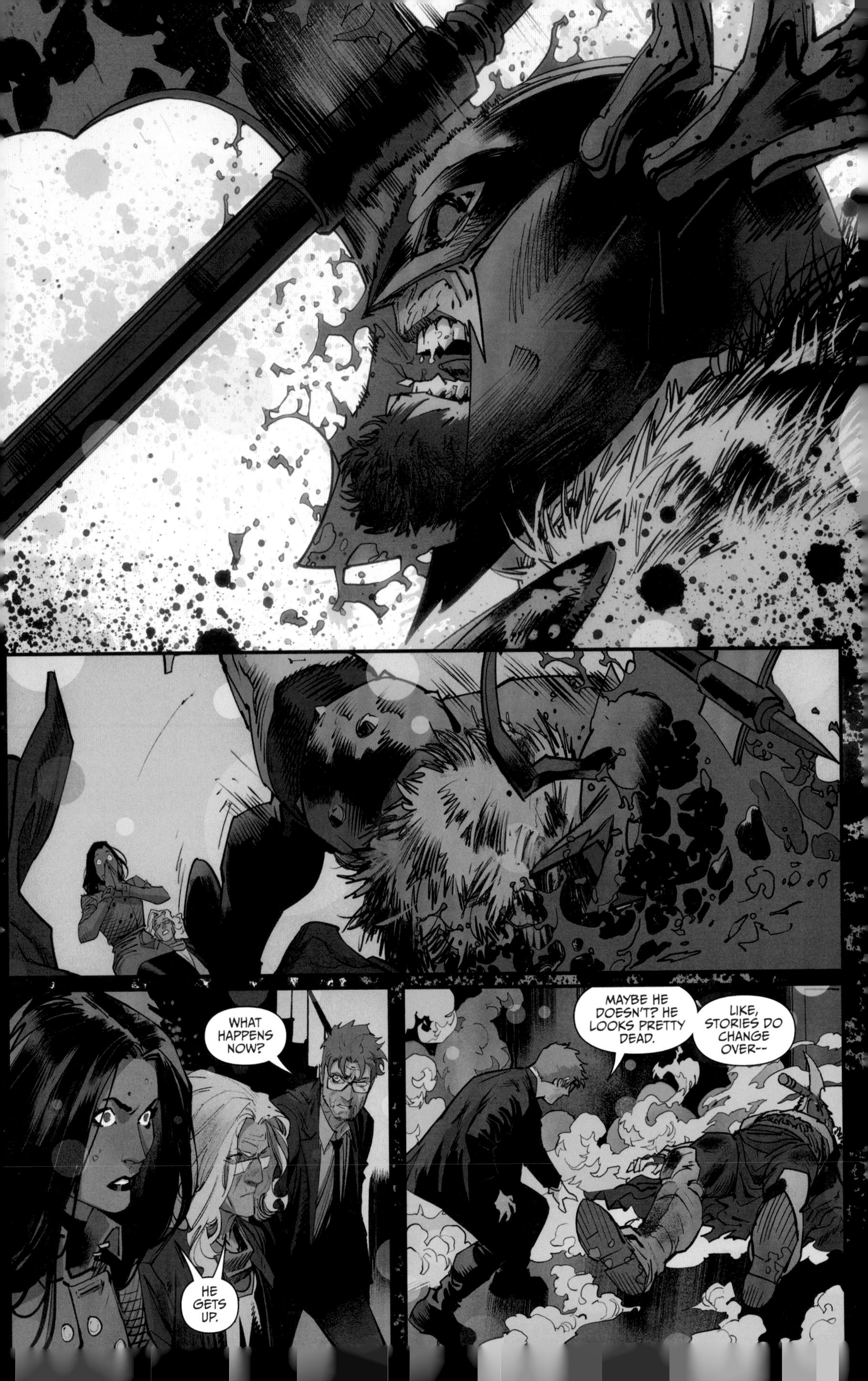
WHAT HAPPENS NOW?
HE GETS UP.
MAYBE HE DOESN'T? HE LOOKS PRETTY DEAD.
LIKE, STORIES DO CHANGE OVER--

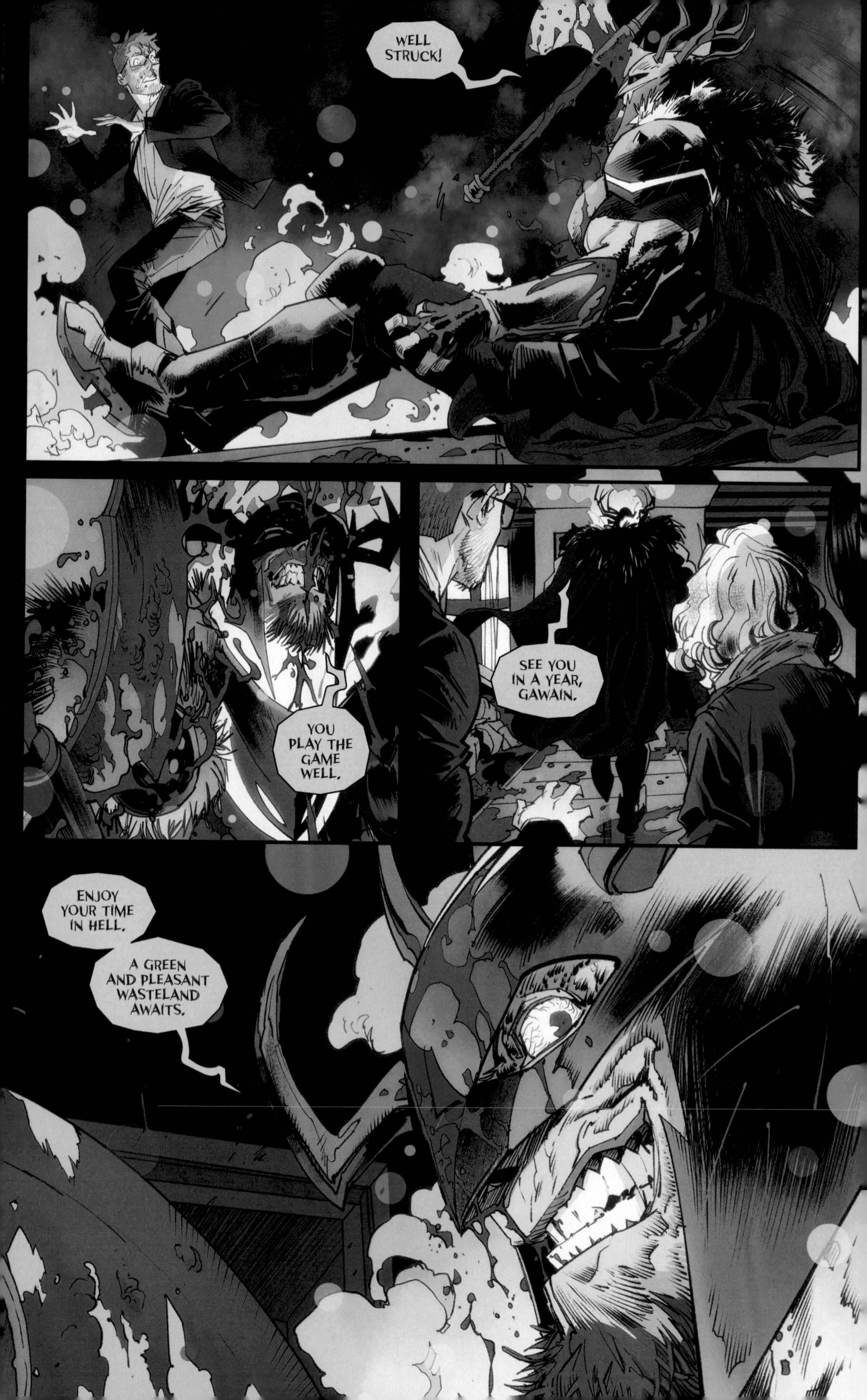
WELL STRUCK!
YOU PLAY THE GAME WELL,
SEE YOU IN A YEAR, GAWAIN.
ENJOY YOUR TIME IN HELL,
A GREEN AND PLEASANT WASTELAND AWAITS.

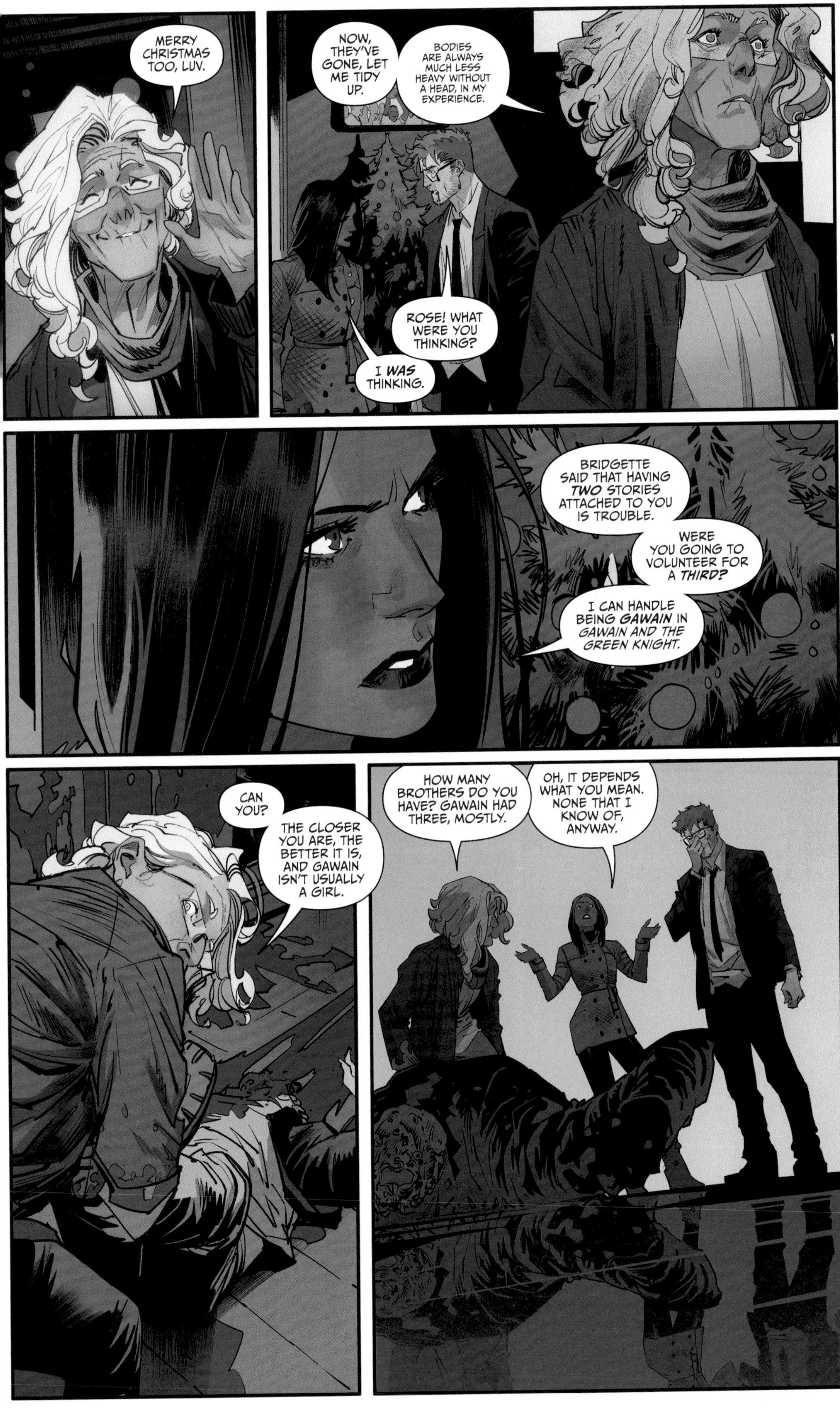
MERRY CHRISTMAS TOO, LUV.
NOW, THEY'VE GONE, LET ME TIDY UP.
BODIES ARE ALWAYS MUCH LESS HEAVY WITHOUT A HEAD, IN MY EXPERIENCE.
ROSE! WHAT WERE YOU THINKING?
I *WAS* THINKING.
BRIDGETTE SAID THAT HAVING *TWO* STORIES ATTACHED TO YOU IS TROUBLE.
WERE YOU GOING TO VOLUNTEER FOR A *THIRD?*
I CAN HANDLE BEING *GAWAIN* IN *GAWAIN AND THE GREEN KNIGHT.*
CAN YOU?
THE CLOSER YOU ARE, THE BETTER IT IS, AND GAWAIN ISN'T USUALLY A GIRL.
HOW MANY BROTHERS DO YOU HAVE? GAWAIN HAD THREE, MOSTLY.
OH, IT DEPENDS WHAT YOU MEAN. NONE THAT I KNOW OF, ANYWAY.

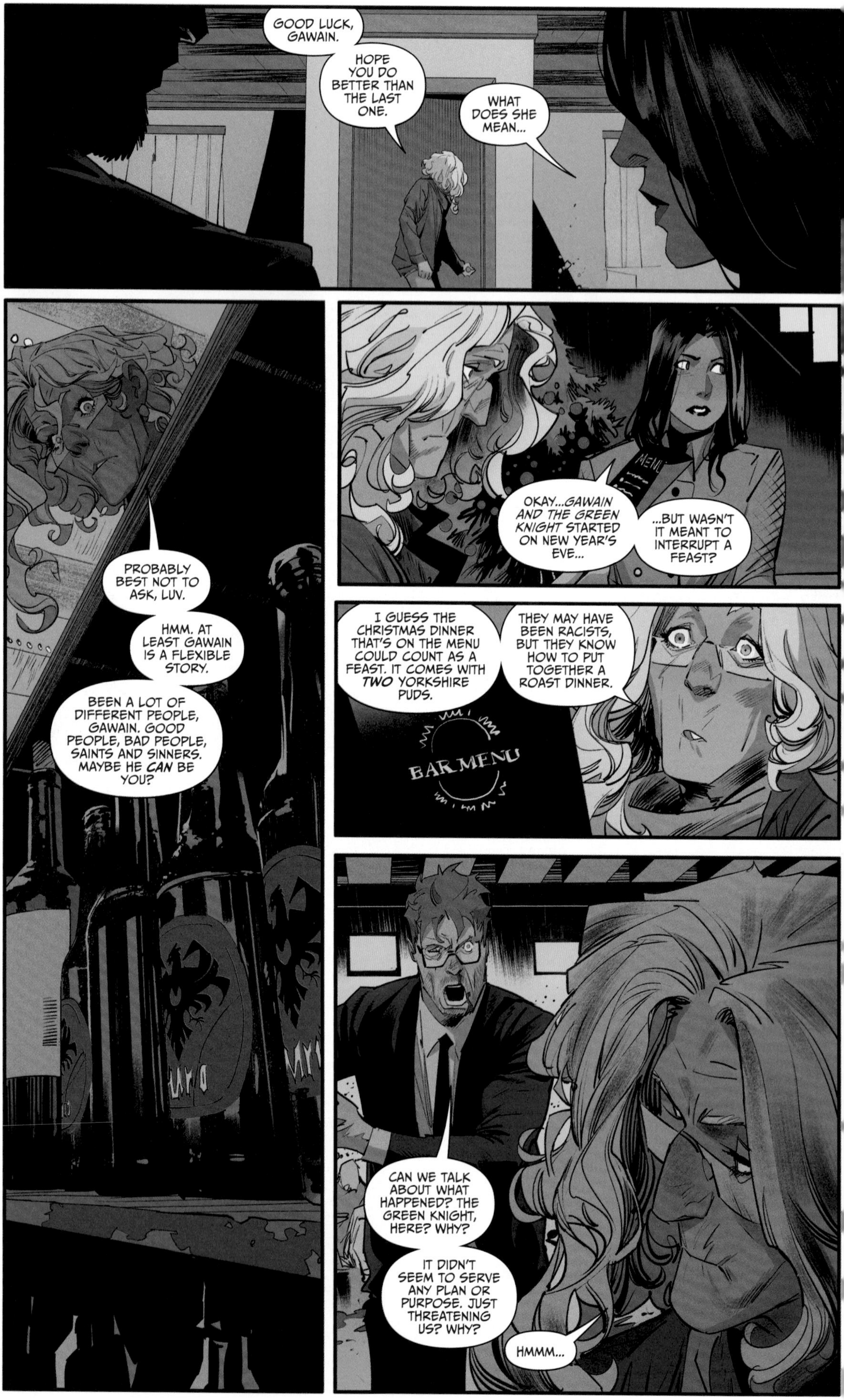

GOOD LUCK, GAWAIN.
HOPE YOU DO BETTER THAN THE LAST ONE.
WHAT DOES SHE MEAN...
PROBABLY BEST NOT TO ASK, LUV.
HMM. AT LEAST GAWAIN IS A FLEXIBLE STORY.
BEEN A LOT OF DIFFERENT PEOPLE, GAWAIN. GOOD PEOPLE, BAD PEOPLE, SAINTS AND SINNERS. MAYBE HE *CAN* BE YOU?
OKAY...*GAWAIN AND THE GREEN KNIGHT* STARTED ON NEW YEAR'S EVE...
...BUT WASN'T IT MEANT TO INTERRUPT A FEAST?
I GUESS THE CHRISTMAS DINNER THAT'S ON THE MENU COULD COUNT AS A FEAST. IT COMES WITH *TWO* YORKSHIRE PUDS.
THEY MAY HAVE BEEN RACISTS, BUT THEY KNOW HOW TO PUT TOGETHER A ROAST DINNER.
BAR MENU
CAN WE TALK ABOUT WHAT HAPPENED? THE GREEN KNIGHT, HERE? WHY?
IT DIDN'T SEEM TO SERVE ANY PLAN OR PURPOSE. JUST THREATENING US? WHY?
HMMM...

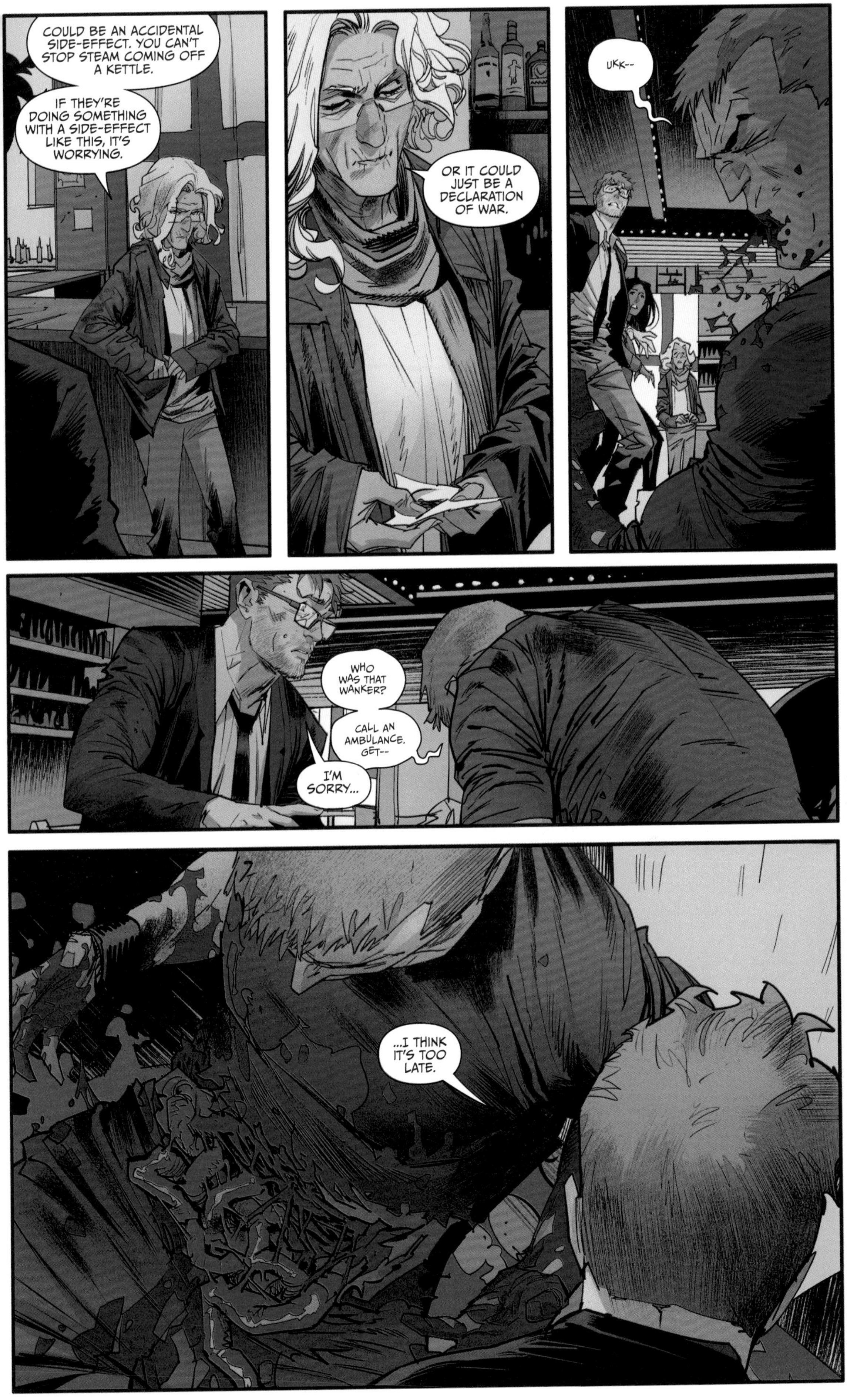
COULD BE AN ACCIDENTAL SIDE-EFFECT. YOU CAN'T STOP STEAM COMING OFF A KETTLE.
IF THEY'RE DOING SOMETHING WITH A SIDE-EFFECT LIKE THIS, IT'S WORRYING.
OR IT COULD JUST BE A DECLARATION OF WAR.
UKK--
WHO WAS THAT WANKER?
CALL AN AMBULANCE. GET--
I'M SORRY...
...I THINK IT'S TOO LATE.

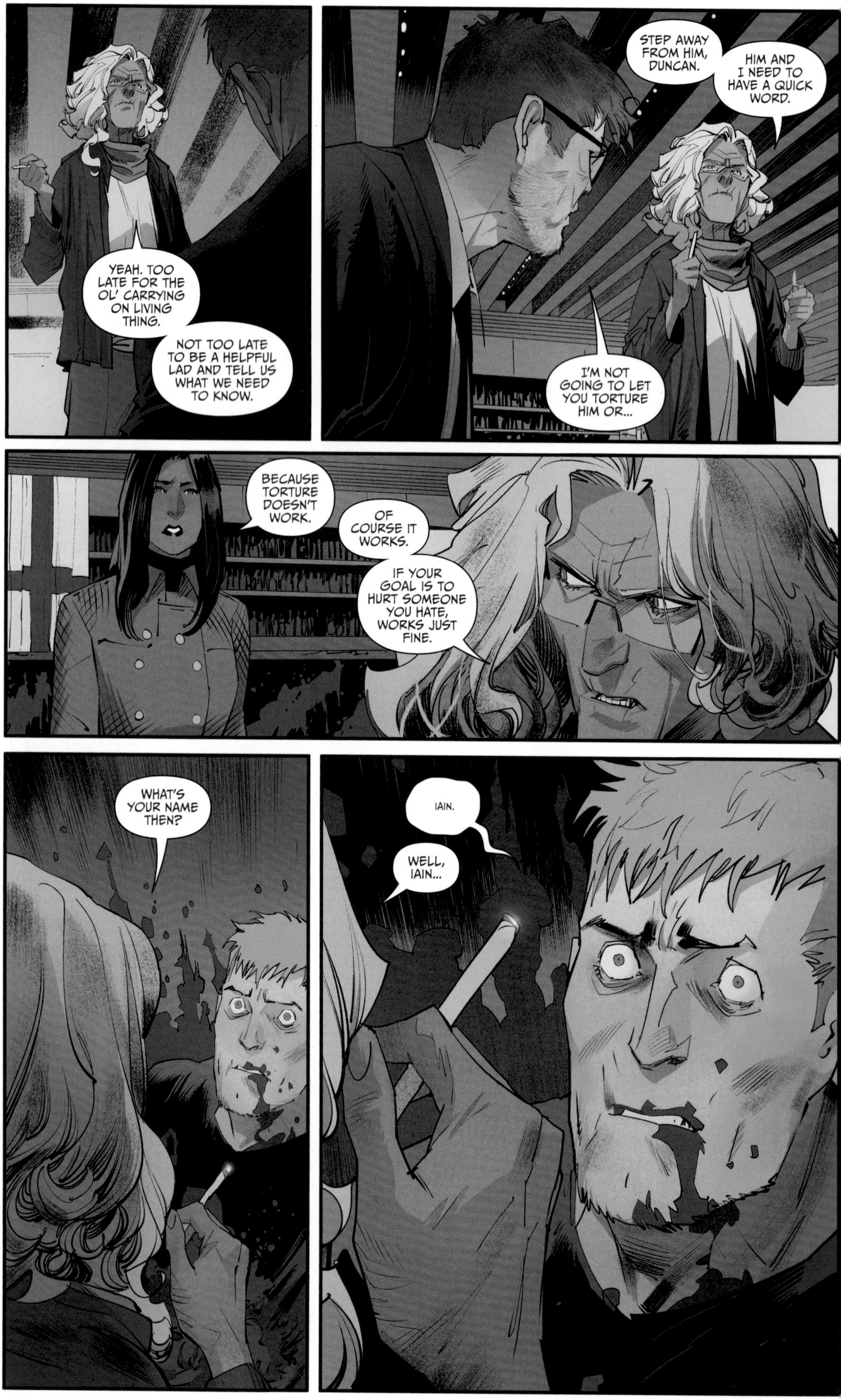
YEAH. TOO LATE FOR THE OL' CARRYING ON LIVING THING.
NOT TOO LATE TO BE A HELPFUL LAD AND TELL US WHAT WE NEED TO KNOW.
STEP AWAY FROM HIM, DUNCAN.
HIM AND I NEED TO HAVE A QUICK WORD.
I'M NOT GOING TO LET YOU TORTURE HIM OR...
BECAUSE TORTURE DOESN'T WORK.
OF COURSE IT WORKS.
IF YOUR GOAL IS TO HURT SOMEONE YOU HATE, WORKS JUST FINE.
WHAT'S YOUR NAME THEN?
IAIN.
WELL, IAIN...

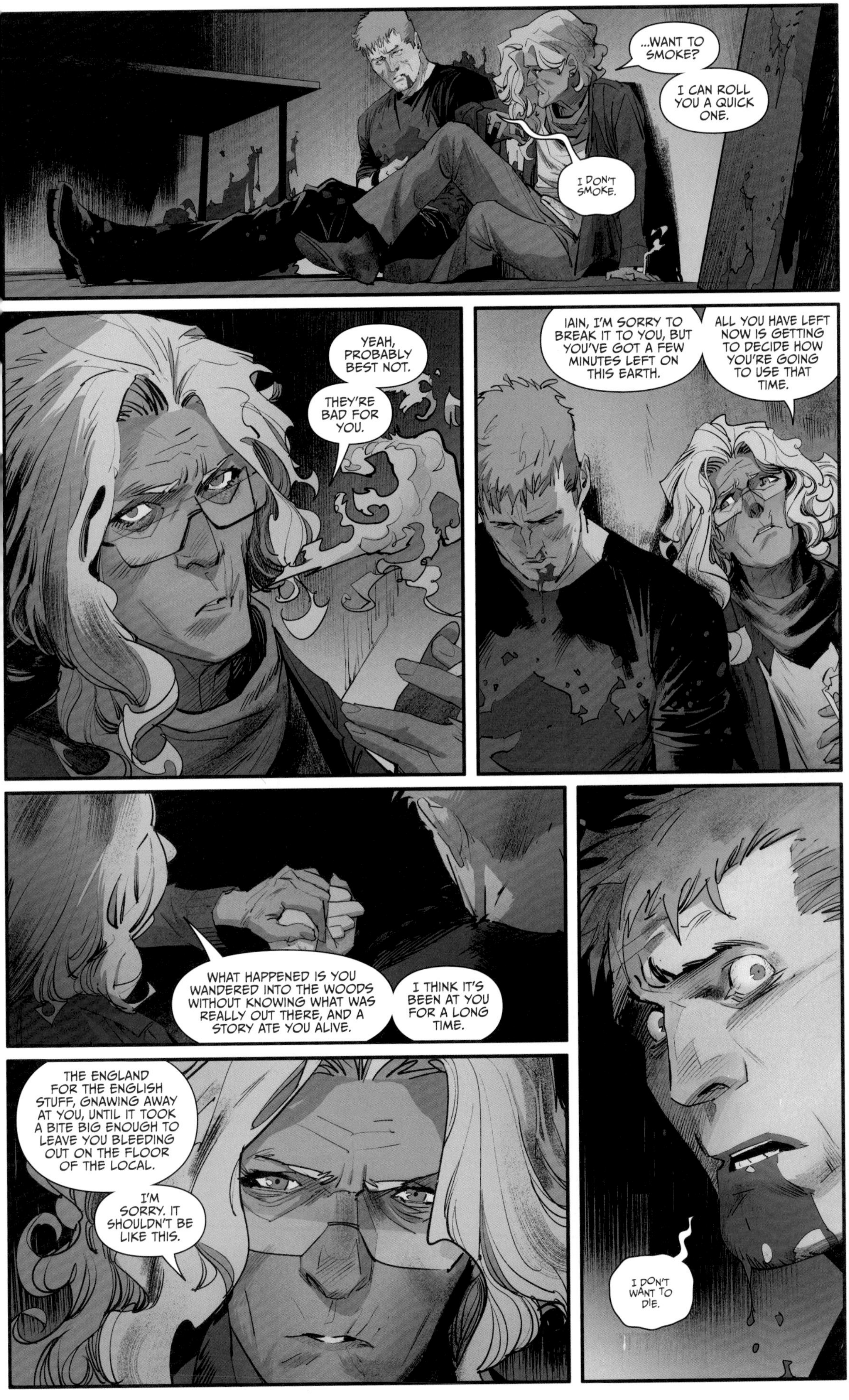
...WANT TO SMOKE?
I CAN ROLL YOU A QUICK ONE.
I DON'T SMOKE.
YEAH, PROBABLY BEST NOT.
THEY'RE BAD FOR YOU.
IAIN, I'M SORRY TO BREAK IT TO YOU, BUT YOU'VE GOT A FEW MINUTES LEFT ON THIS EARTH.
ALL YOU HAVE LEFT NOW IS GETTING TO DECIDE HOW YOU'RE GOING TO USE THAT TIME.
WHAT HAPPENED IS YOU WANDERED INTO THE WOODS WITHOUT KNOWING WHAT WAS REALLY OUT THERE, AND A STORY ATE YOU ALIVE.
I THINK IT'S BEEN AT YOU FOR A LONG TIME.
THE ENGLAND FOR THE ENGLISH STUFF, GNAWING AWAY AT YOU, UNTIL IT TOOK A BITE BIG ENOUGH TO LEAVE YOU BLEEDING OUT ON THE FLOOR OF THE LOCAL.
I'M SORRY. IT SHOULDN'T BE LIKE THIS.
I DON'T WANT TO DIE.

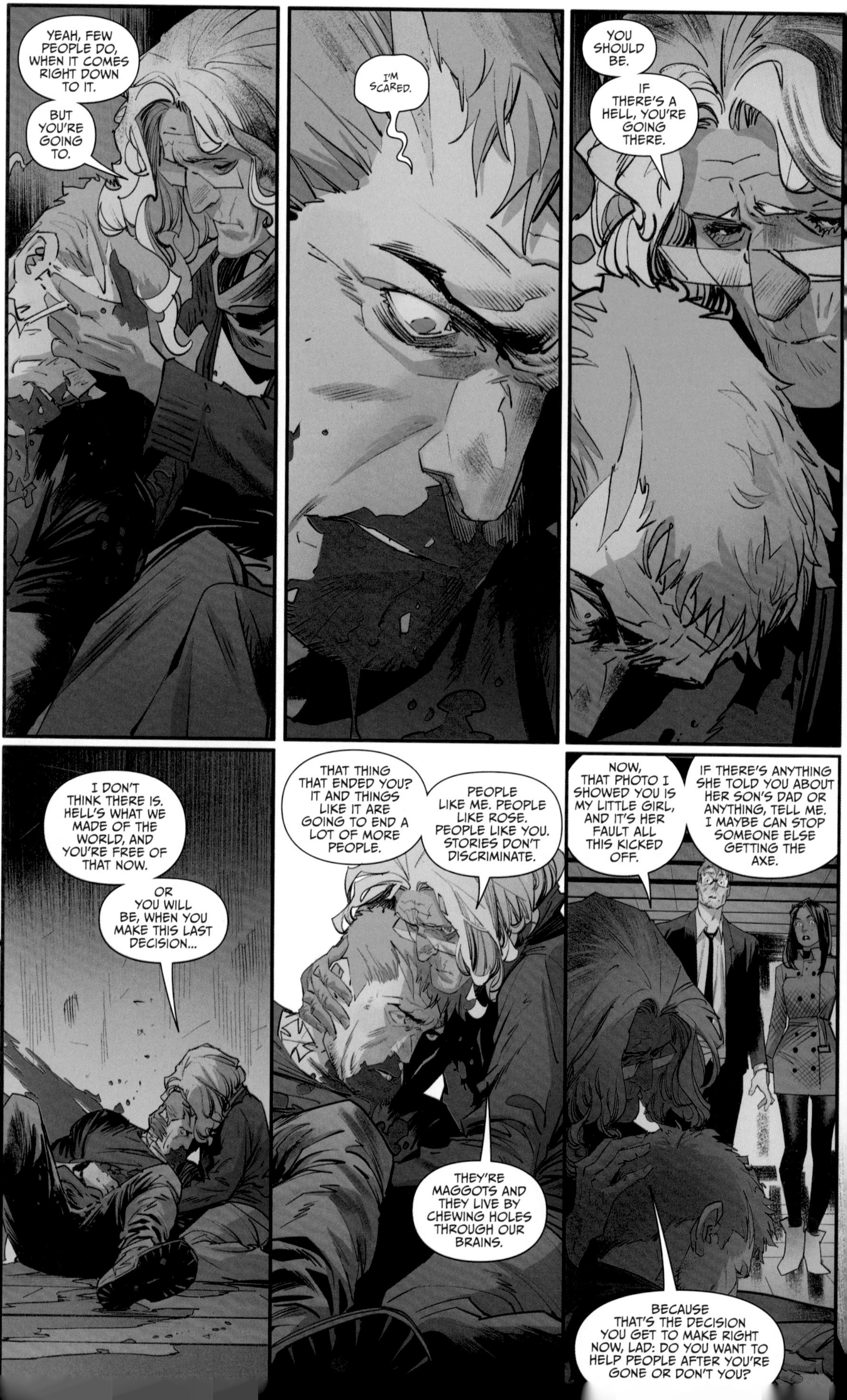
YEAH, FEW PEOPLE DO, WHEN IT COMES RIGHT DOWN TO IT.
BUT YOU'RE GOING TO.
I'M SCARED.
YOU SHOULD BE.
IF THERE'S A HELL, YOU'RE GOING THERE.
I DON'T THINK THERE IS. HELL'S WHAT WE MADE OF THE WORLD, AND YOU'RE FREE OF THAT NOW.
OR YOU WILL BE, WHEN YOU MAKE THIS LAST DECISION...
THAT THING THAT ENDED YOU? IT AND THINGS LIKE IT ARE GOING TO END A LOT OF MORE PEOPLE.
PEOPLE LIKE ME. PEOPLE LIKE ROSE. PEOPLE LIKE YOU. STORIES DON'T DISCRIMINATE.
THEY'RE MAGGOTS AND THEY LIVE BY CHEWING HOLES THROUGH OUR BRAINS.
NOW, THAT PHOTO I SHOWED YOU IS MY LITTLE GIRL, AND IT'S HER FAULT ALL THIS KICKED OFF.
IF THERE'S ANYTHING SHE TOLD YOU ABOUT HER SON'S DAD OR ANYTHING, TELL ME. I MAYBE CAN STOP SOMEONE ELSE GETTING THE AXE.
BECAUSE THAT'S THE DECISION YOU GET TO MAKE RIGHT NOW, LAD: DO YOU WANT TO HELP PEOPLE AFTER YOU'RE GONE OR DON'T YOU?

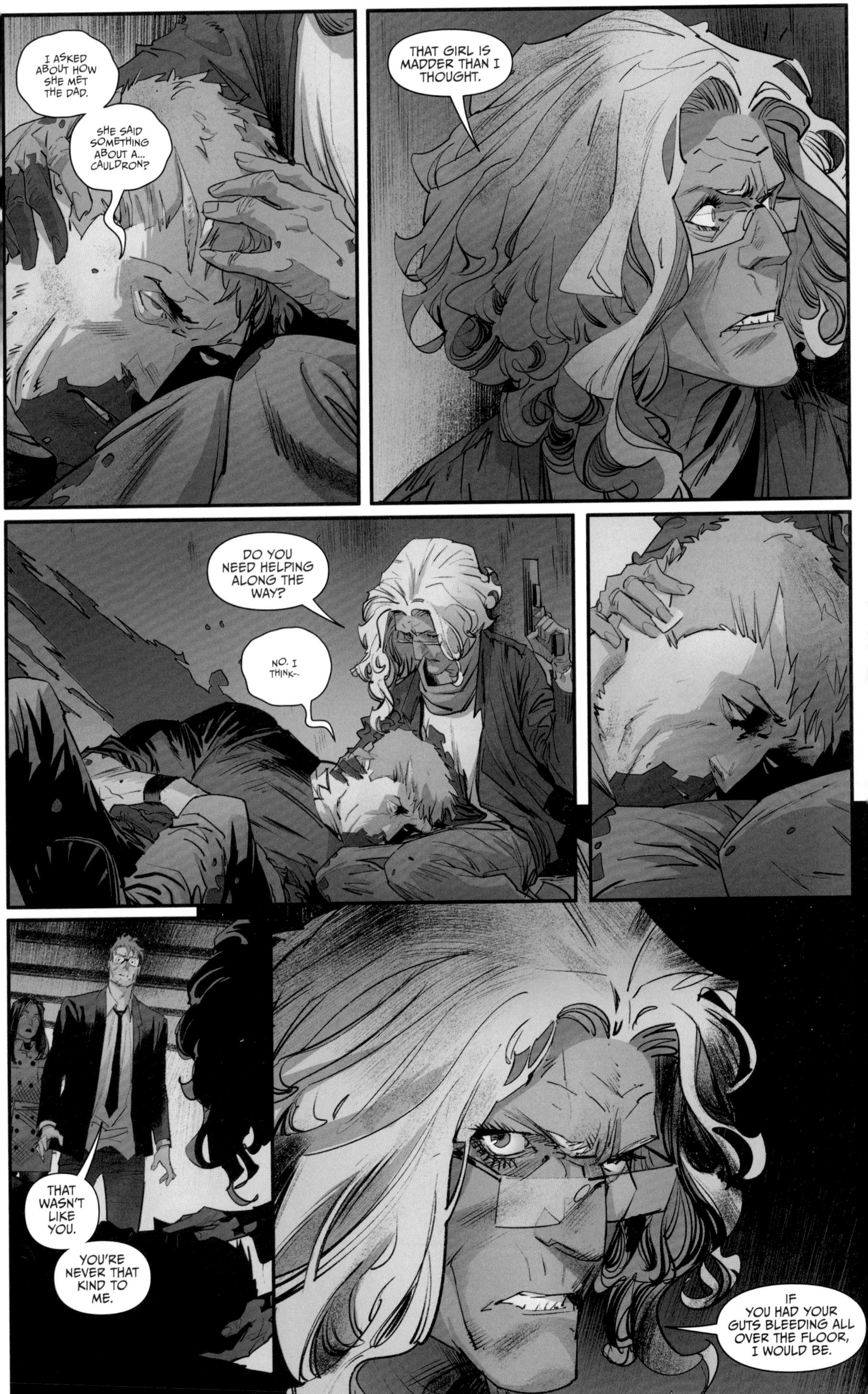
I ASKED ABOUT HOW SHE MET THE DAD.
SHE SAID SOMETHING ABOUT A... CAULDRON?
THAT GIRL IS MADDER THAN I THOUGHT.
DO YOU NEED HELPING ALONG THE WAY?
NO. I THINK--
THAT WASN'T LIKE YOU.
YOU'RE NEVER THAT KIND TO ME.
IF YOU HAD YOUR GUTS BLEEDING ALL OVER THE FLOOR, I WOULD BE.

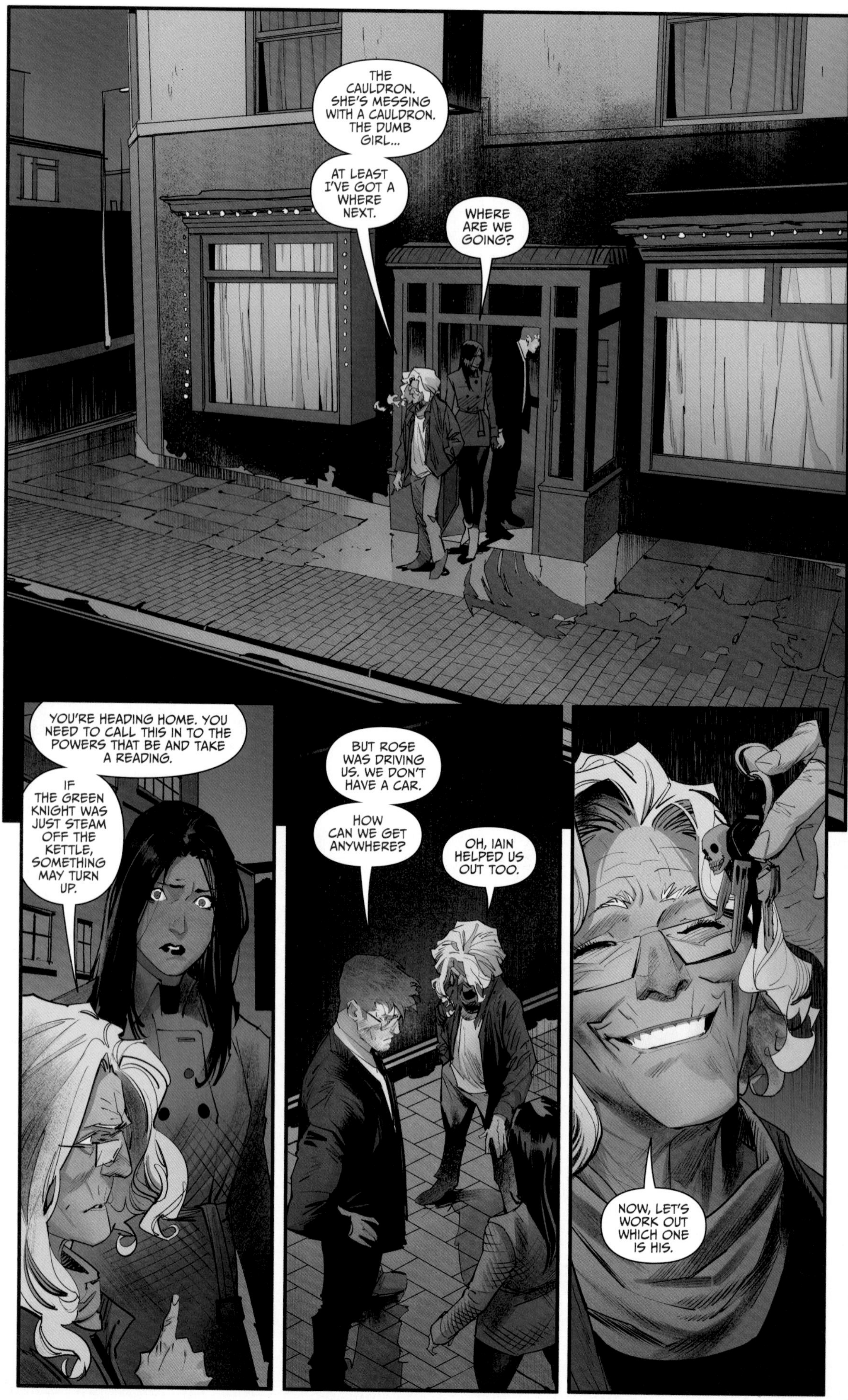
THE CAULDRON. SHE'S MESSING WITH A CAULDRON. THE DUMB GIRL...
AT LEAST I'VE GOT A WHERE NEXT.
WHERE ARE WE GOING?
YOU'RE HEADING HOME. YOU NEED TO CALL THIS IN TO THE POWERS THAT BE AND TAKE A READING.
IF THE GREEN KNIGHT WAS JUST STEAM OFF THE KETTLE, SOMETHING MAY TURN UP.
BUT ROSE WAS DRIVING US. WE DON'T HAVE A CAR.
HOW CAN WE GET ANYWHERE?
OH, IAIN HELPED US OUT TOO.
NOW, LET'S WORK OUT WHICH ONE IS HIS.

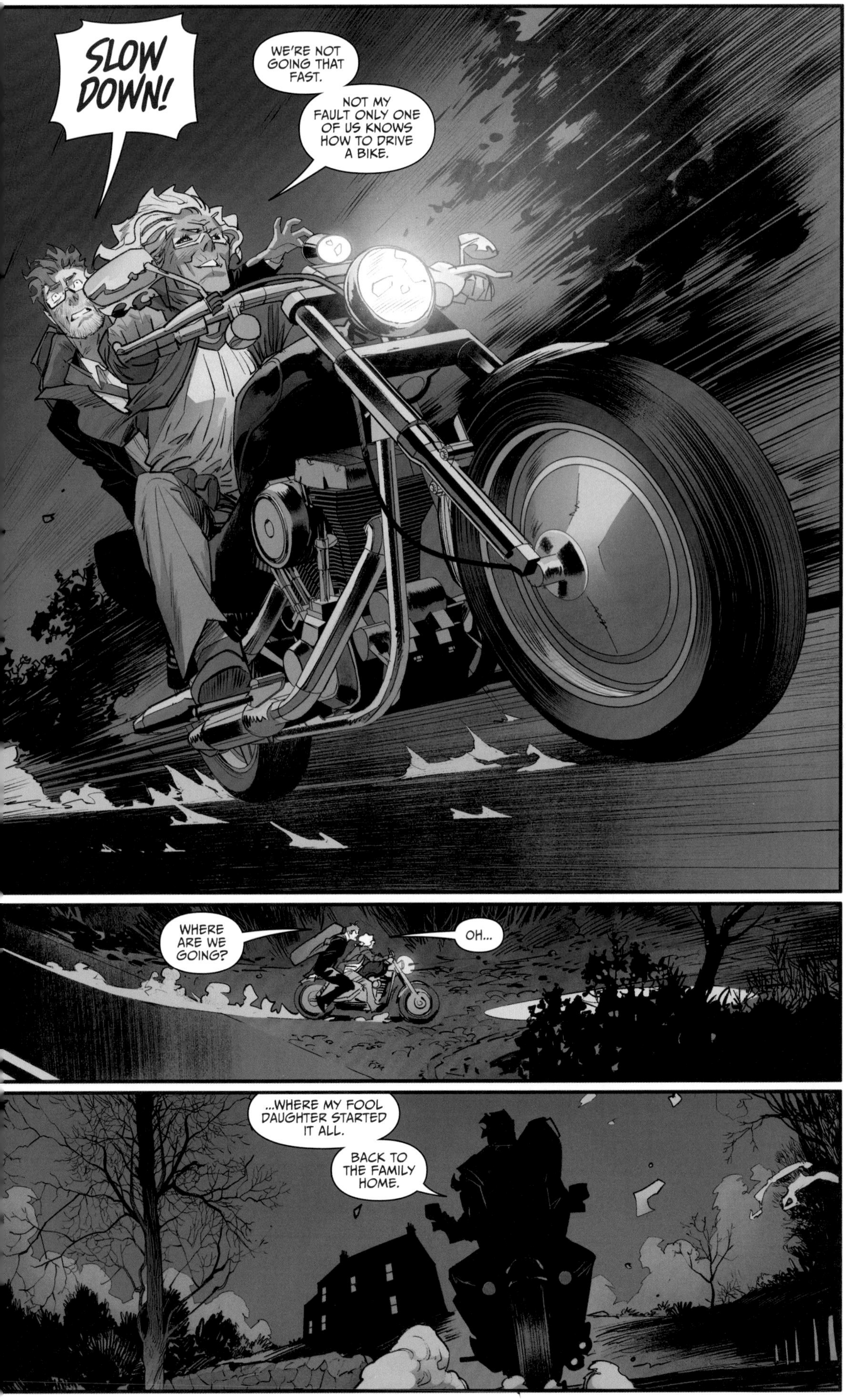
SLOW DOWN!
WE'RE NOT GOING THAT FAST.
NOT MY FAULT ONLY ONE OF US KNOWS HOW TO DRIVE A BIKE.
WHERE ARE WE GOING?
OH...
...WHERE MY FOOL DAUGHTER STARTED IT ALL.
BACK TO THE FAMILY HOME.

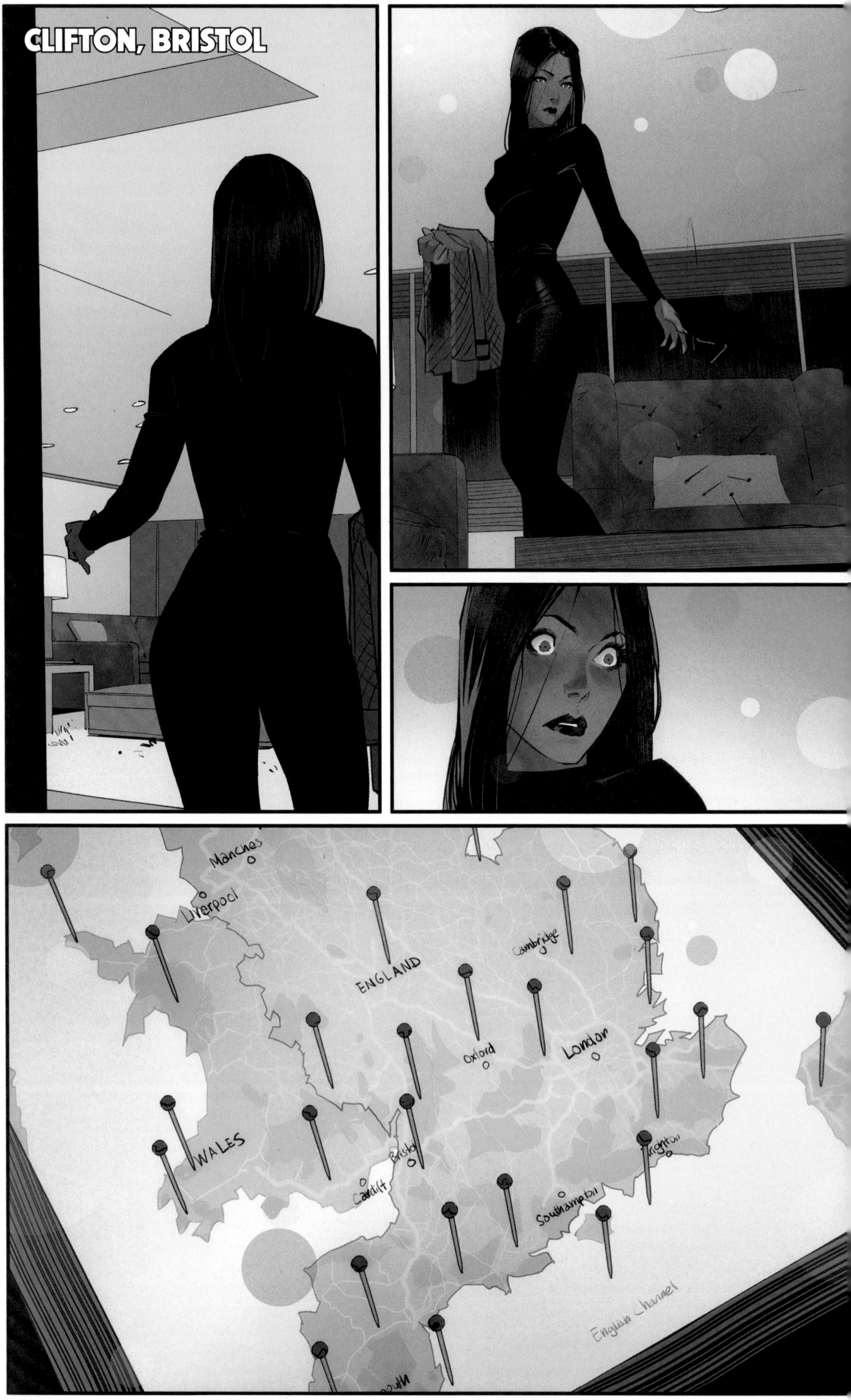
CLIFTON, BRISTOL
Manches
Liverpool
Cambridge
ENGLAND
Oxford
London
WALES
Bristol
Cardiff
Southampton
English Channel

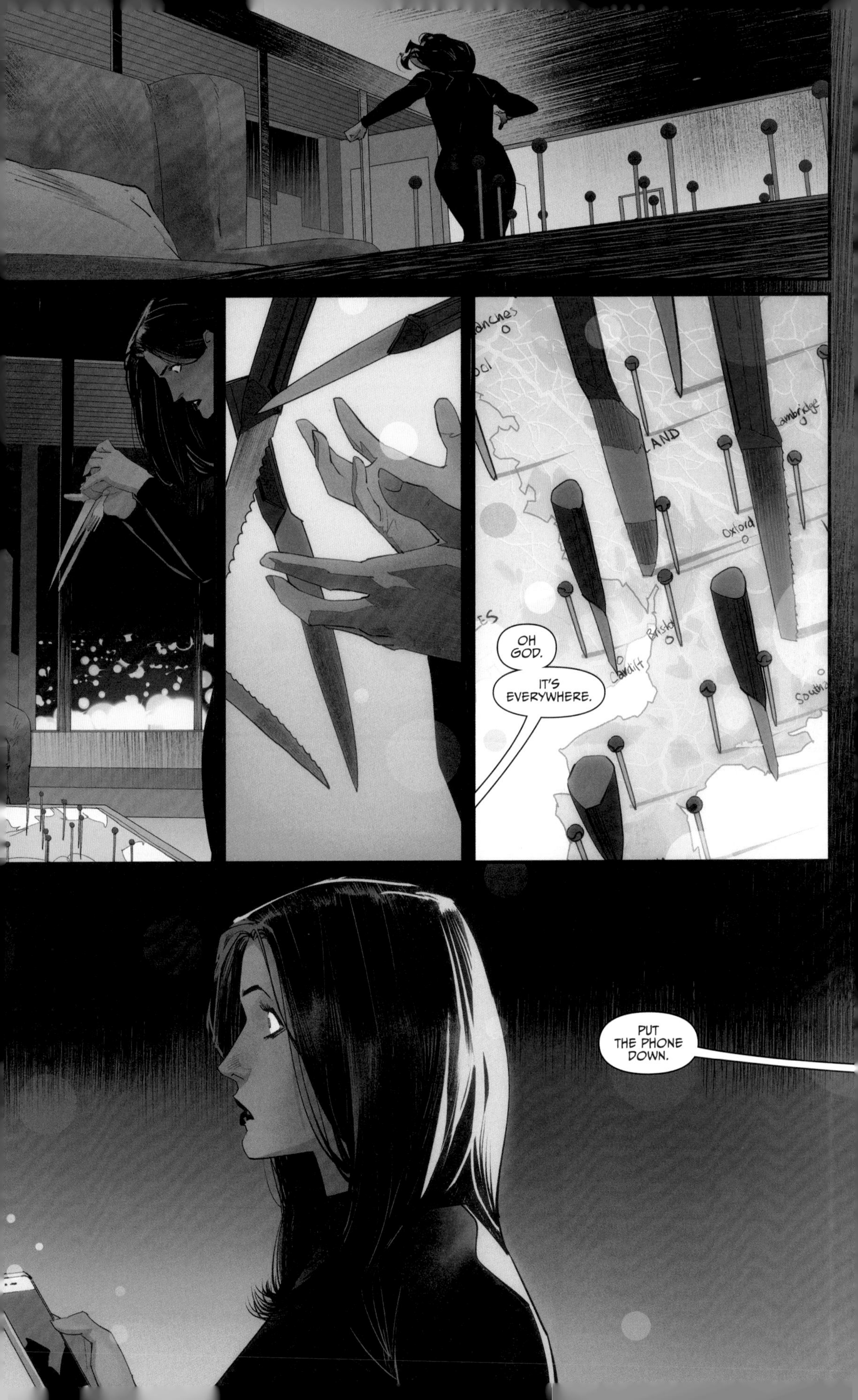
OH GOD.
IT'S EVERYWHERE.
PUT THE PHONE DOWN.

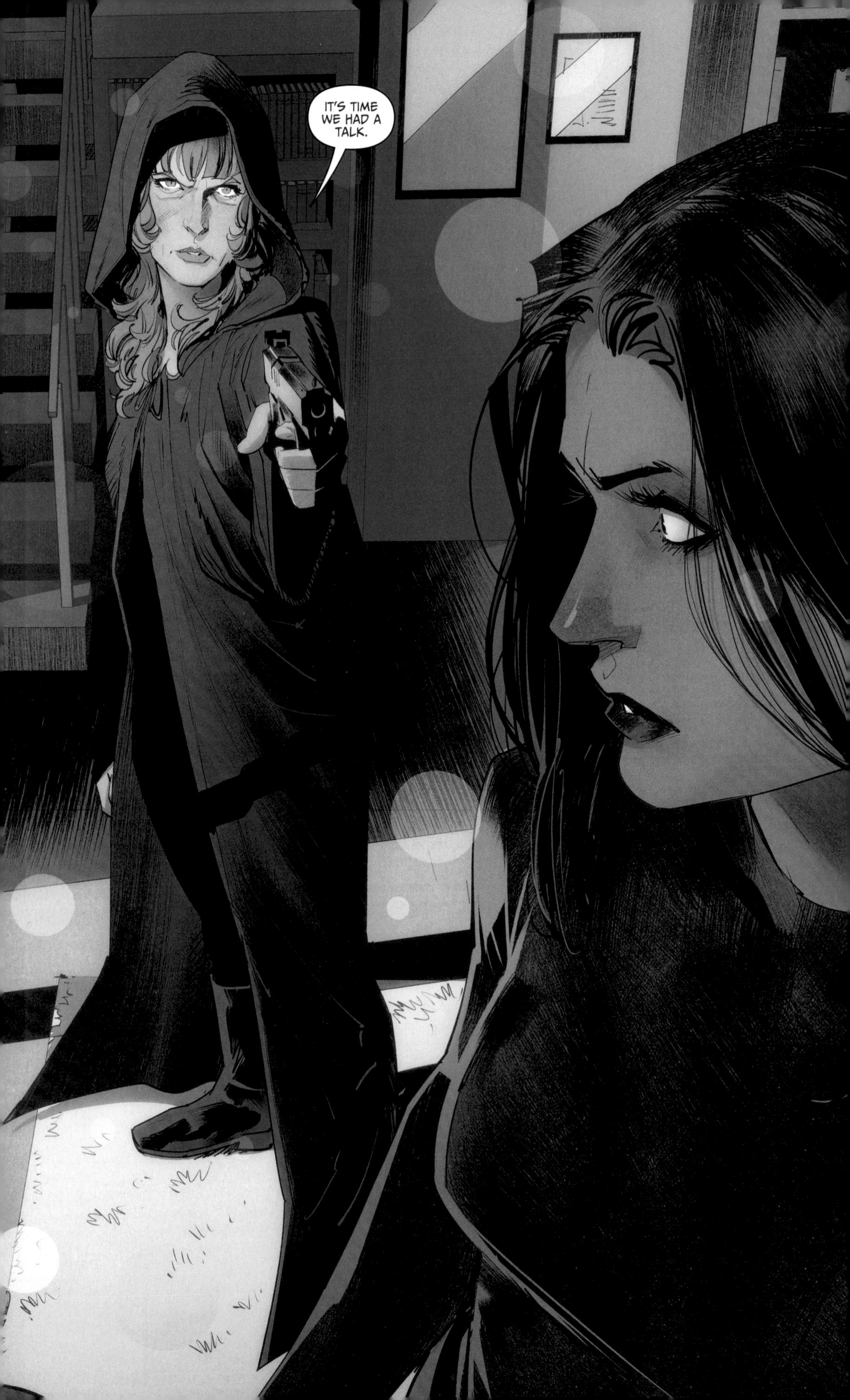
IT'S TIME WE HAD A TALK.

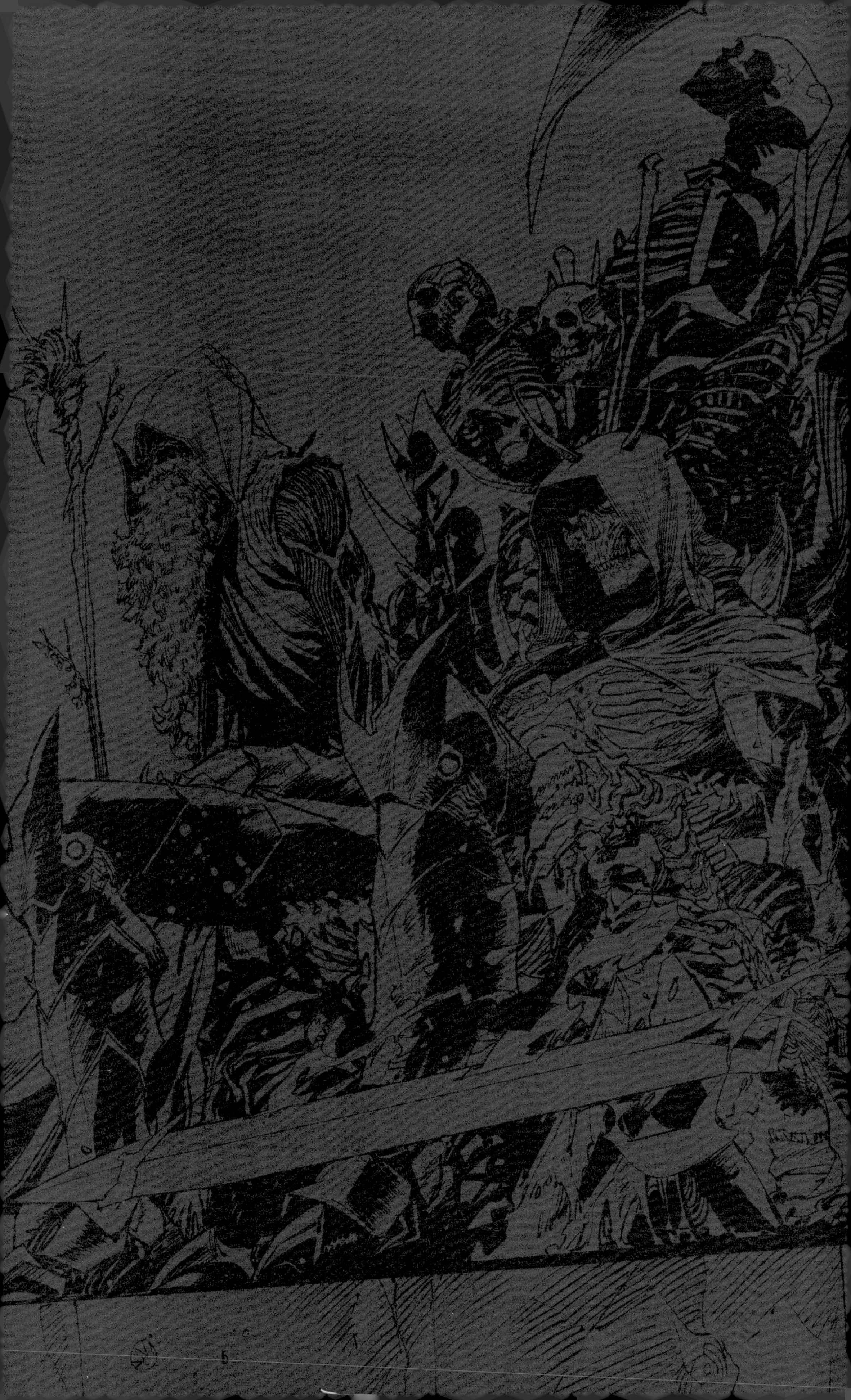

CHAPTER FIFTEEN

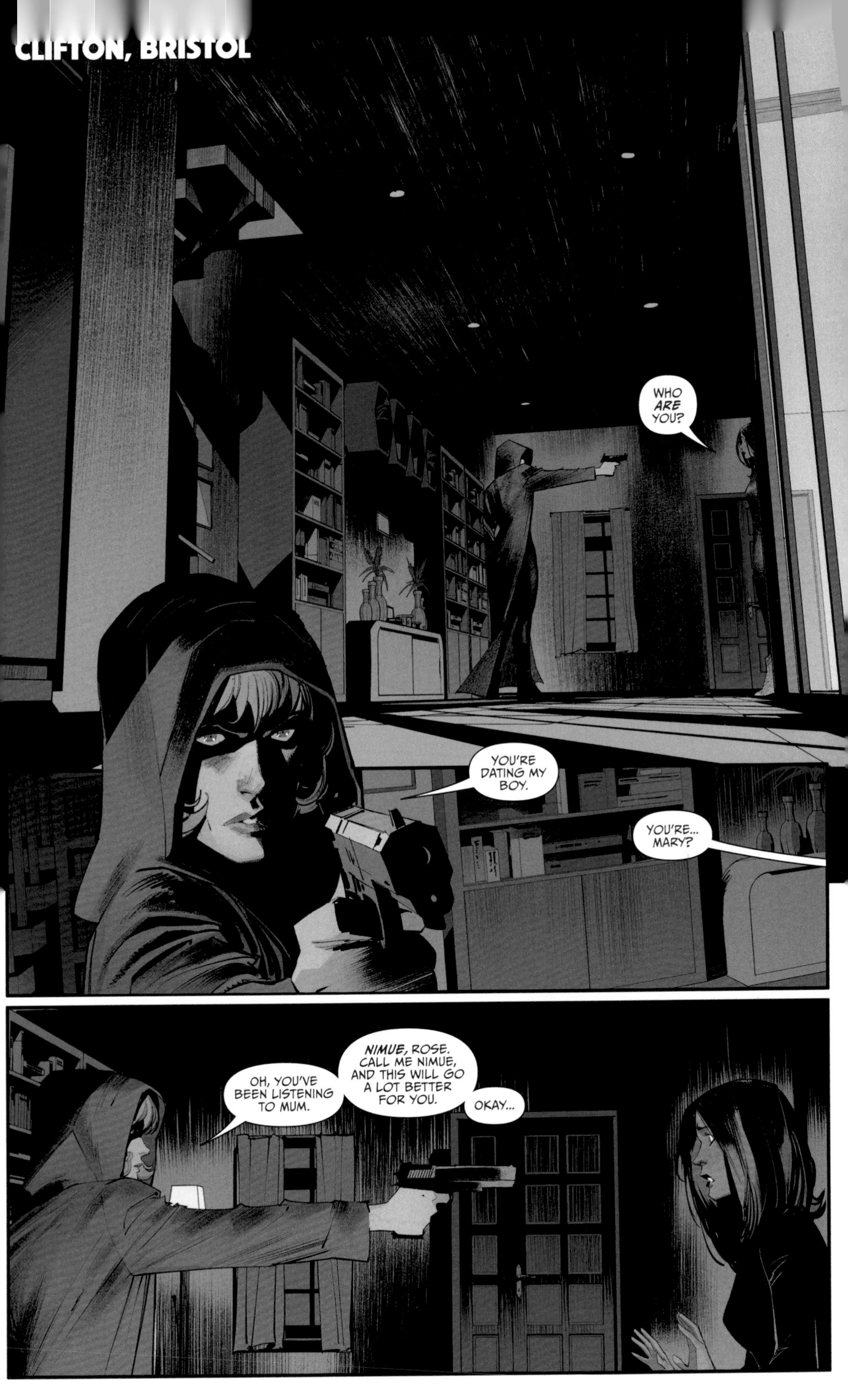
CLIFTON, BRISTOL
WHO *ARE* YOU?
YOU'RE DATING MY BOY.
YOU'RE... MARY?
OH, YOU'VE BEEN LISTENING TO MUM.
NIMUE, ROSE. CALL ME NIMUE, AND THIS WILL GO A LOT BETTER FOR YOU.
OKAY...

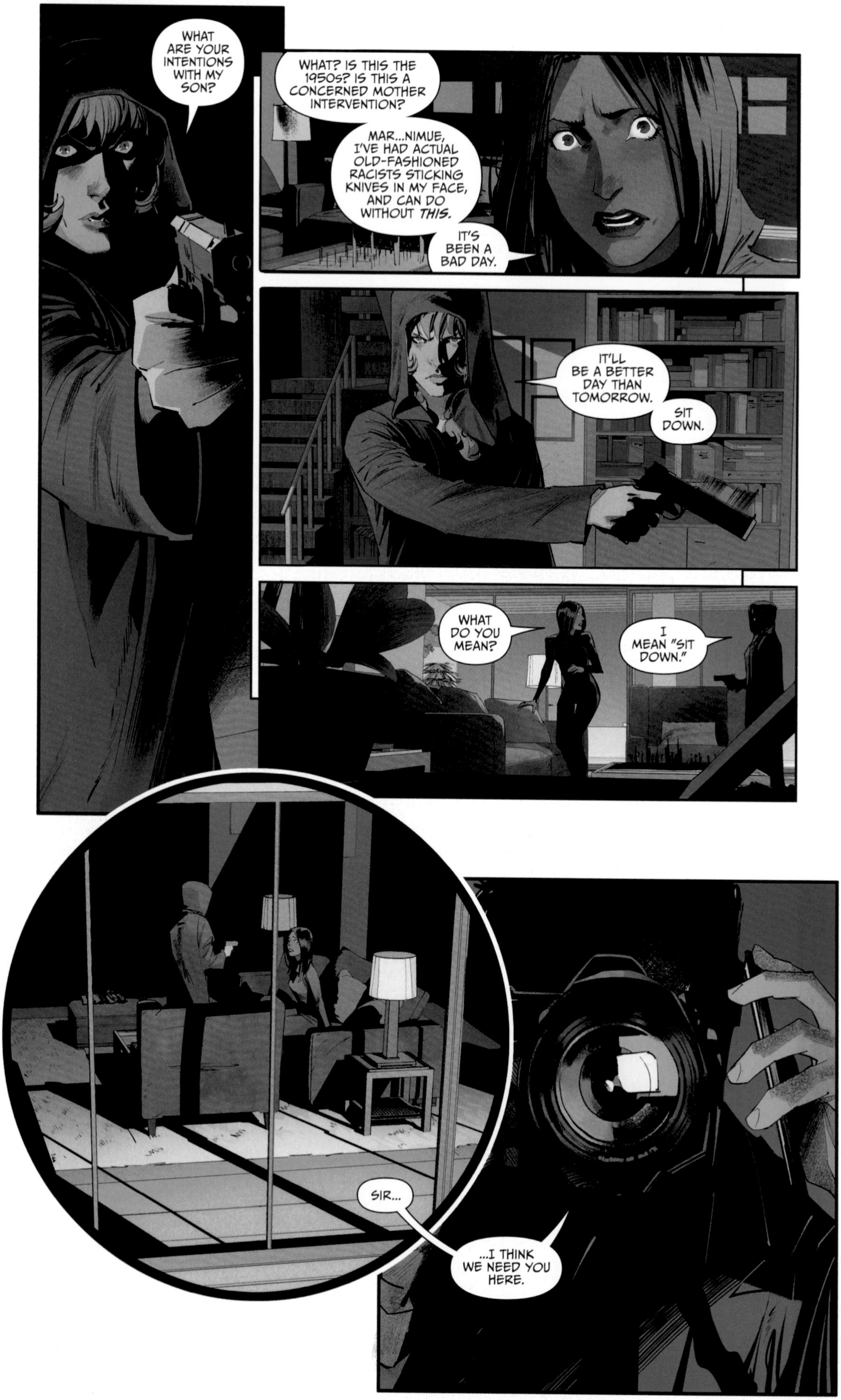
WHAT ARE YOUR INTENTIONS WITH MY SON?
WHAT? IS THIS THE 1950s? IS THIS A CONCERNED MOTHER INTERVENTION?
MAR...NIMUE, I'VE HAD ACTUAL OLD-FASHIONED RACISTS STICKING KNIVES IN MY FACE, AND CAN DO WITHOUT *THIS.*
IT'S BEEN A BAD DAY.
IT'LL BE A BETTER DAY THAN TOMORROW.
SIT DOWN.
WHAT DO YOU MEAN?
I MEAN "SIT DOWN."
SIR...
...I THINK WE NEED YOU HERE.

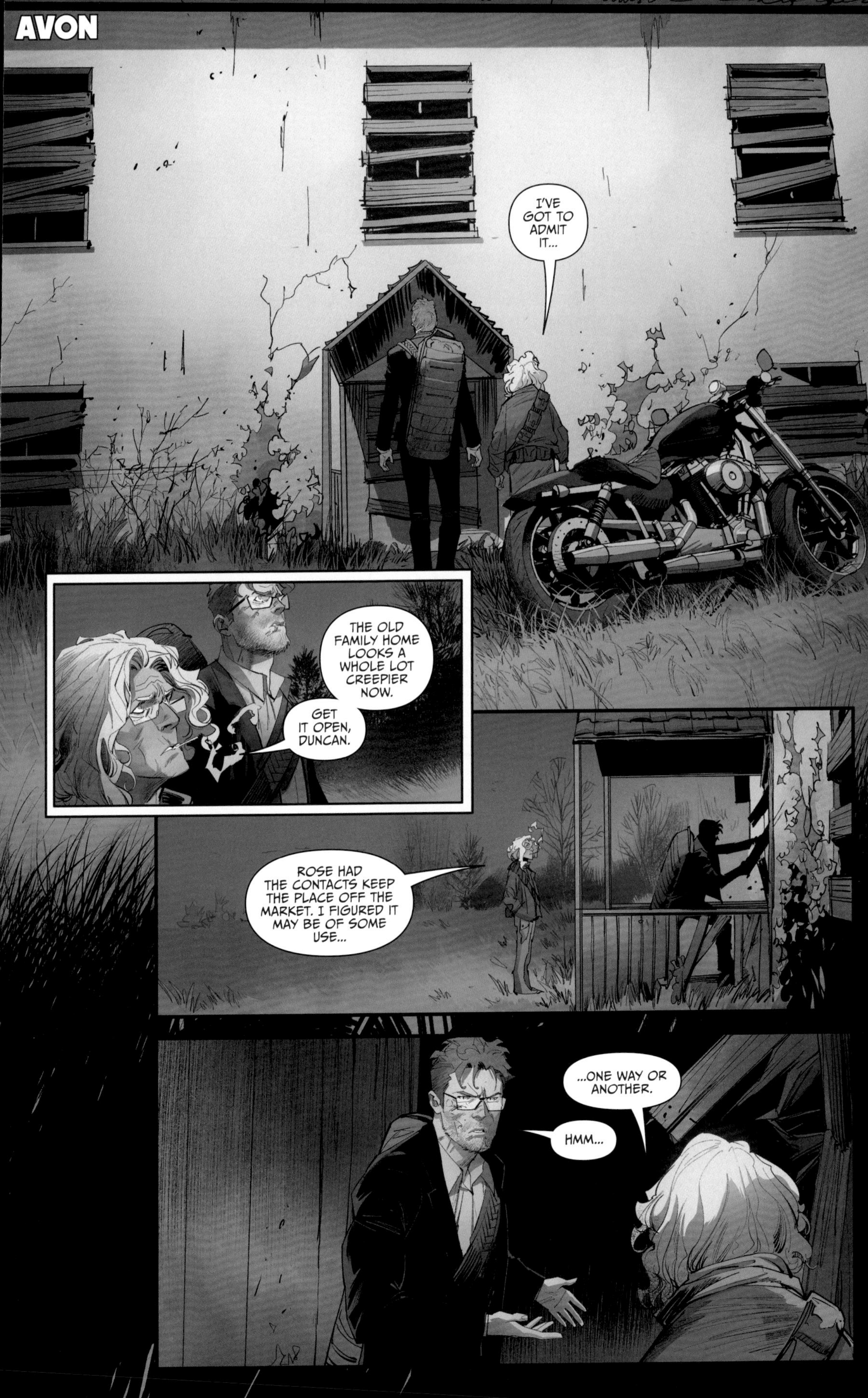
AVON
I'VE GOT TO ADMIT IT...
THE OLD FAMILY HOME LOOKS A WHOLE LOT CREEPIER NOW.
GET IT OPEN, DUNCAN.
ROSE HAD THE CONTACTS KEEP THE PLACE OFF THE MARKET. I FIGURED IT MAY BE OF SOME USE...
...ONE WAY OR ANOTHER.
HMM...

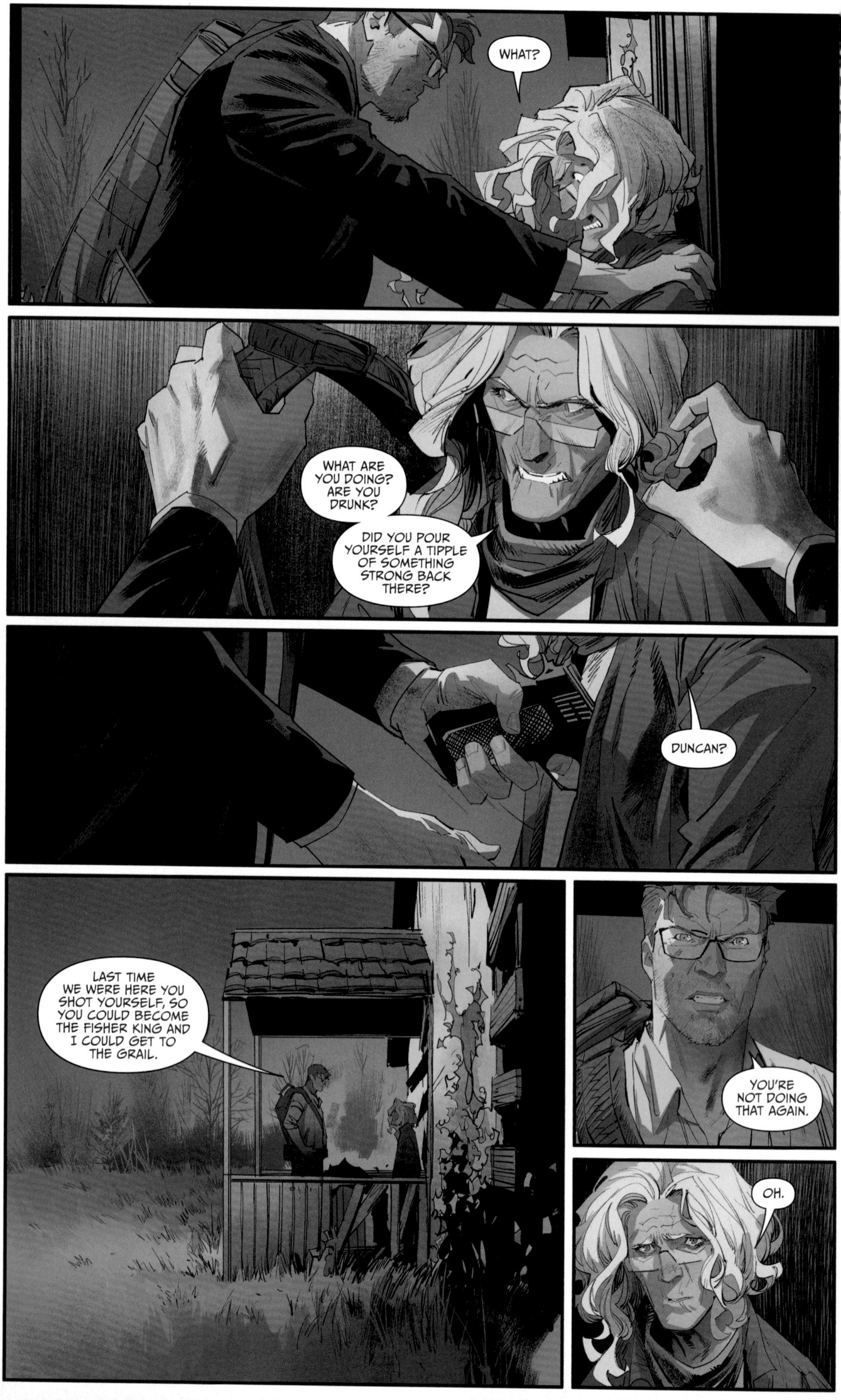
WHAT?
WHAT ARE YOU DOING? ARE YOU DRUNK?
DID YOU POUR YOURSELF A TIPPLE OF SOMETHING STRONG BACK THERE?
DUNCAN?
LAST TIME WE WERE HERE YOU SHOT YOURSELF, SO YOU COULD BECOME THE FISHER KING AND I COULD GET TO THE GRAIL.
YOU'RE NOT DOING THAT AGAIN.
OH.

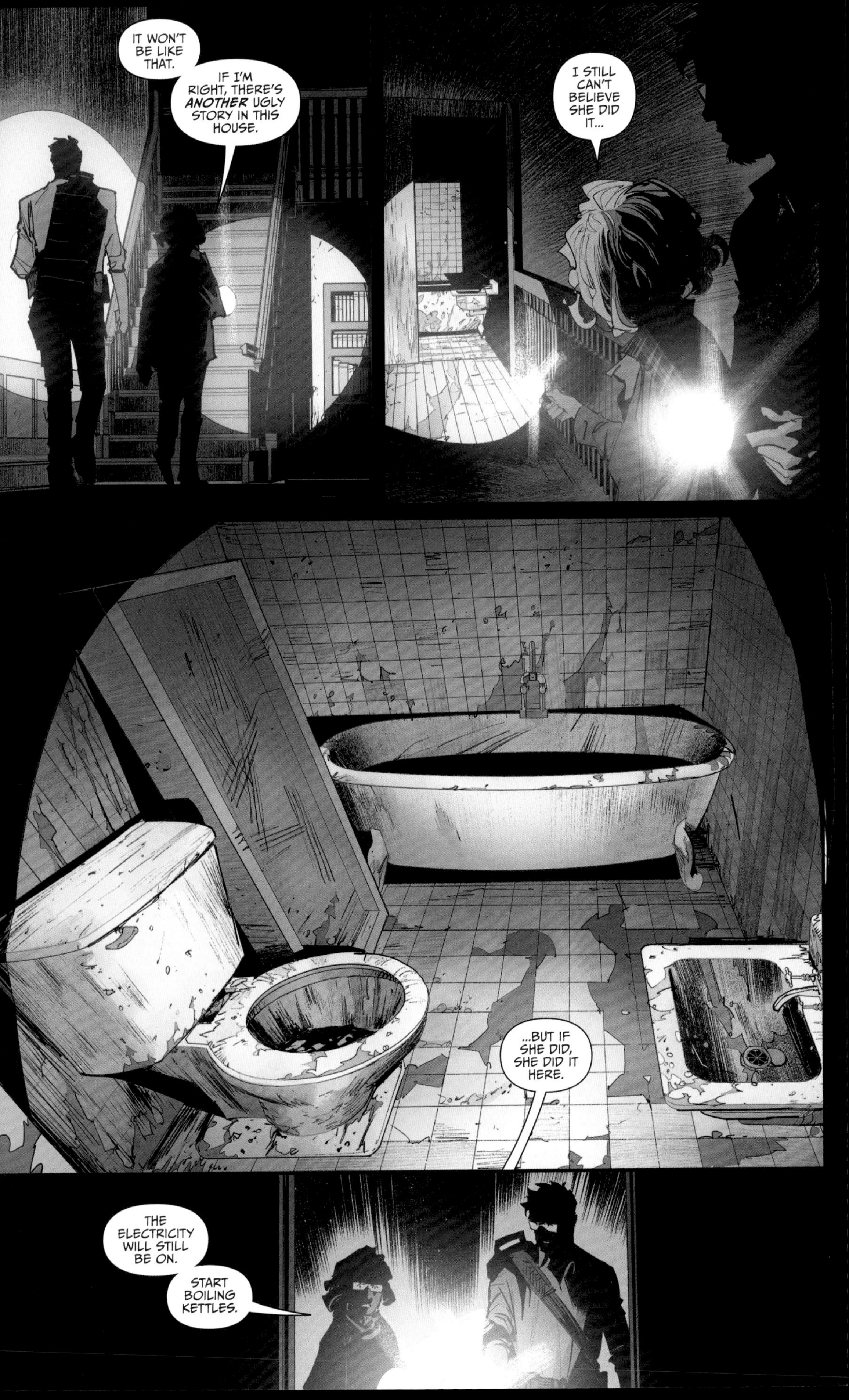
IT WON'T BE LIKE THAT.
IF I'M RIGHT, THERE'S ANOTHER UGLY STORY IN THIS HOUSE.
I STILL CAN'T BELIEVE SHE DID IT...
...BUT IF SHE DID, SHE DID IT HERE.
THE ELECTRICITY WILL STILL BE ON.
START BOILING KETTLES.

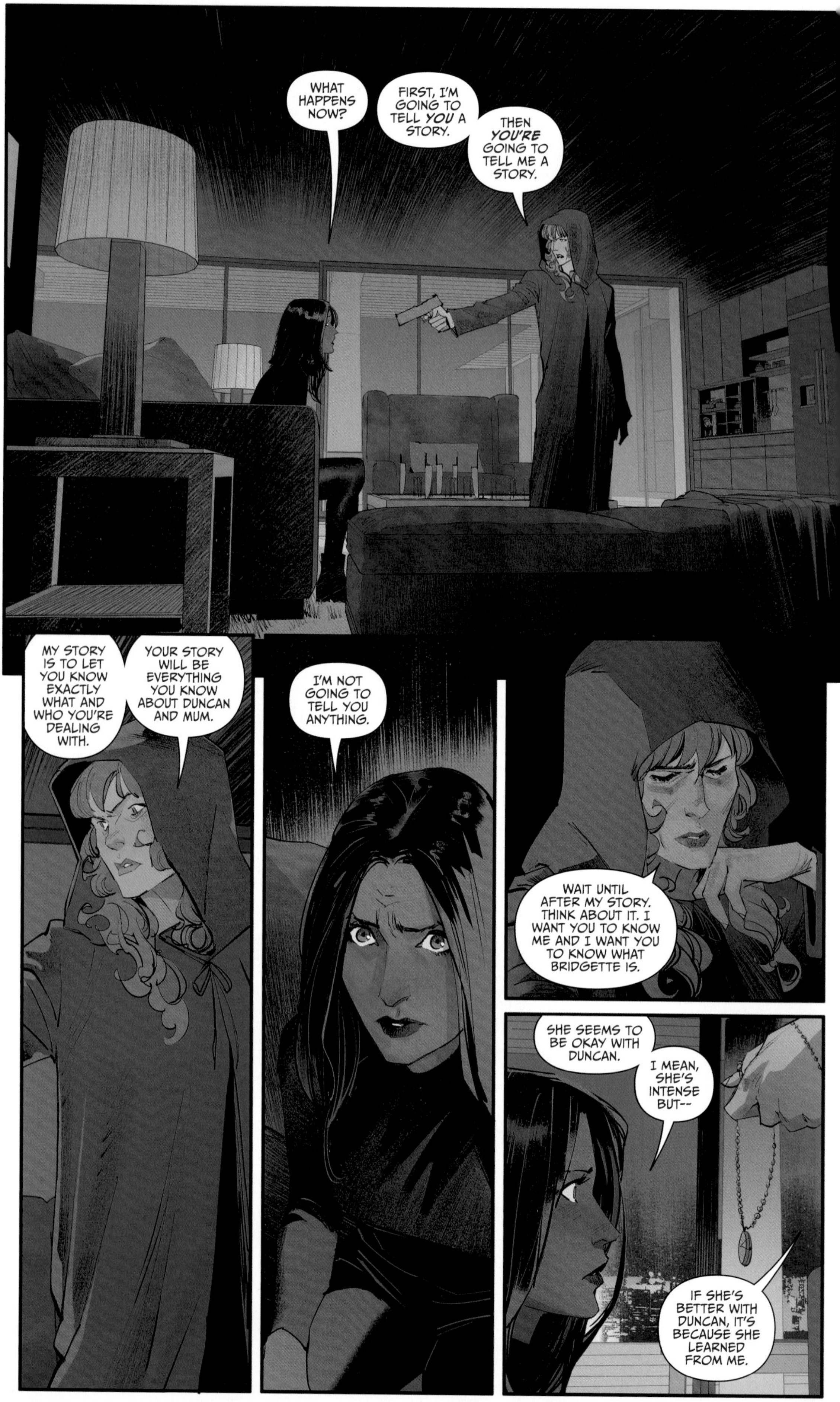
WHAT HAPPENS NOW?
FIRST, I'M GOING TO TELL *YOU* A STORY.
THEN *YOU'RE* GOING TO TELL ME A STORY.
MY STORY IS TO LET YOU KNOW EXACTLY WHAT AND WHO YOU'RE DEALING WITH.
YOUR STORY WILL BE EVERYTHING YOU KNOW ABOUT DUNCAN AND MUM.
I'M NOT GOING TO TELL YOU ANYTHING.
WAIT UNTIL AFTER MY STORY. THINK ABOUT IT. I WANT YOU TO KNOW ME AND I WANT YOU TO KNOW WHAT BRIDGETTE IS.
SHE SEEMS TO BE OKAY WITH DUNCAN.
I MEAN, SHE'S INTENSE BUT--
IF SHE'S BETTER WITH DUNCAN, IT'S BECAUSE SHE LEARNED FROM ME.

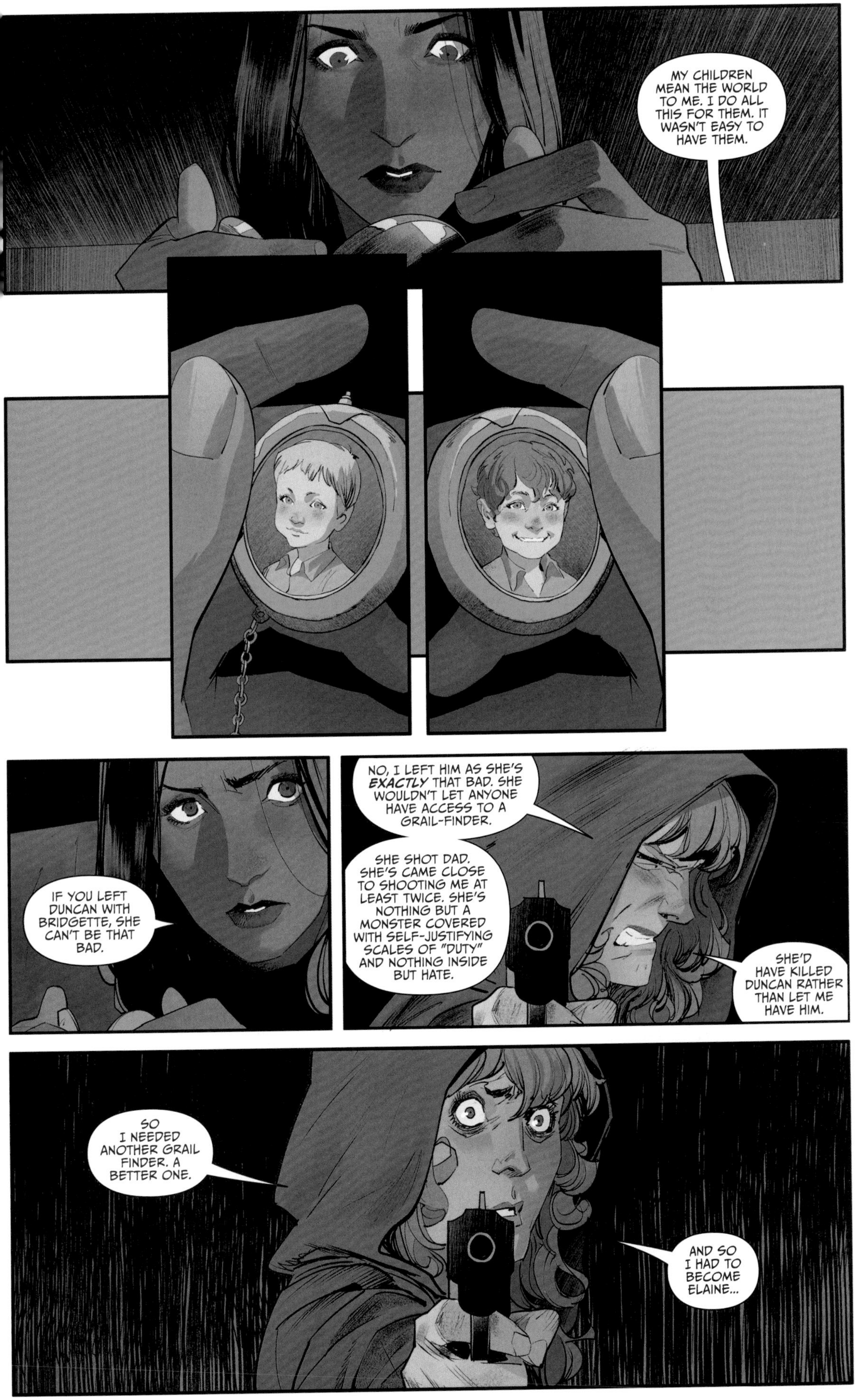
MY CHILDREN MEAN THE WORLD TO ME. I DO ALL THIS FOR THEM. IT WASN'T EASY TO HAVE THEM.
IF YOU LEFT DUNCAN WITH BRIDGETTE, SHE CAN'T BE THAT BAD.
NO, I LEFT HIM AS SHE'S *EXACTLY* THAT BAD. SHE WOULDN'T LET ANYONE HAVE ACCESS TO A GRAIL-FINDER.
SHE SHOT DAD. SHE'S CAME CLOSE TO SHOOTING ME AT LEAST TWICE. SHE'S NOTHING BUT A MONSTER COVERED WITH SELF-JUSTIFYING SCALES OF "DUTY" AND NOTHING INSIDE BUT HATE.
SHE'D HAVE KILLED DUNCAN RATHER THAN LET ME HAVE HIM.
SO I NEEDED ANOTHER GRAIL FINDER. A BETTER ONE.
AND SO I HAD TO BECOME ELAINE...

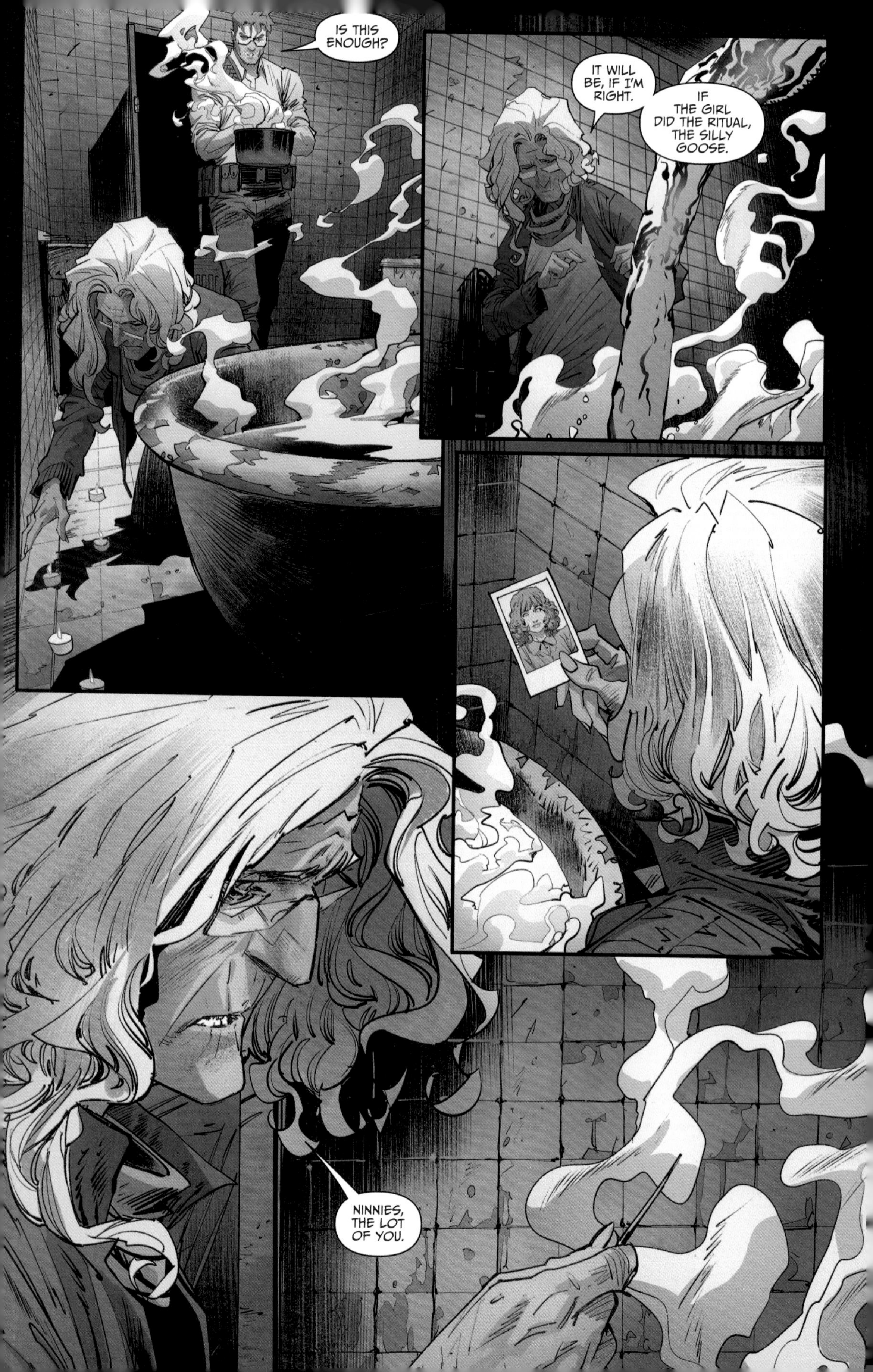
IS THIS ENOUGH?
IT WILL BE, IF I'M RIGHT.
IF THE GIRL DID THE RITUAL, THE SILLY GOOSE.
NINNIES, THE LOT OF YOU.

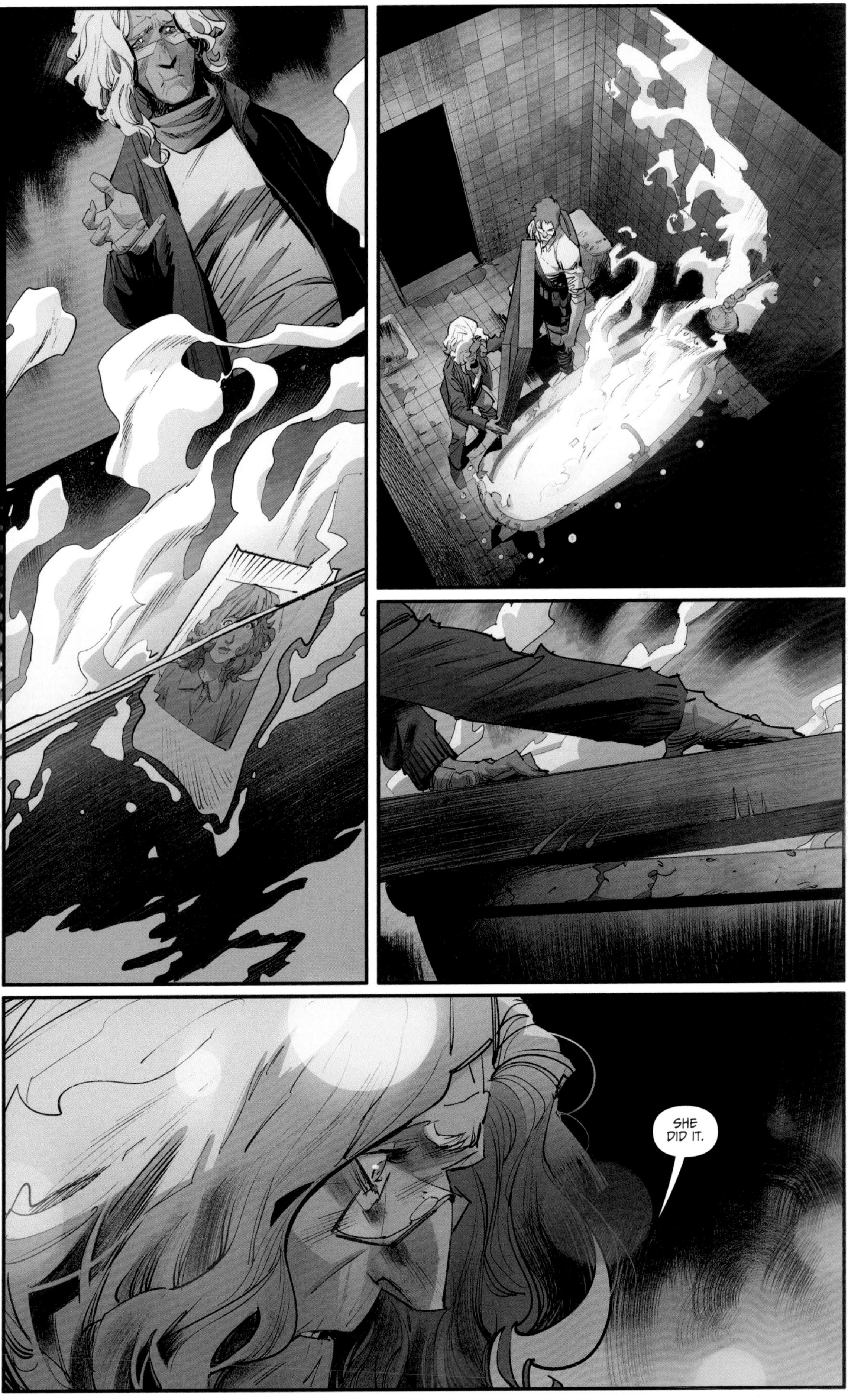
SHE DID IT.

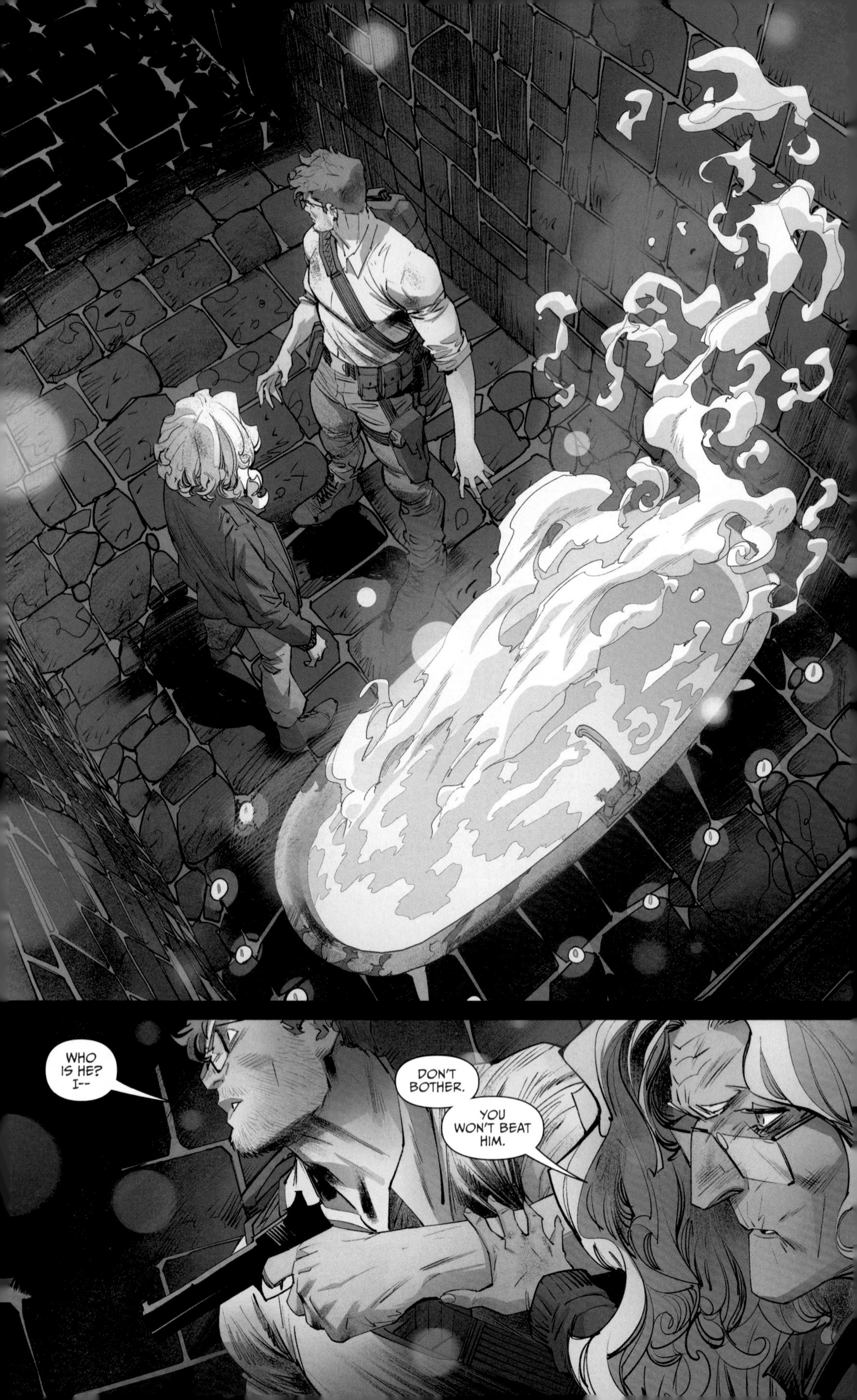
WHO IS HE? I--
DON'T BOTHER.
YOU WON'T BEAT HIM.

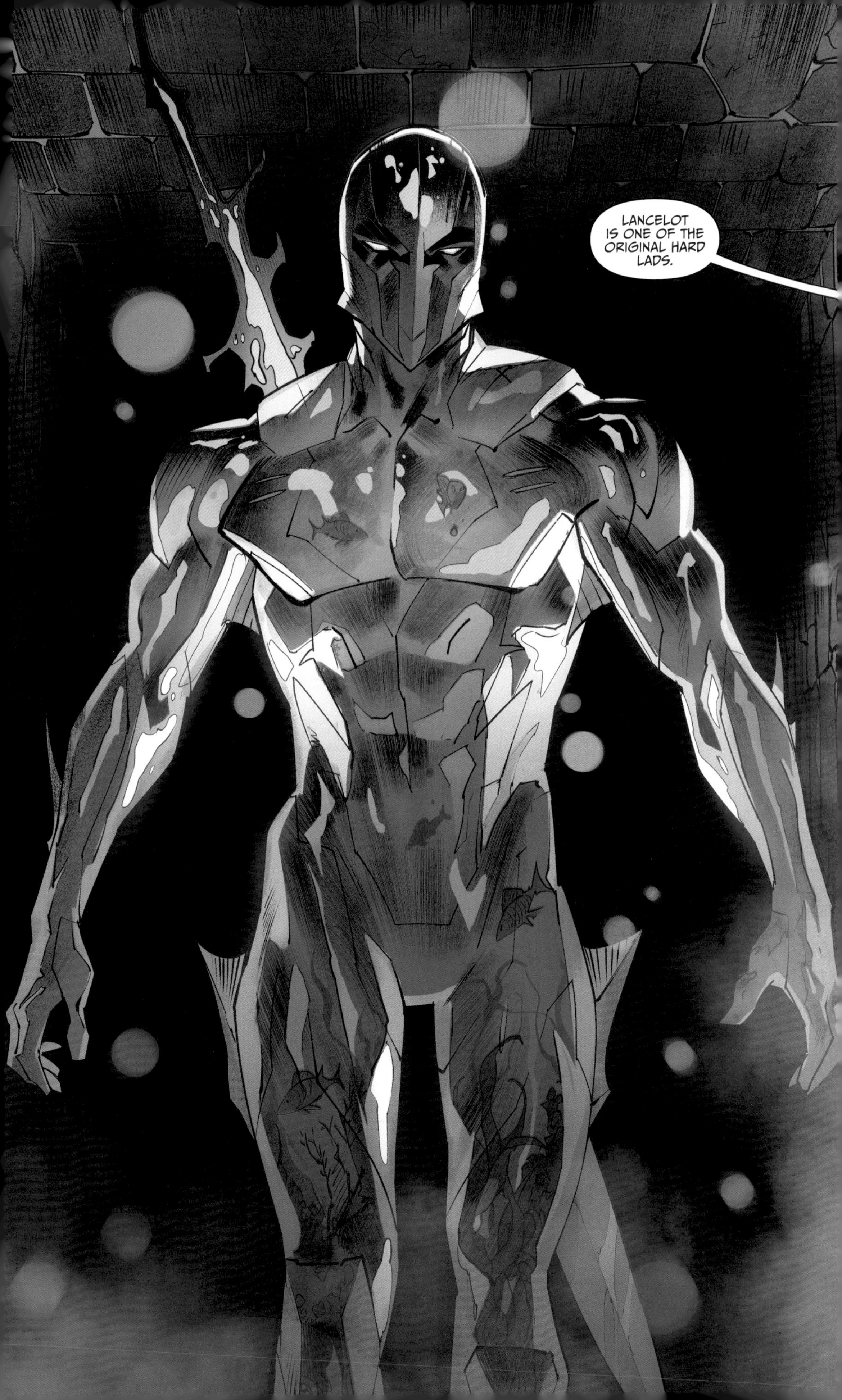
LANCELOT IS ONE OF THE ORIGINAL HARD LADS.

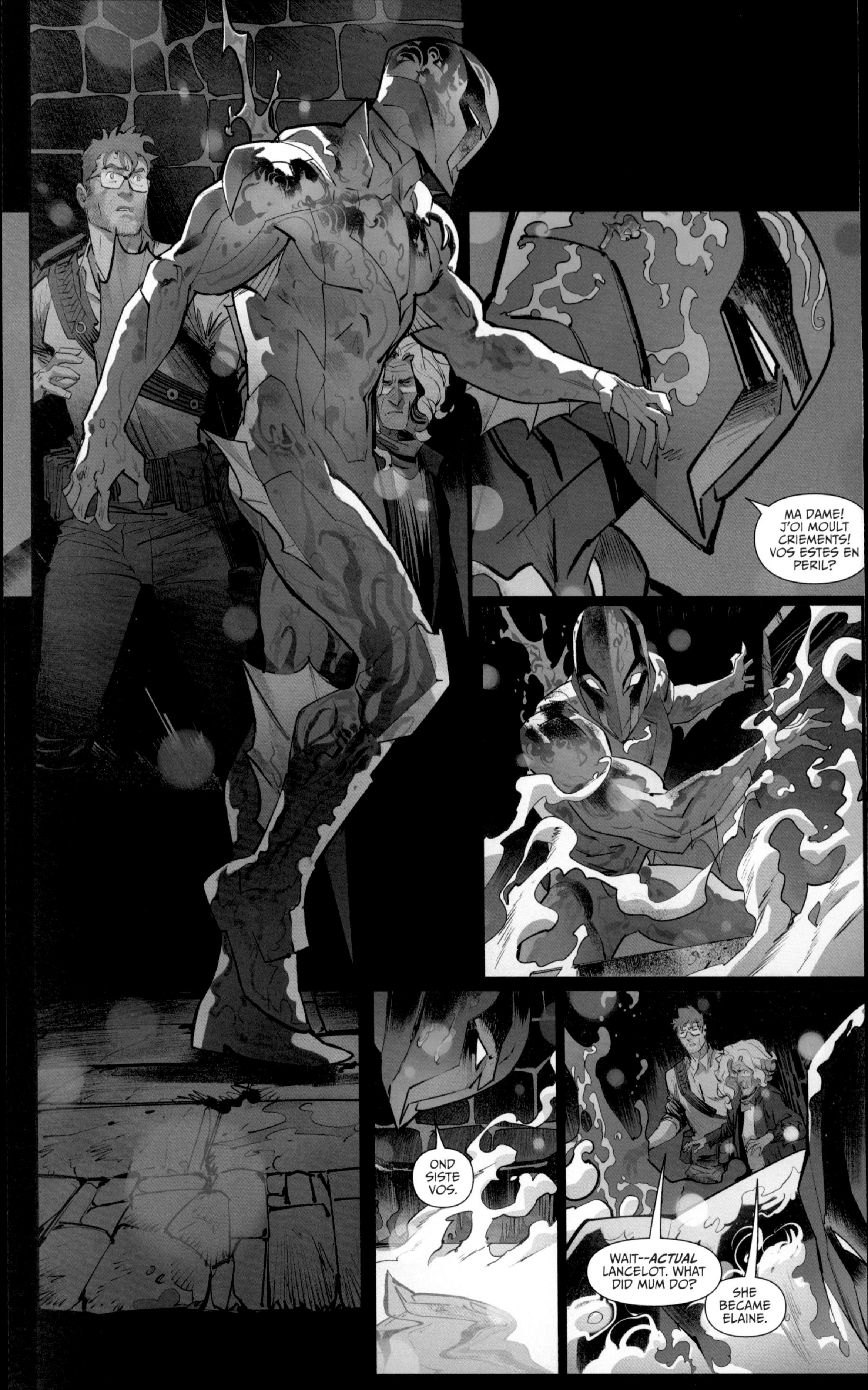
MA DAME! J'OI MOULT CRIEMENTS! VOS ESTES EN PERIL?
OND SISTE VOS.
WAIT--*ACTUAL* LANCELOT. WHAT DID MUM DO?
SHE BECAME ELAINE.

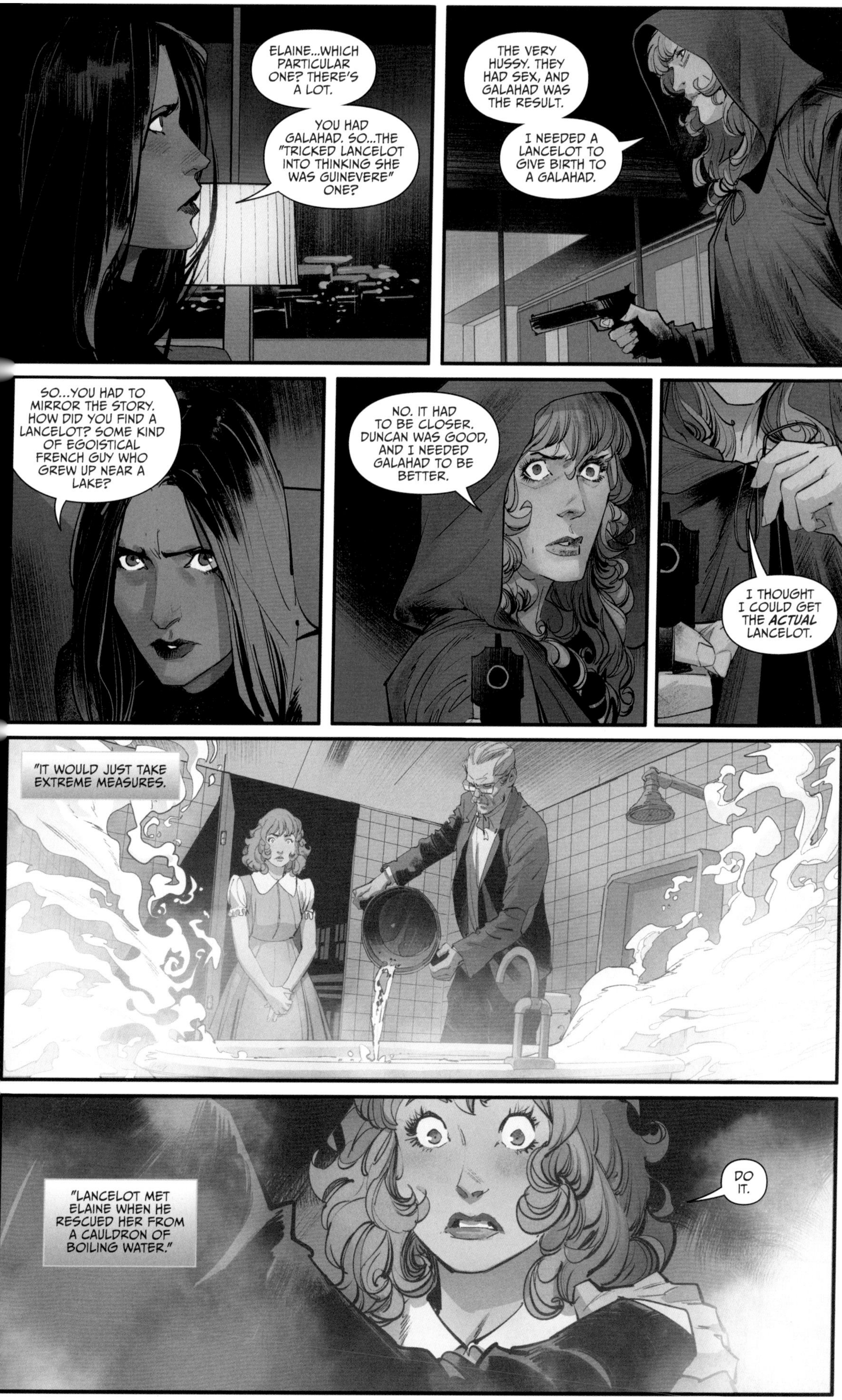
ELAINE...WHICH PARTICULAR ONE? THERE'S A LOT.
YOU HAD GALAHAD. SO...THE "TRICKED LANCELOT INTO THINKING SHE WAS GUINEVERE" ONE?
THE VERY HUSSY. THEY HAD SEX, AND GALAHAD WAS THE RESULT.
I NEEDED A LANCELOT TO GIVE BIRTH TO A GALAHAD.
SO...YOU HAD TO MIRROR THE STORY. HOW DID YOU FIND A LANCELOT? SOME KIND OF EGOISTICAL FRENCH GUY WHO GREW UP NEAR A LAKE?
NO. IT HAD TO BE CLOSER. DUNCAN WAS GOOD, AND I NEEDED GALAHAD TO BE BETTER.
I THOUGHT I COULD GET THE *ACTUAL* LANCELOT.
"IT WOULD JUST TAKE EXTREME MEASURES.
"LANCELOT MET ELAINE WHEN HE RESCUED HER FROM A CAULDRON OF BOILING WATER."
DO IT.

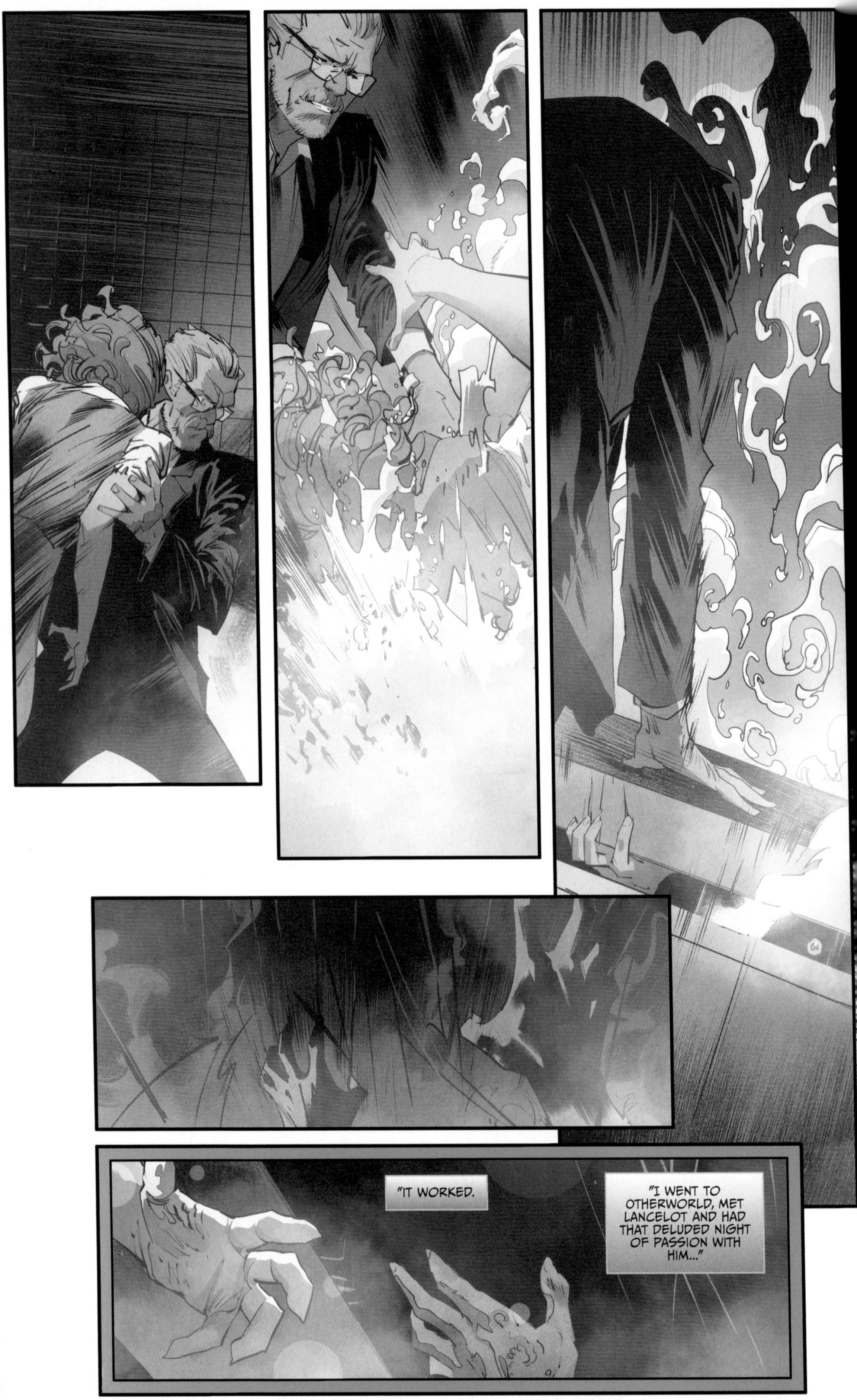

"IT WORKED.
"I WENT TO OTHERWORLD, MET LANCELOT AND HAD THAT DELUDED NIGHT OF PASSION WITH HIM..."

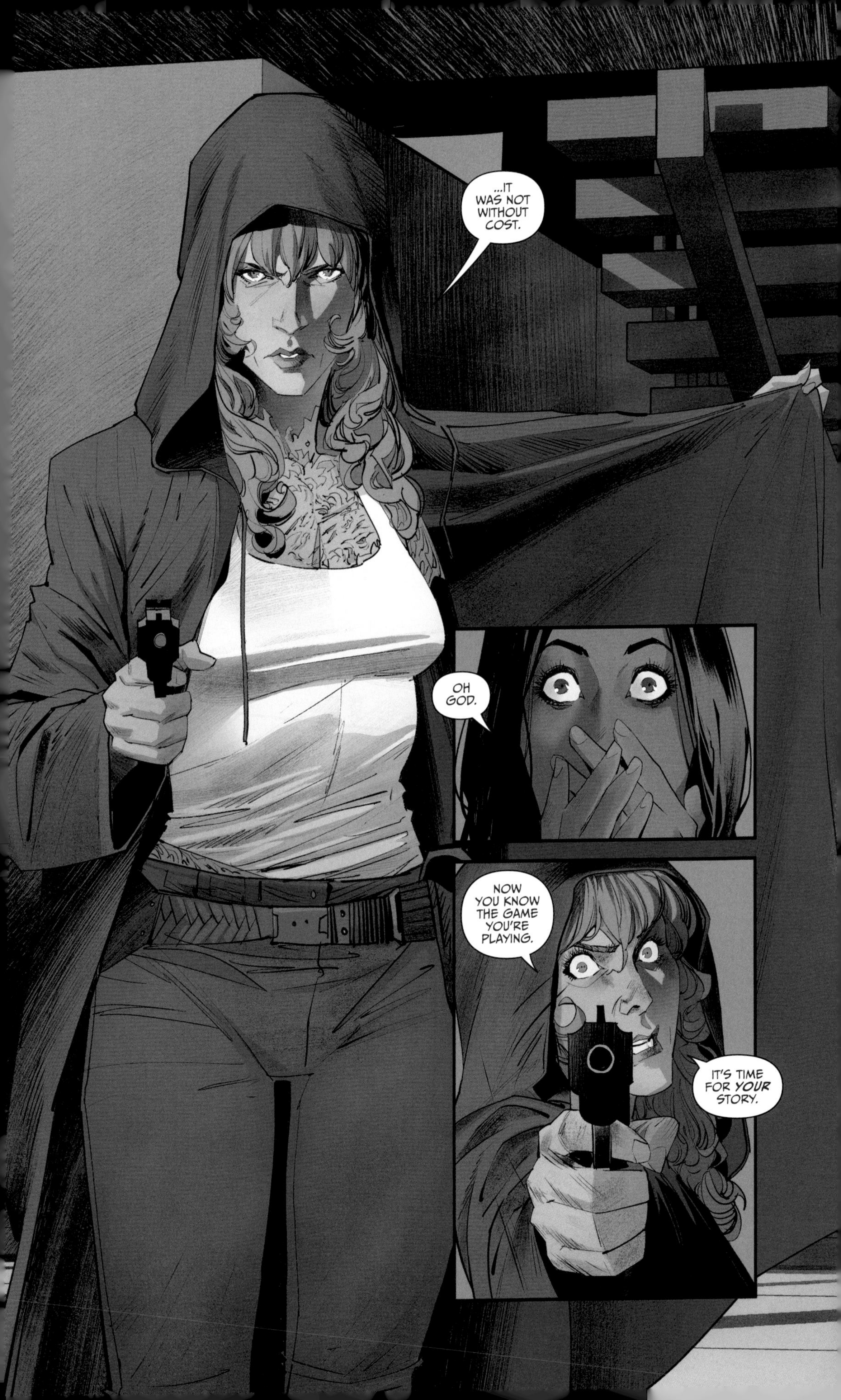
...IT WAS NOT WITHOUT COST.
OH GOD.
NOW YOU KNOW THE GAME YOU'RE PLAYING.
IT'S TIME FOR *YOUR* STORY.

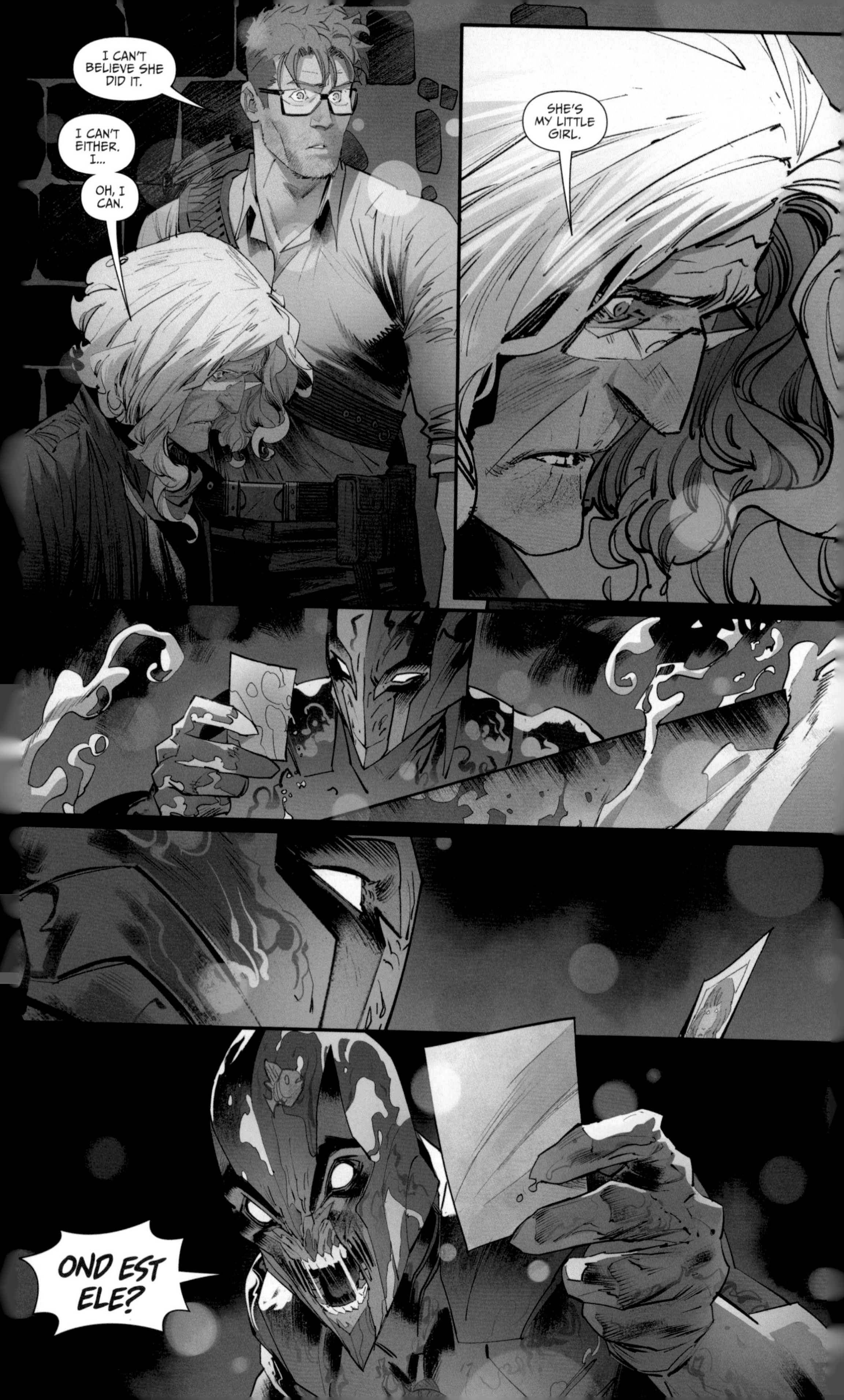
I CAN'T BELIEVE SHE DID IT.
I CAN'T EITHER. I...
OH, I CAN.
SHE'S MY LITTLE GIRL.
OND EST ELE?

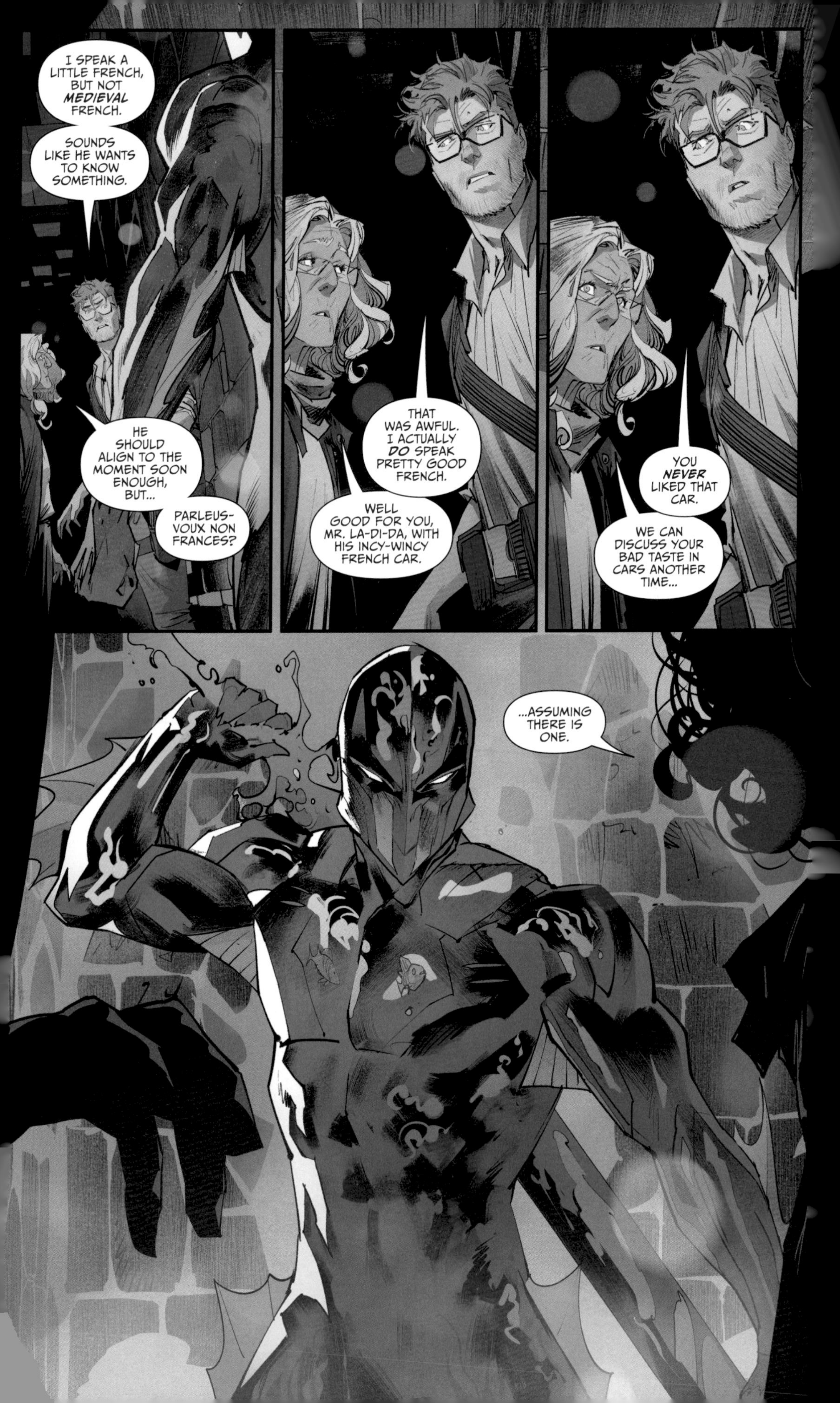
I SPEAK A LITTLE FRENCH, BUT NOT *MEDIEVAL* FRENCH.
SOUNDS LIKE HE WANTS TO KNOW SOMETHING.
HE SHOULD ALIGN TO THE MOMENT SOON ENOUGH, BUT...
PARLEUS-VOUX NON FRANCES?
THAT WAS AWFUL. I ACTUALLY *DO* SPEAK PRETTY GOOD FRENCH.
WELL GOOD FOR YOU, MR. LA-DI-DA, WITH HIS INCY-WINCY FRENCH CAR.
YOU *NEVER* LIKED THAT CAR.
WE CAN DISCUSS YOUR BAD TASTE IN CARS ANOTHER TIME...
...ASSUMING THERE IS ONE.

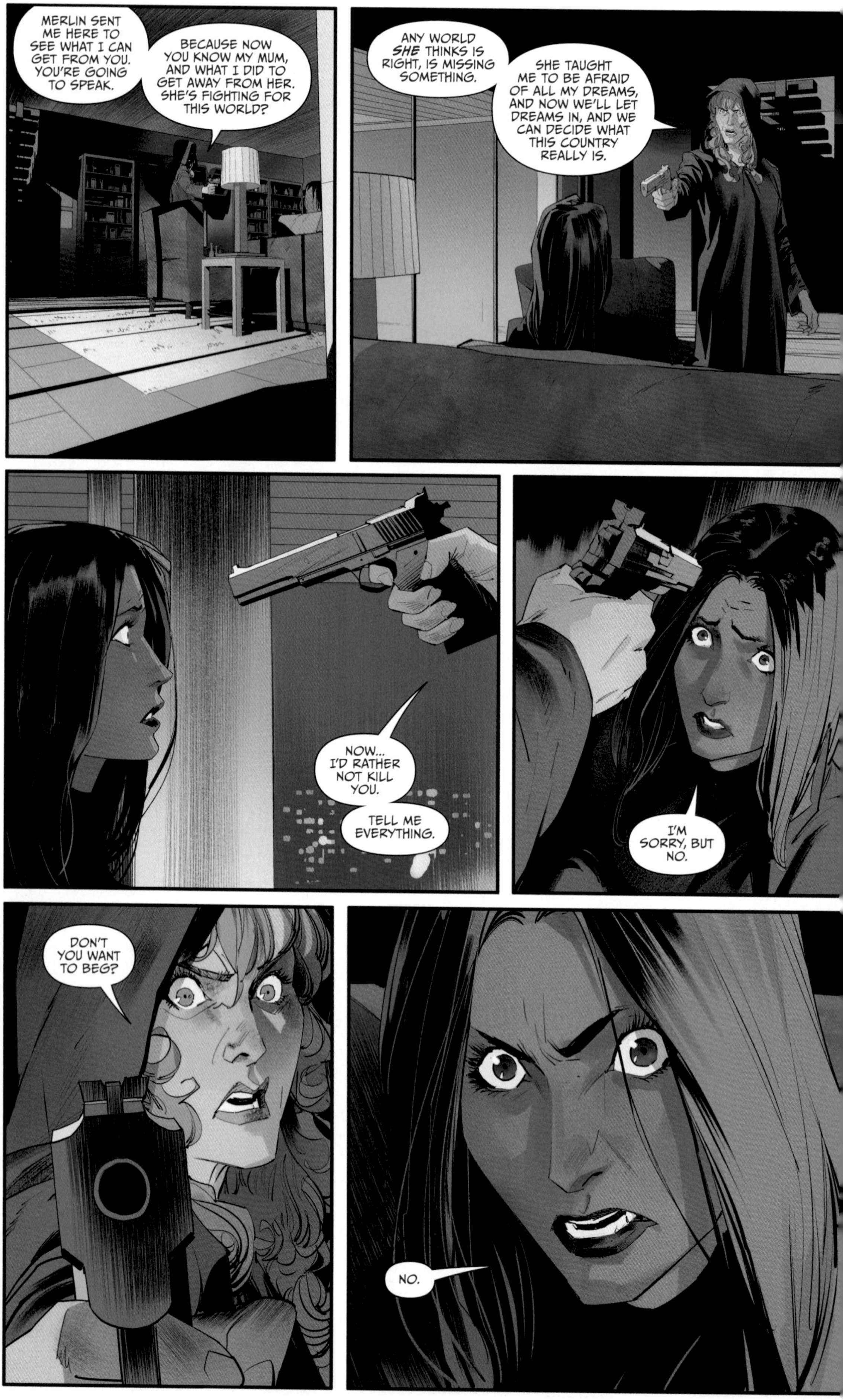
MERLIN SENT ME HERE TO SEE WHAT I CAN GET FROM YOU. YOU'RE GOING TO SPEAK.
BECAUSE NOW YOU KNOW MY MUM, AND WHAT I DID TO GET AWAY FROM HER. SHE'S FIGHTING FOR THIS WORLD?
ANY WORLD *SHE* THINKS IS RIGHT, IS MISSING SOMETHING.
SHE TAUGHT ME TO BE AFRAID OF ALL MY DREAMS, AND NOW WE'LL LET DREAMS IN, AND WE CAN DECIDE WHAT THIS COUNTRY REALLY IS.
NOW... I'D RATHER NOT KILL YOU.
TELL ME EVERYTHING.
I'M SORRY, BUT NO.
DON'T YOU WANT TO BEG?
NO.

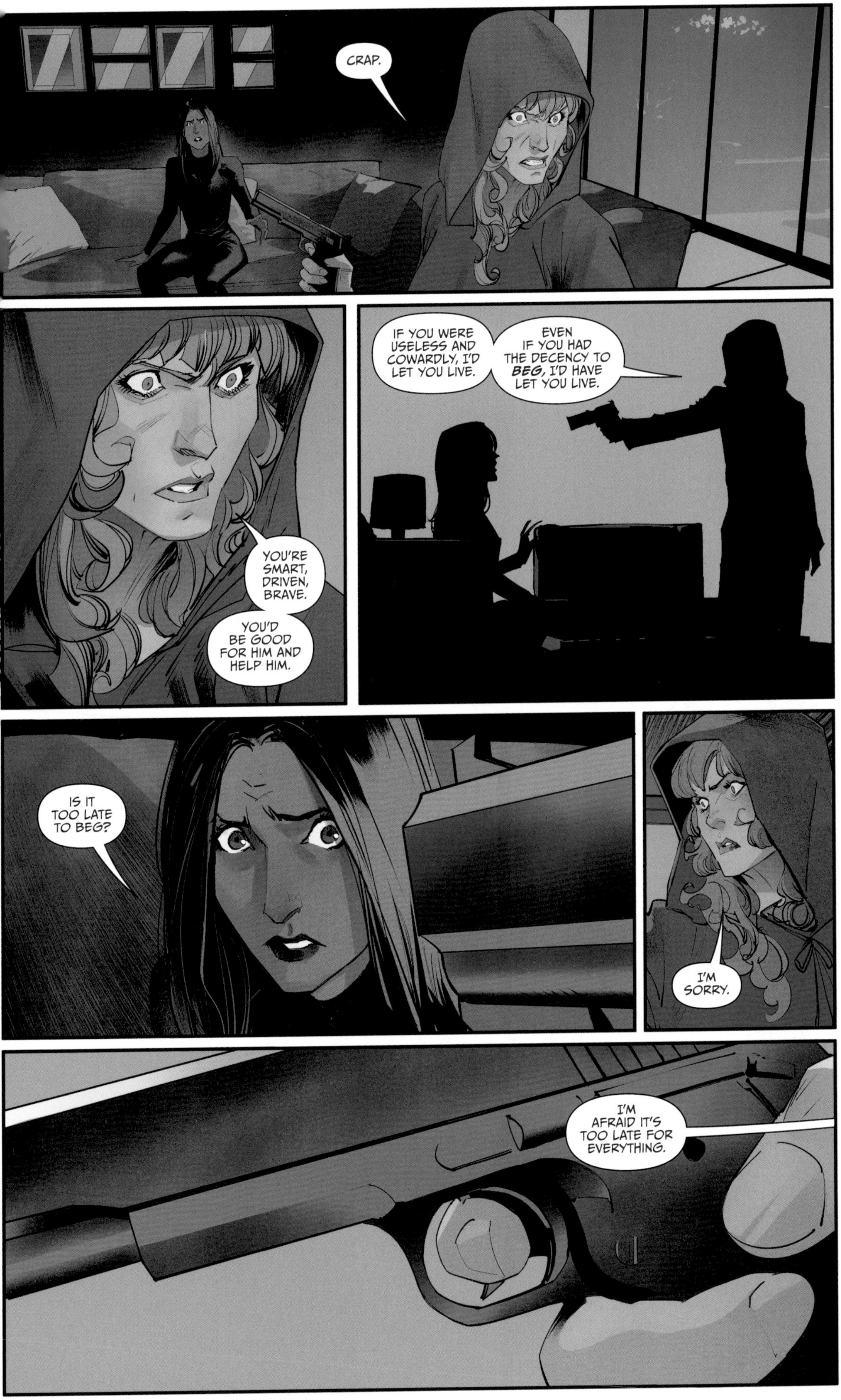
CRAP.
YOU'RE SMART, DRIVEN, BRAVE.
YOU'D BE GOOD FOR HIM AND HELP HIM.
IF YOU WERE USELESS AND COWARDLY, I'D LET YOU LIVE.
EVEN IF YOU HAD THE DECENCY TO BEG, I'D HAVE LET YOU LIVE.
IS IT TOO LATE TO BEG?
I'M SORRY.
I'M AFRAID IT'S TOO LATE FOR EVERYTHING.

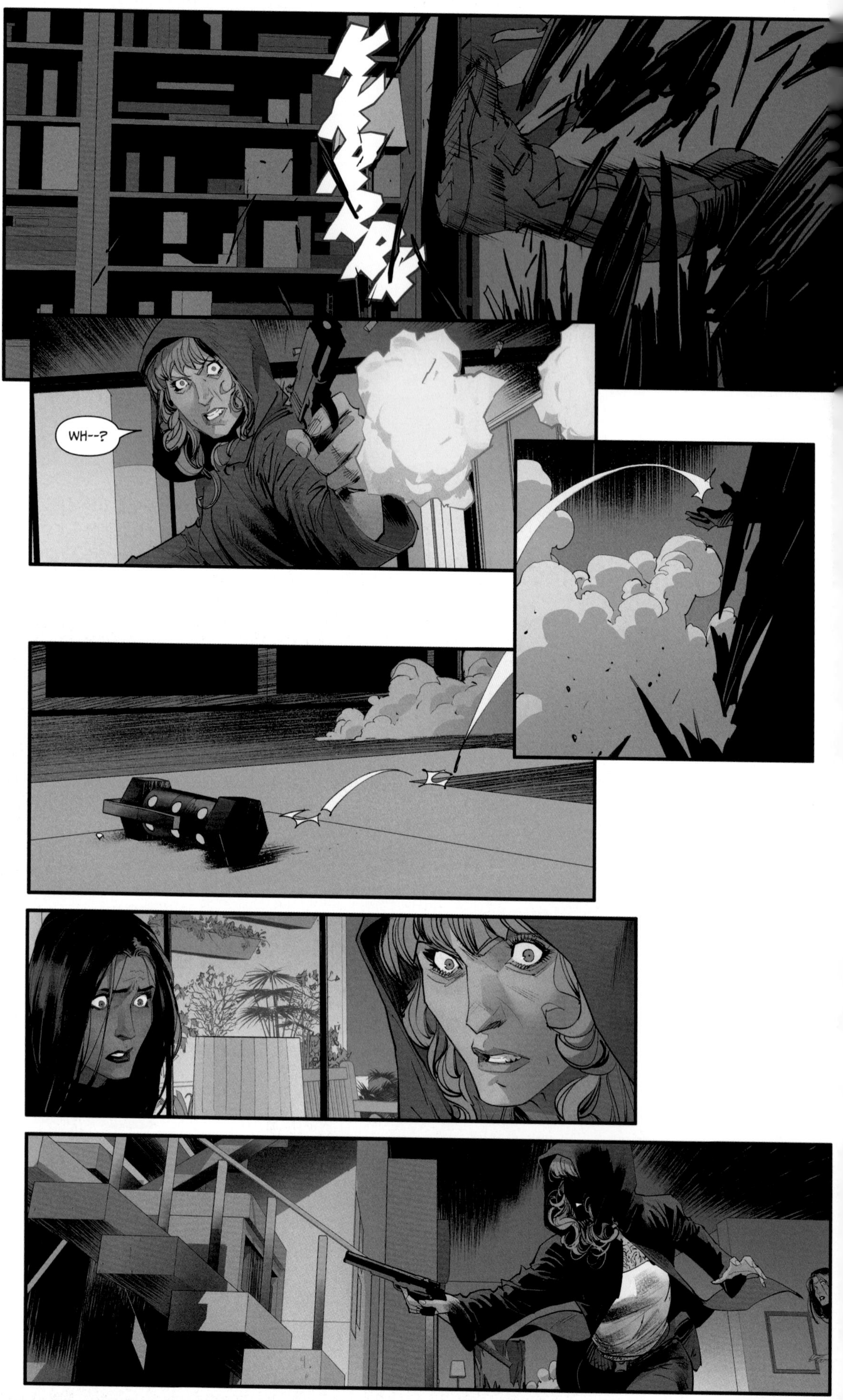
WH--?

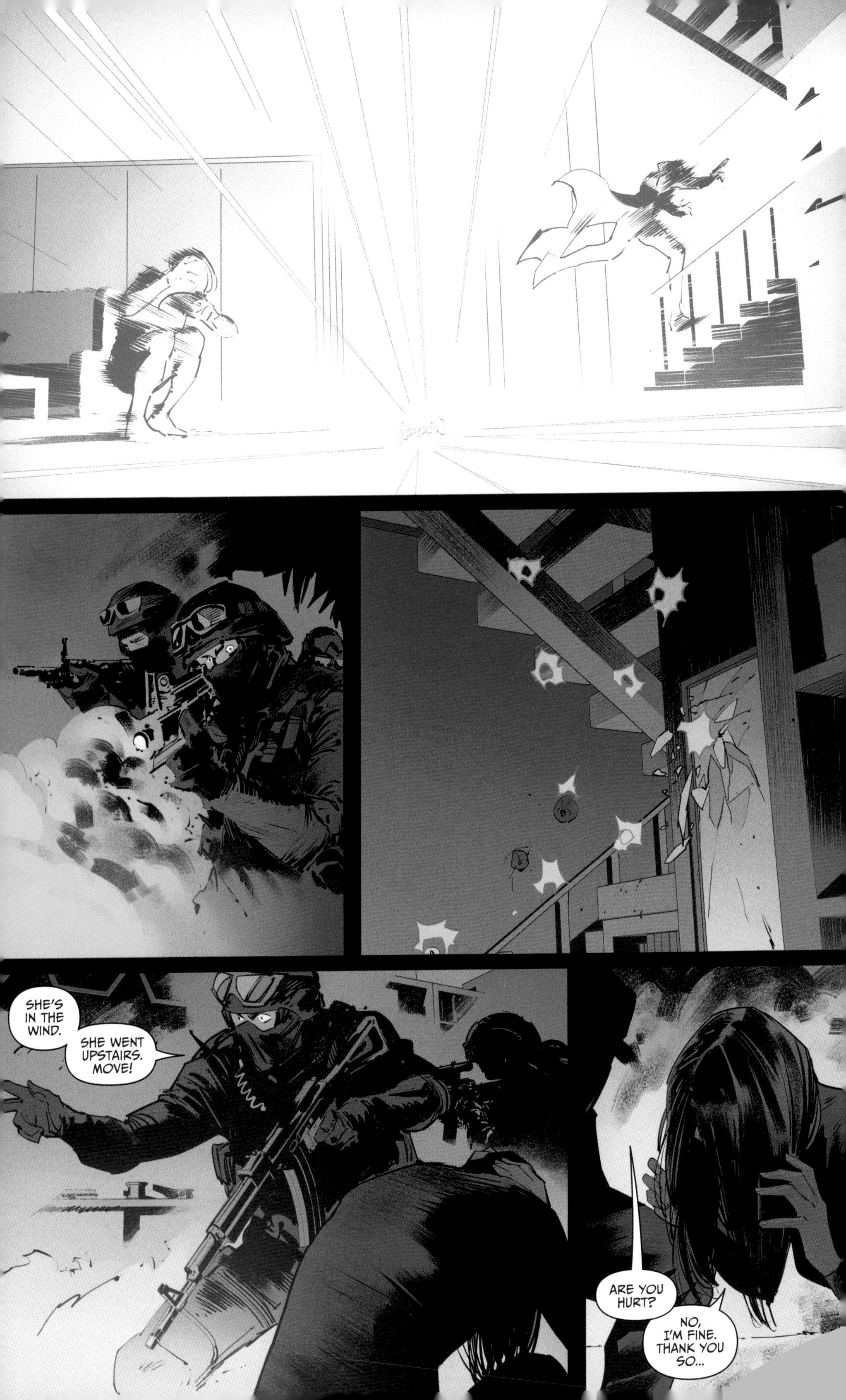
SHE'S IN THE WIND.
SHE WENT UPSTAIRS. MOVE!
ARE YOU HURT?
NO, I'M FINE. THANK YOU SO...

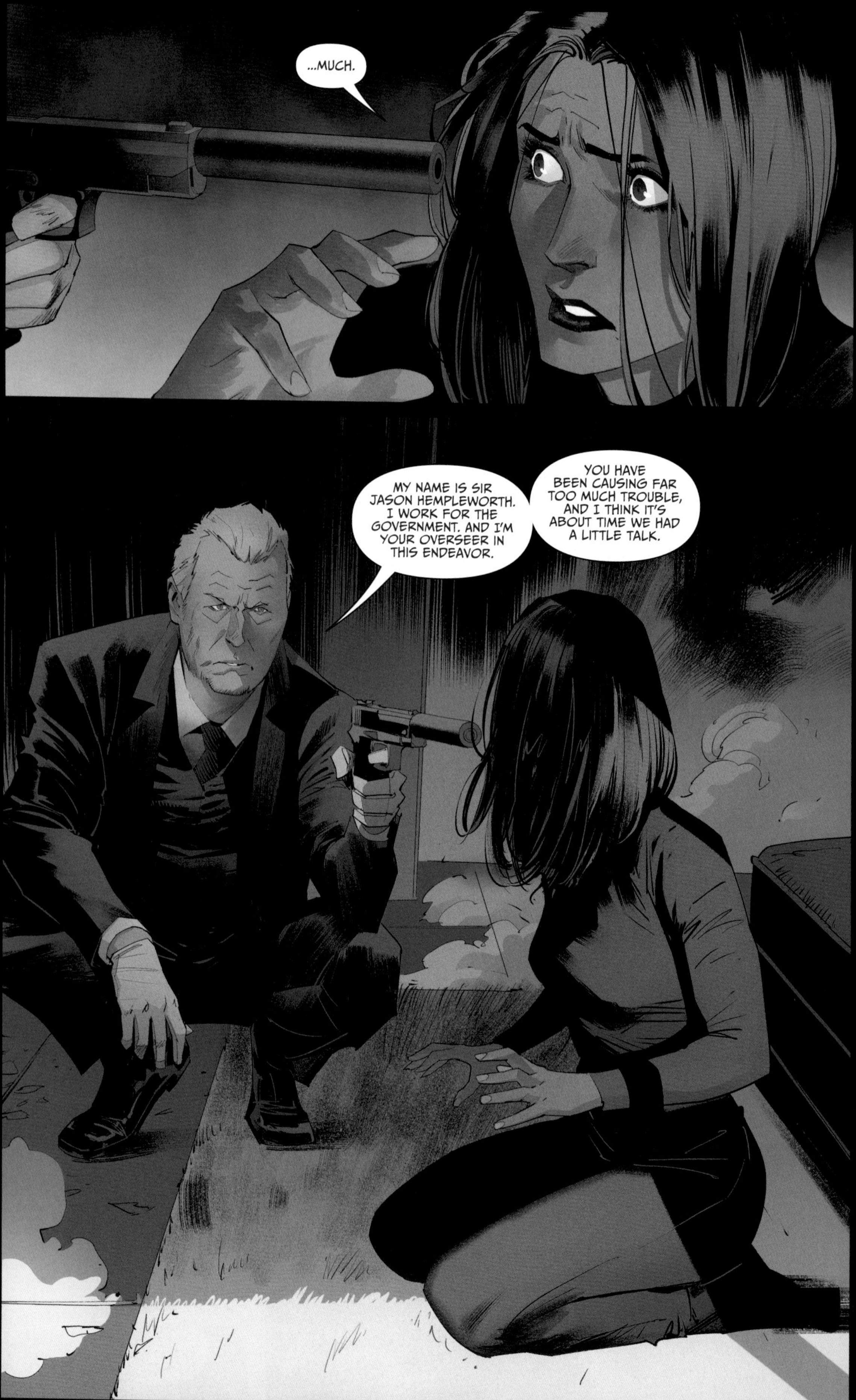
...MUCH.
MY NAME IS SIR JASON HEMPLEWORTH. I WORK FOR THE GOVERNMENT. AND I'M YOUR OVERSEER IN THIS ENDEAVOR.
YOU HAVE BEEN CAUSING FAR TOO MUCH TROUBLE, AND I THINK IT'S ABOUT TIME WE HAD A LITTLE TALK.

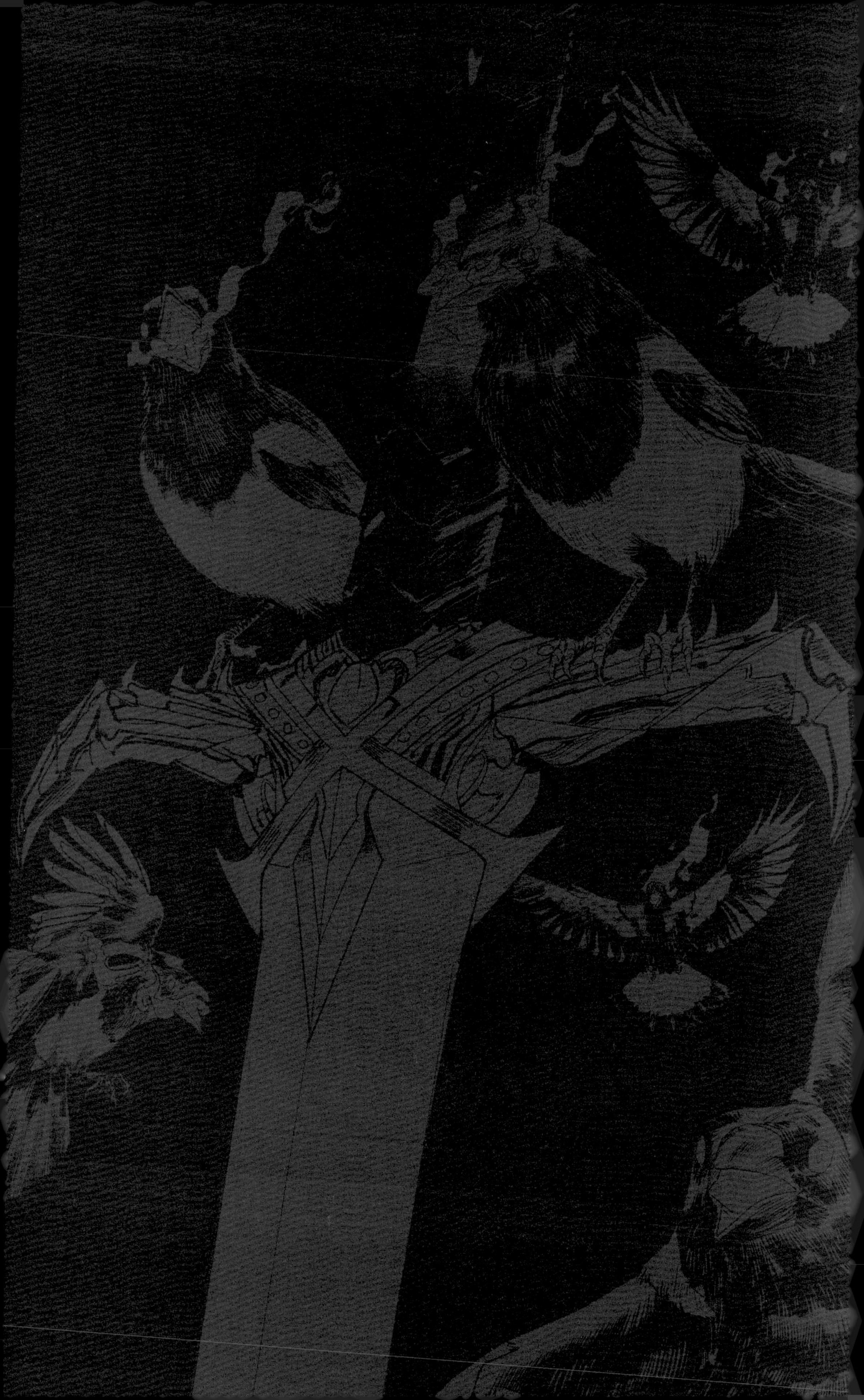

CHAPTER SIXTEEN

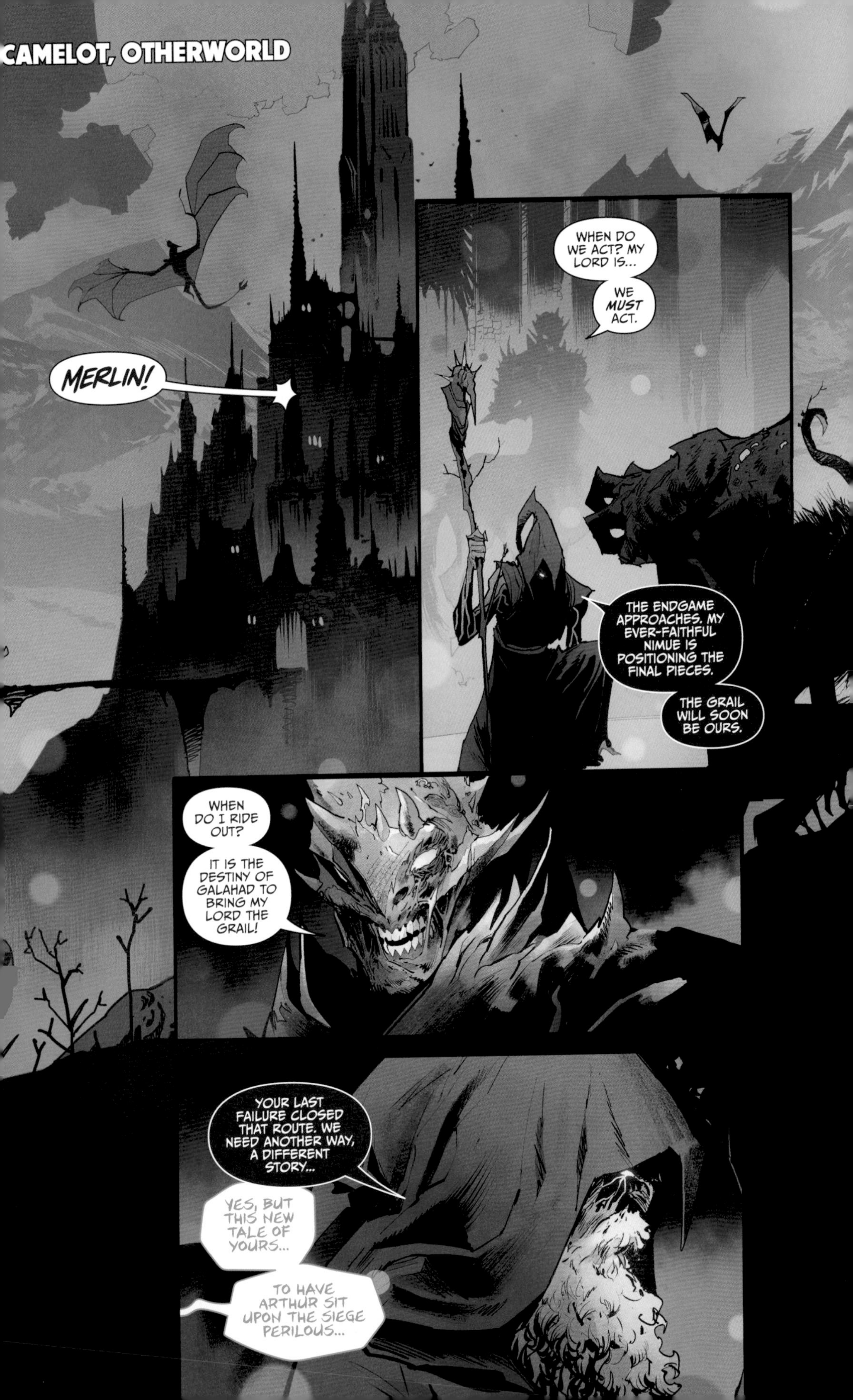
CAMELOT, OTHERWORLD
MERLIN!
WHEN DO WE ACT? MY LORD IS...
WE MUST ACT.
THE ENDGAME APPROACHES. MY EVER-FAITHFUL NIMUE IS POSITIONING THE FINAL PIECES.
THE GRAIL WILL SOON BE OURS.
WHEN DO I RIDE OUT?
IT IS THE DESTINY OF GALAHAD TO BRING MY LORD THE GRAIL!
YOUR LAST FAILURE CLOSED THAT ROUTE. WE NEED ANOTHER WAY, A DIFFERENT STORY...
YES, BUT THIS NEW TALE OF YOURS...
TO HAVE ARTHUR SIT UPON THE SIEGE PERILOUS...

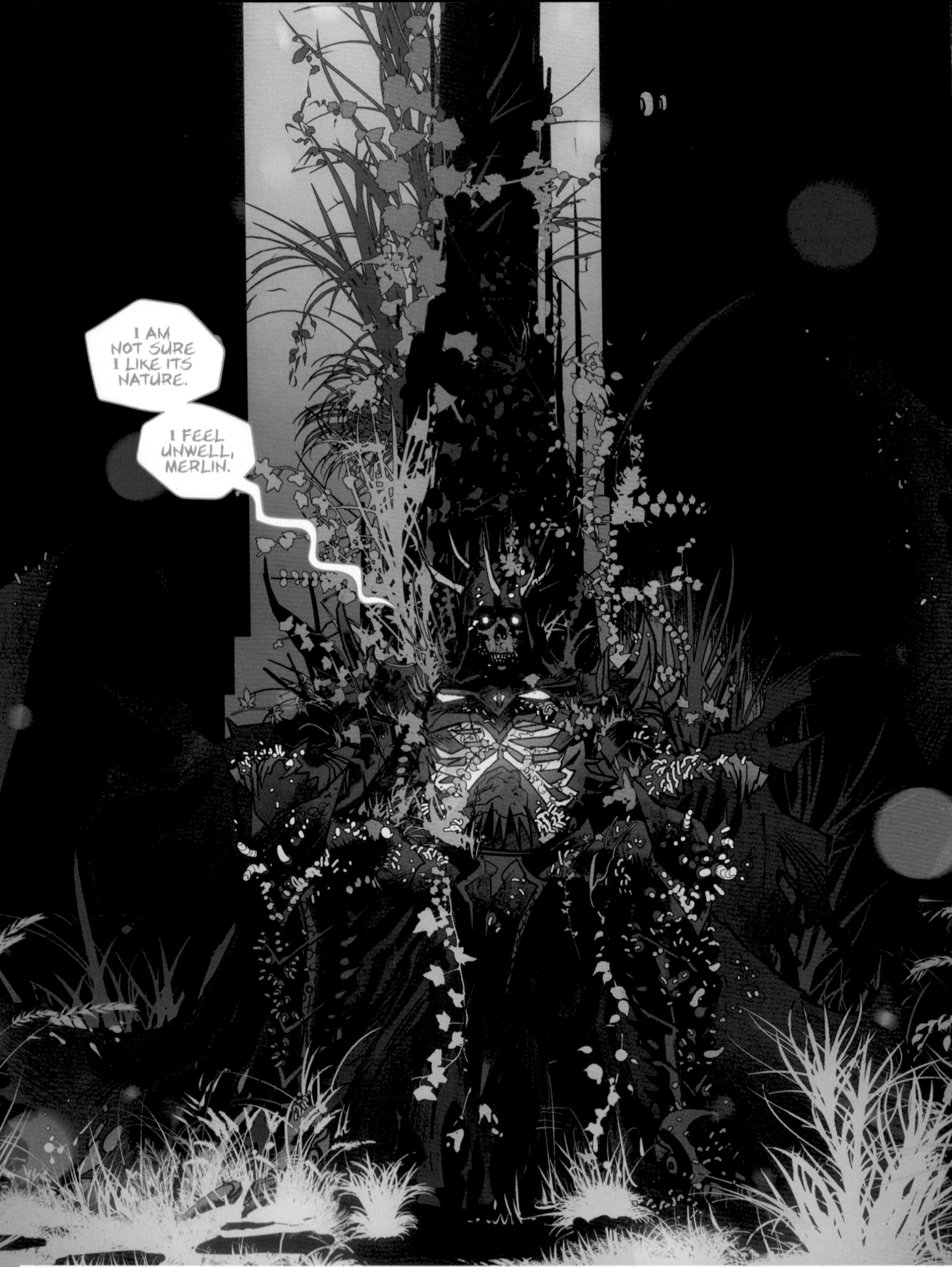
I AM NOT SURE I LIKE ITS NATURE.
I FEEL UNWELL, MERLIN.

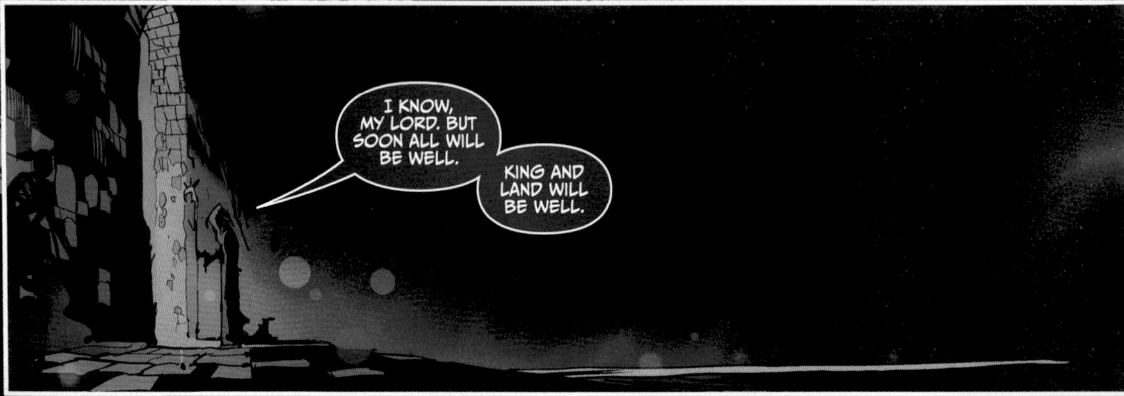
I KNOW, MY LORD. BUT SOON ALL WILL BE WELL.
KING AND LAND WILL BE WELL.

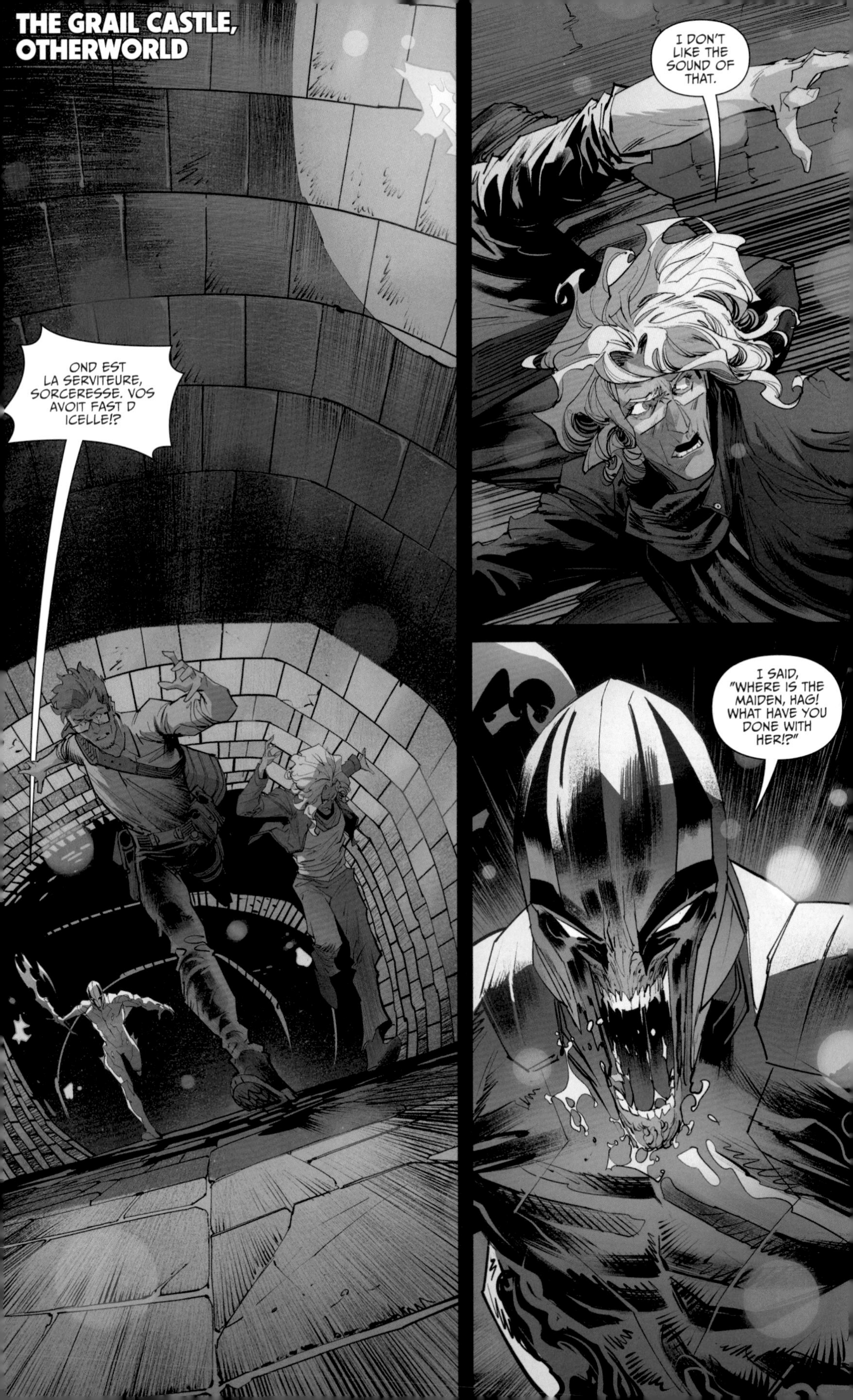
THE GRAIL CASTLE, OTHERWORLD
OND EST LA SERVITEURE, SORCERESSE. VOS AVOIT FAST D ICELLE!?
I DON'T LIKE THE SOUND OF THAT.
I SAID, "WHERE IS THE MAIDEN, HAG! WHAT HAVE YOU DONE WITH HER!?"

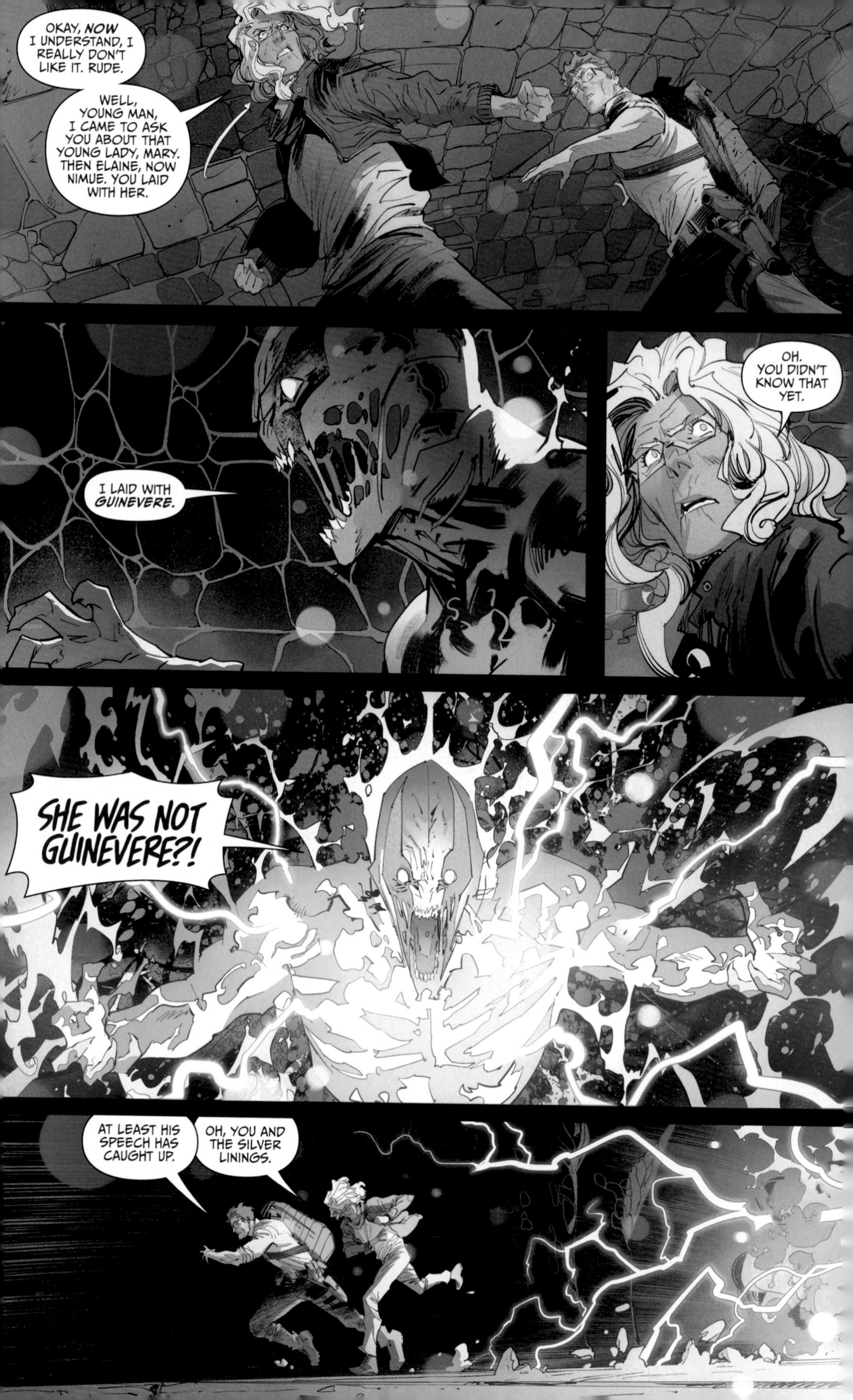
OKAY, NOW I UNDERSTAND, I REALLY DON'T LIKE IT. RUDE.
WELL, YOUNG MAN, I CAME TO ASK YOU ABOUT THAT YOUNG LADY, MARY. THEN ELAINE, NOW NIMUE. YOU LAID WITH HER.
I LAID WITH GUINEVERE.
OH. YOU DIDN'T KNOW THAT YET.
SHE WAS NOT GUINEVERE?!
AT LEAST HIS SPEECH HAS CAUGHT UP.
OH, YOU AND THE SILVER LININGS.

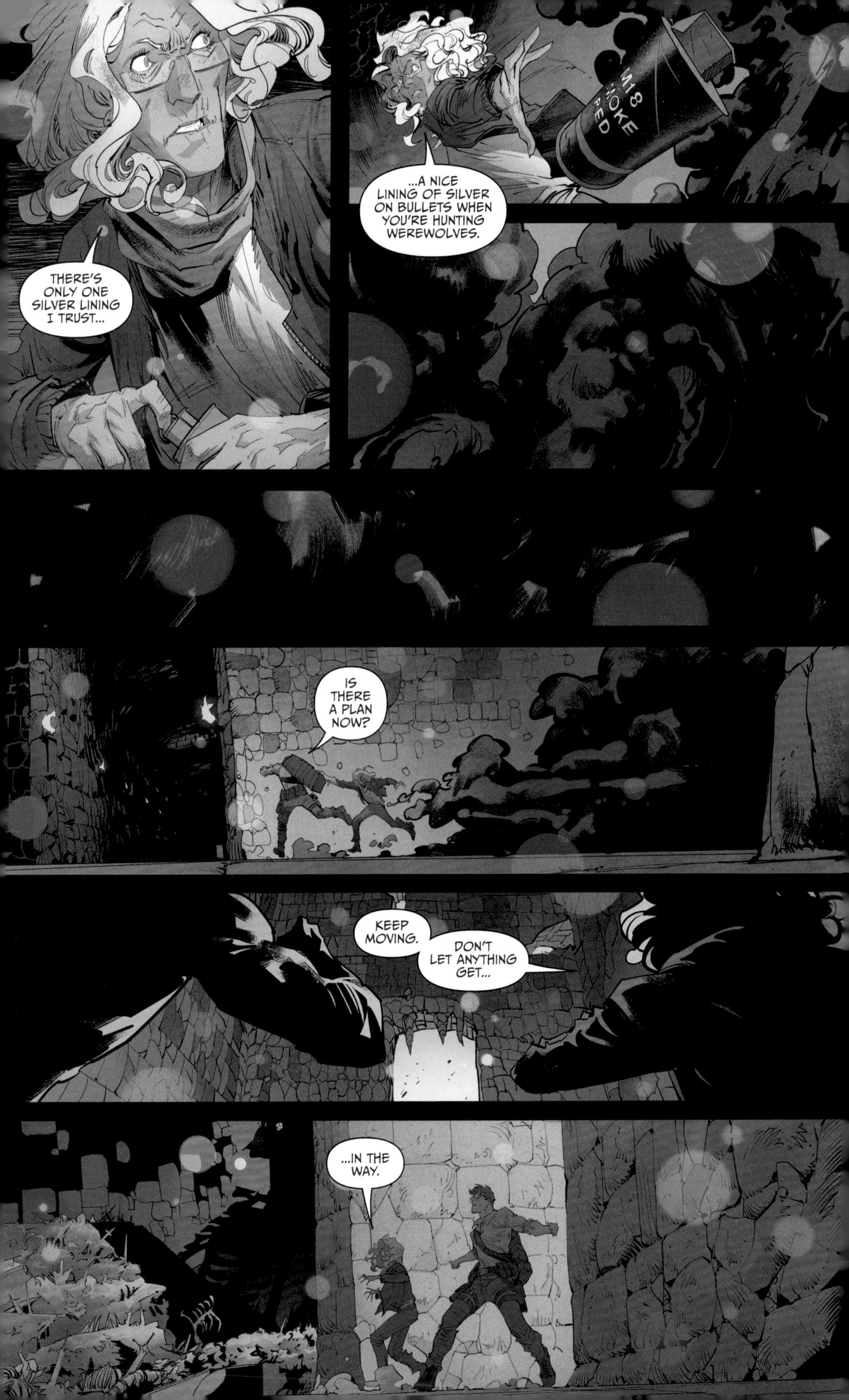
THERE'S ONLY ONE SILVER LINING I TRUST...
M18 SMOKE RED
...A NICE LINING OF SILVER ON BULLETS WHEN YOU'RE HUNTING WEREWOLVES.
IS THERE A PLAN NOW?
KEEP MOVING.
DON'T LET ANYTHING GET...
...IN THE WAY.

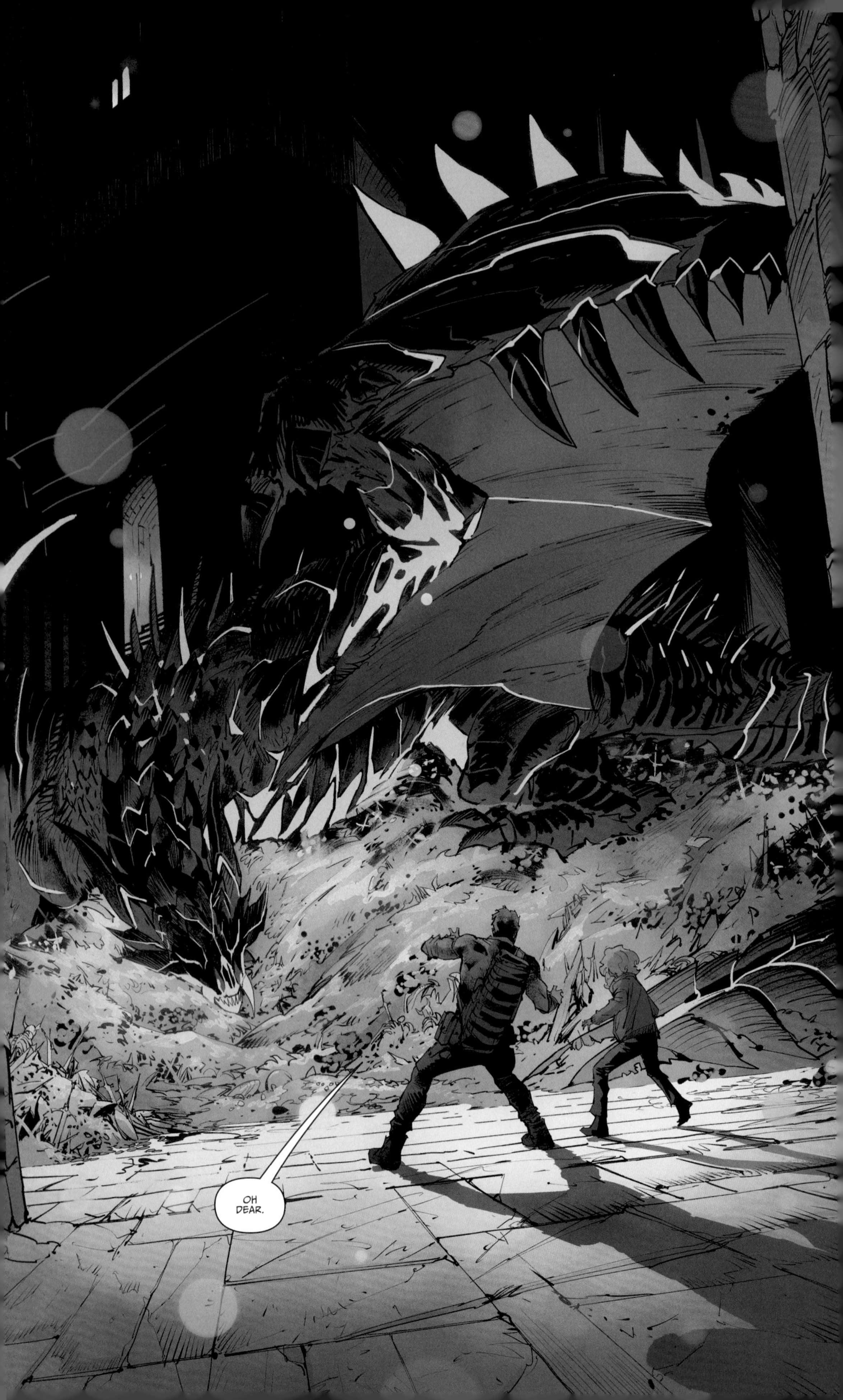
OH DEAR.

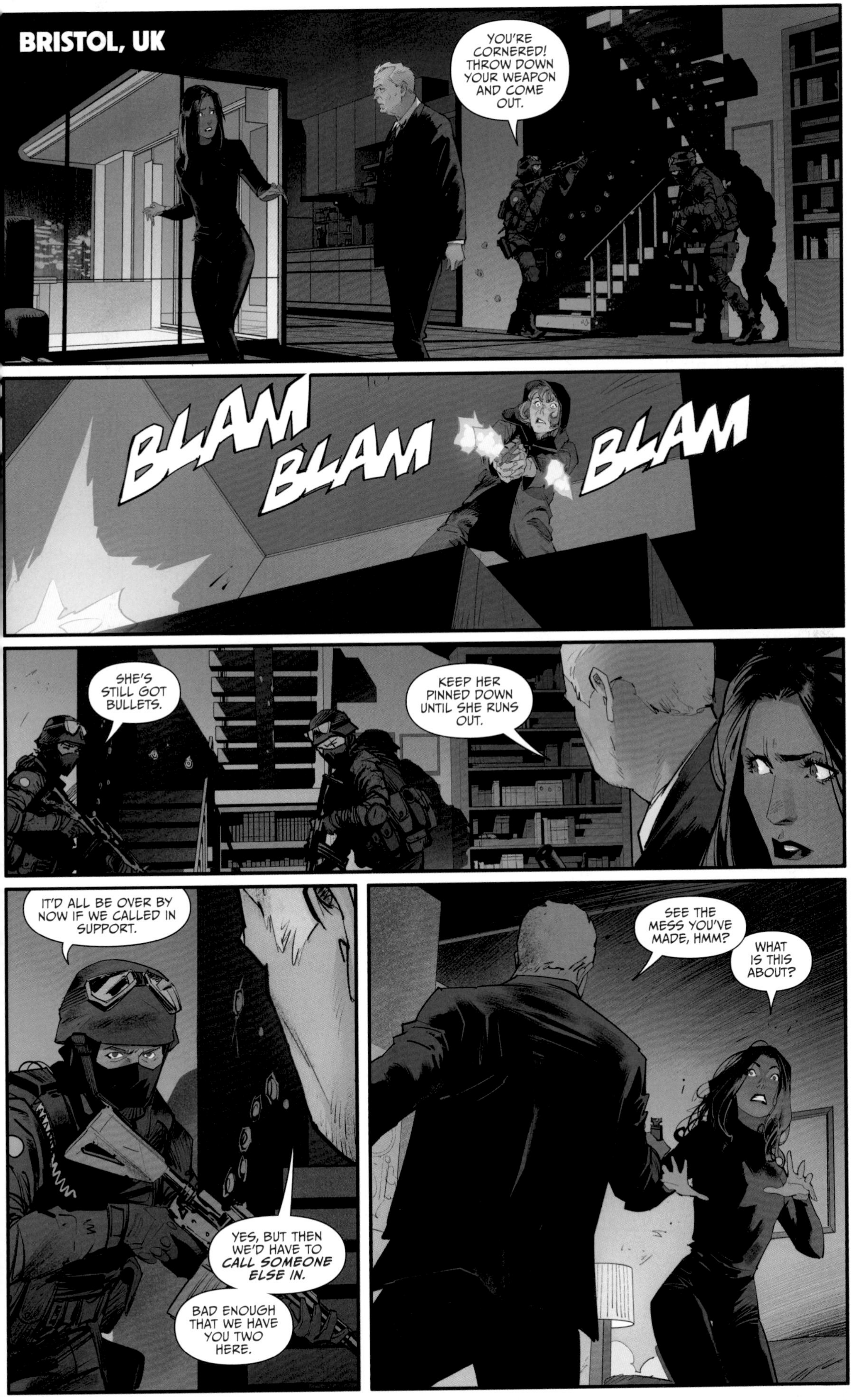
BRISTOL, UK
YOU'RE CORNERED! THROW DOWN YOUR WEAPON AND COME OUT.
BLAM
BLAM
BLAM
SHE'S STILL GOT BULLETS.
KEEP HER PINNED DOWN UNTIL SHE RUNS OUT.
IT'D ALL BE OVER BY NOW IF WE CALLED IN SUPPORT.
YES, BUT THEN WE'D HAVE TO *CALL SOMEONE ELSE IN.*
BAD ENOUGH THAT WE HAVE YOU TWO HERE.
SEE THE MESS YOU'VE MADE, HMM?
WHAT IS THIS ABOUT?

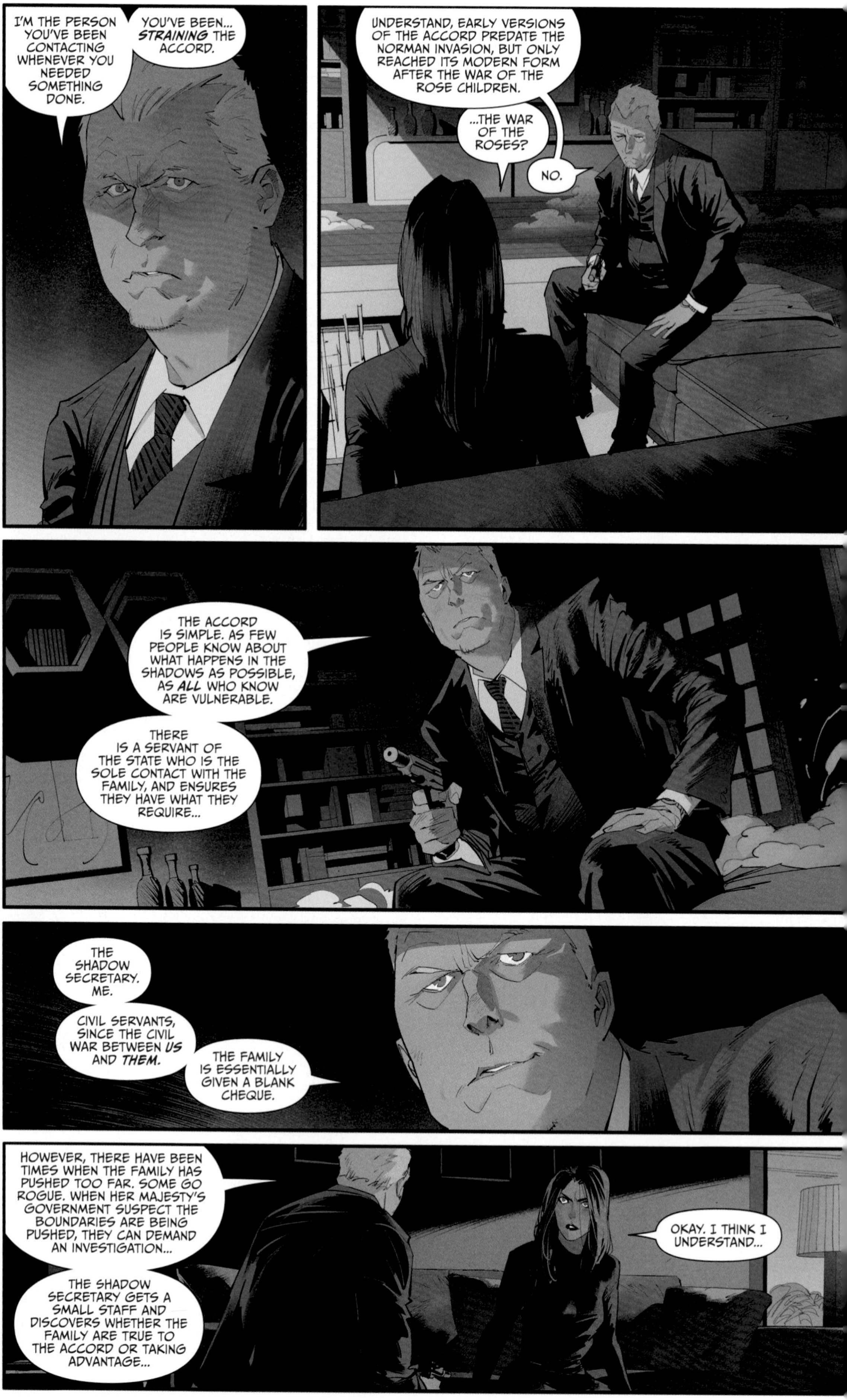
I'M THE PERSON YOU'VE BEEN CONTACTING WHENEVER YOU NEEDED SOMETHING DONE.
YOU'VE BEEN... **STRAINING** THE ACCORD.
UNDERSTAND, EARLY VERSIONS OF THE ACCORD PREDATE THE NORMAN INVASION, BUT ONLY REACHED ITS MODERN FORM AFTER THE WAR OF THE ROSE CHILDREN.
...THE WAR OF THE ROSES?
NO.
THE ACCORD IS SIMPLE. AS FEW PEOPLE KNOW ABOUT WHAT HAPPENS IN THE SHADOWS AS POSSIBLE, AS **ALL** WHO KNOW ARE VULNERABLE.
THERE IS A SERVANT OF THE STATE WHO IS THE SOLE CONTACT WITH THE FAMILY, AND ENSURES THEY HAVE WHAT THEY REQUIRE...
THE SHADOW SECRETARY. ME.
CIVIL SERVANTS, SINCE THE CIVIL WAR BETWEEN **US** AND **THEM.**
THE FAMILY IS ESSENTIALLY GIVEN A BLANK CHEQUE.
HOWEVER, THERE HAVE BEEN TIMES WHEN THE FAMILY HAS PUSHED TOO FAR. SOME GO ROGUE. WHEN HER MAJESTY'S GOVERNMENT SUSPECT THE BOUNDARIES ARE BEING PUSHED, THEY CAN DEMAND AN INVESTIGATION...
THE SHADOW SECRETARY GETS A SMALL STAFF AND DISCOVERS WHETHER THE FAMILY ARE TRUE TO THE ACCORD OR TAKING ADVANTAGE...
OKAY. I THINK I UNDERSTAND...

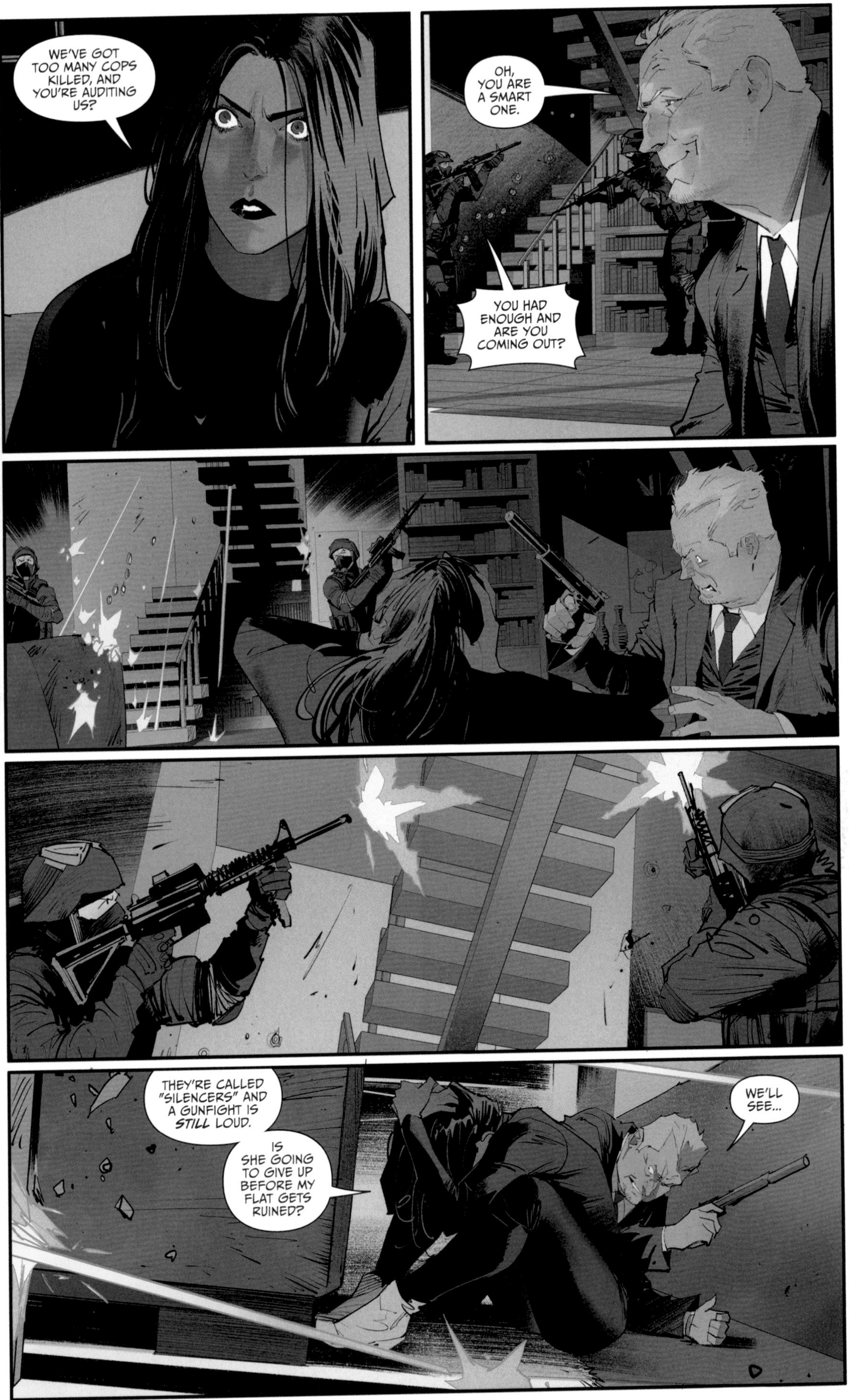
WE'VE GOT TOO MANY COPS KILLED, AND YOU'RE AUDITING US?
OH, YOU ARE A SMART ONE.
YOU HAD ENOUGH AND ARE YOU COMING OUT?
THEY'RE CALLED "SILENCERS" AND A GUNFIGHT IS STILL LOUD.
IS SHE GOING TO GIVE UP BEFORE MY FLAT GETS RUINED?
WE'LL SEE...

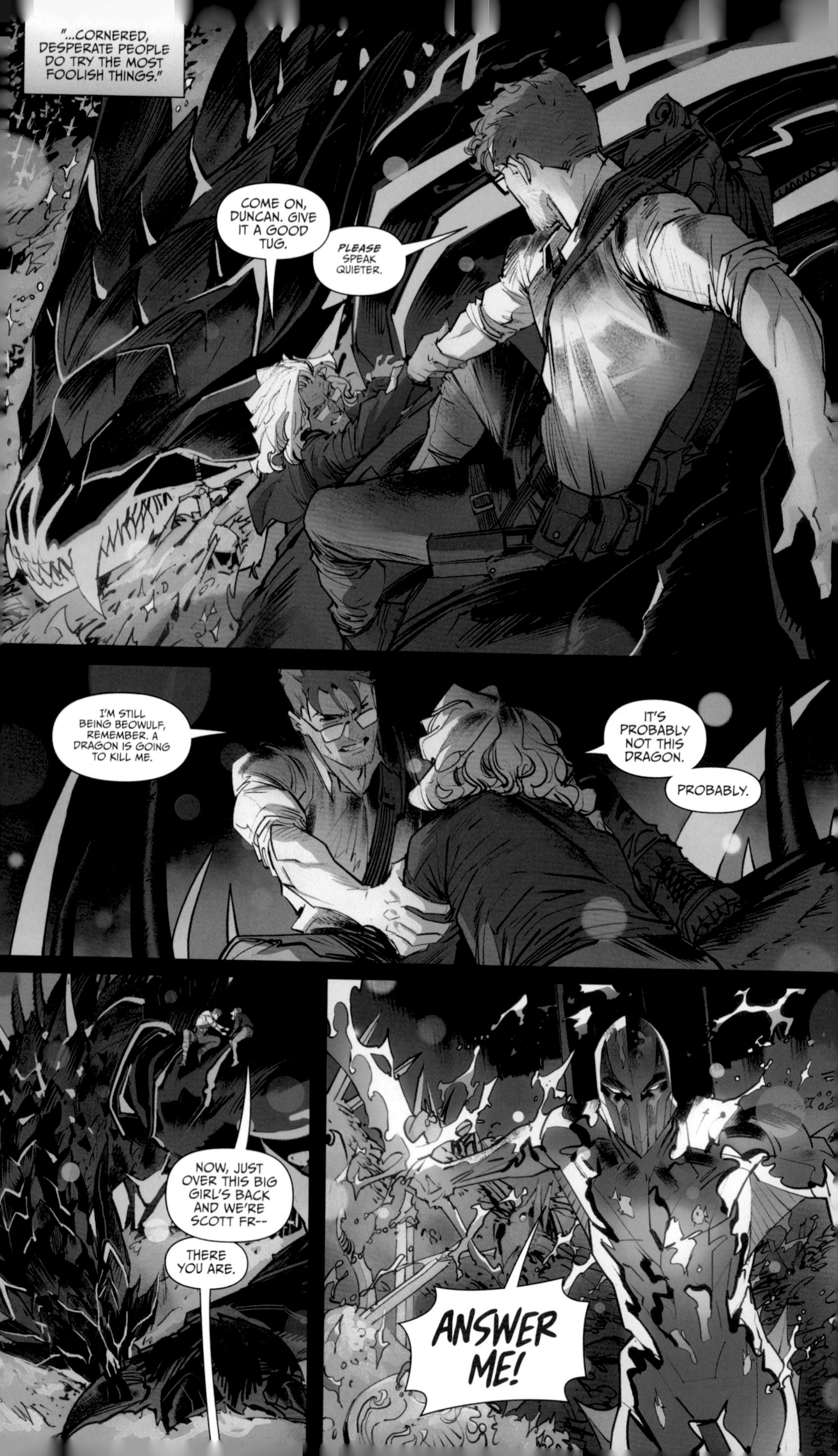
"...CORNERED, DESPERATE PEOPLE DO TRY THE MOST FOOLISH THINGS."
COME ON, DUNCAN. GIVE IT A GOOD TUG.
PLEASE SPEAK QUIETER.
I'M STILL BEING BEOWULF, REMEMBER. A DRAGON IS GOING TO KILL ME.
IT'S PROBABLY NOT THIS DRAGON.
PROBABLY.
NOW, JUST OVER THIS BIG GIRL'S BACK AND WE'RE SCOTT FR--
THERE YOU ARE.
ANSWER ME!

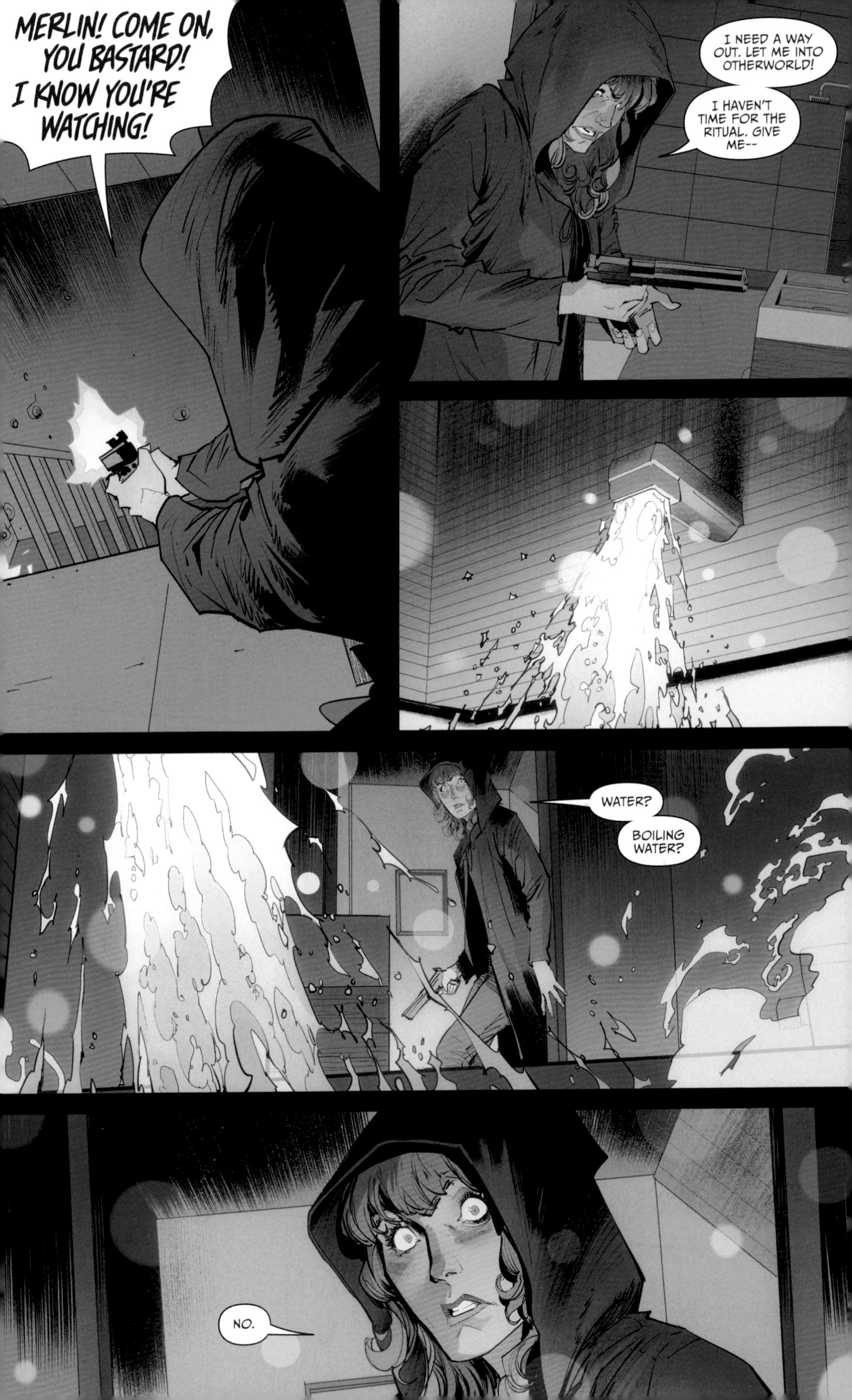
MERLIN! COME ON, YOU BASTARD! I KNOW YOU'RE WATCHING!
I NEED A WAY OUT. LET ME INTO OTHERWORLD!
I HAVEN'T TIME FOR THE RITUAL. GIVE ME--
WATER?
BOILING WATER?
NO.

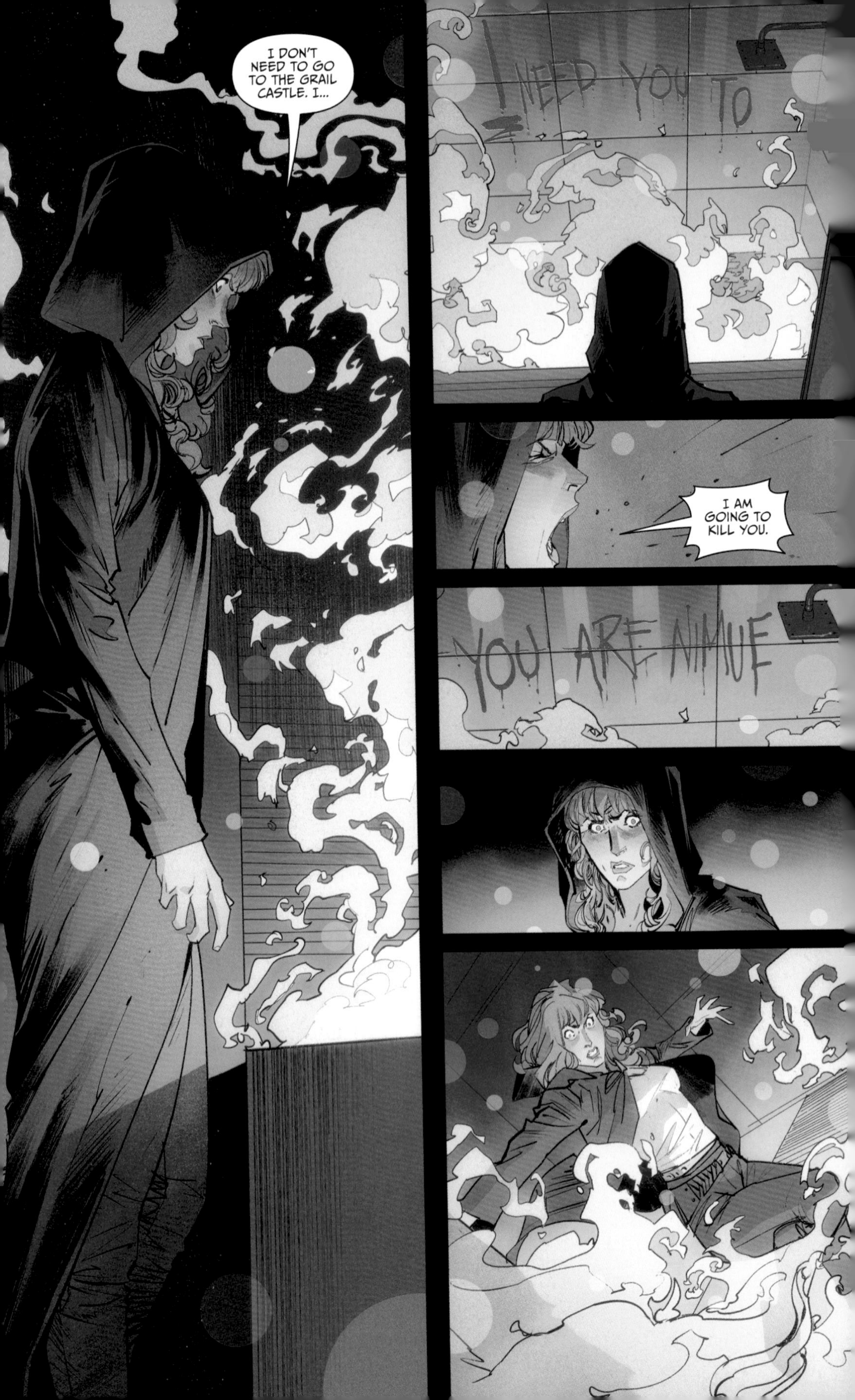
I DON'T NEED TO GO TO THE GRAIL CASTLE. I...
I NEED YOU TO
I AM GOING TO KILL YOU.
YOU ARE NIMUE

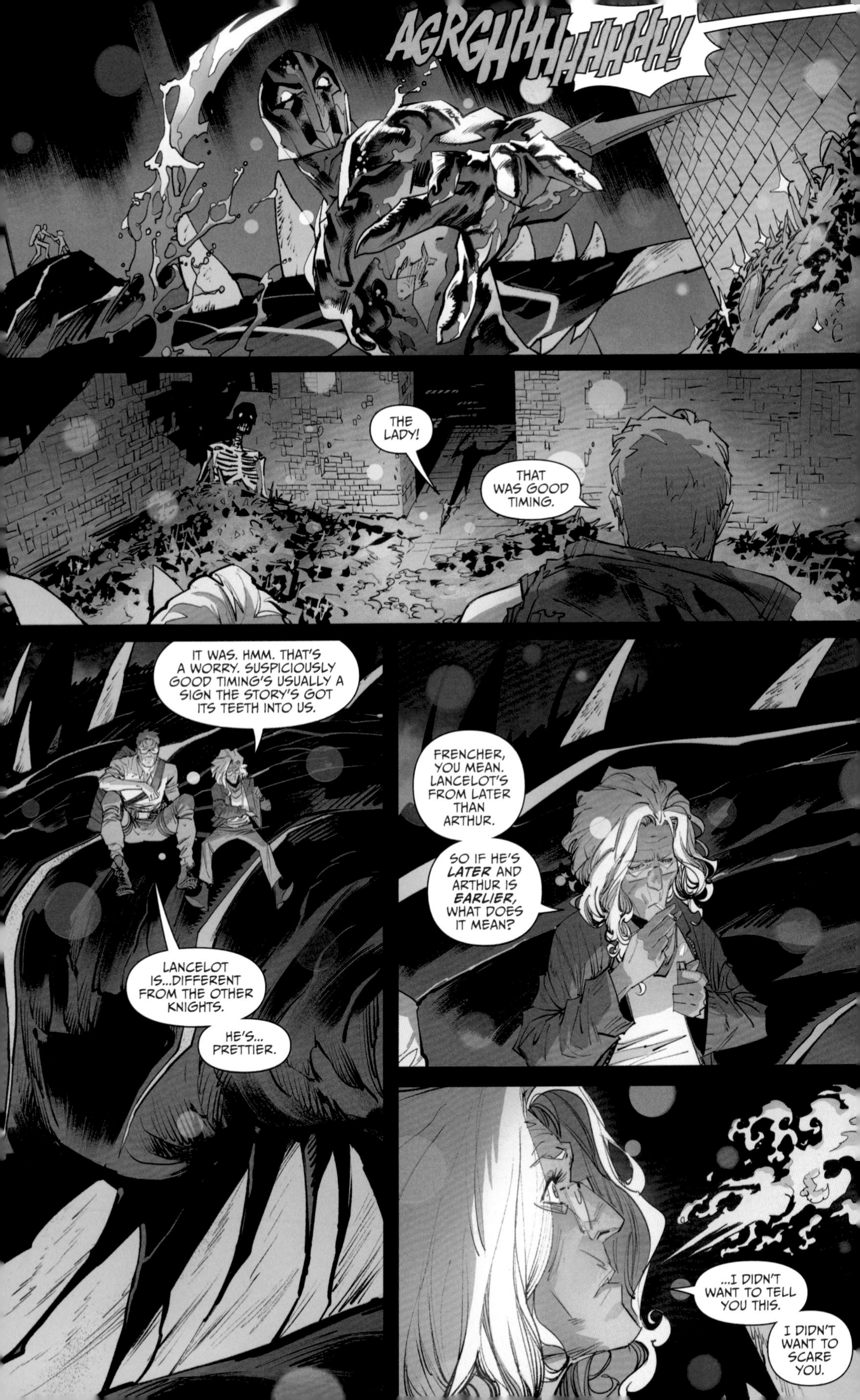
AGRGHHHHHHHH!
THE LADY!
THAT WAS GOOD TIMING.
IT WAS. HMM. THAT'S A WORRY. SUSPICIOUSLY GOOD TIMING'S USUALLY A SIGN THE STORY'S GOT ITS TEETH INTO US.
LANCELOT IS...DIFFERENT FROM THE OTHER KNIGHTS.
HE'S... PRETTIER.
FRENCHER, YOU MEAN. LANCELOT'S FROM LATER THAN ARTHUR.
SO IF HE'S *LATER* AND ARTHUR IS *EARLIER,* WHAT DOES IT MEAN?
...I DIDN'T WANT TO TELL YOU THIS.
I DIDN'T WANT TO SCARE YOU.

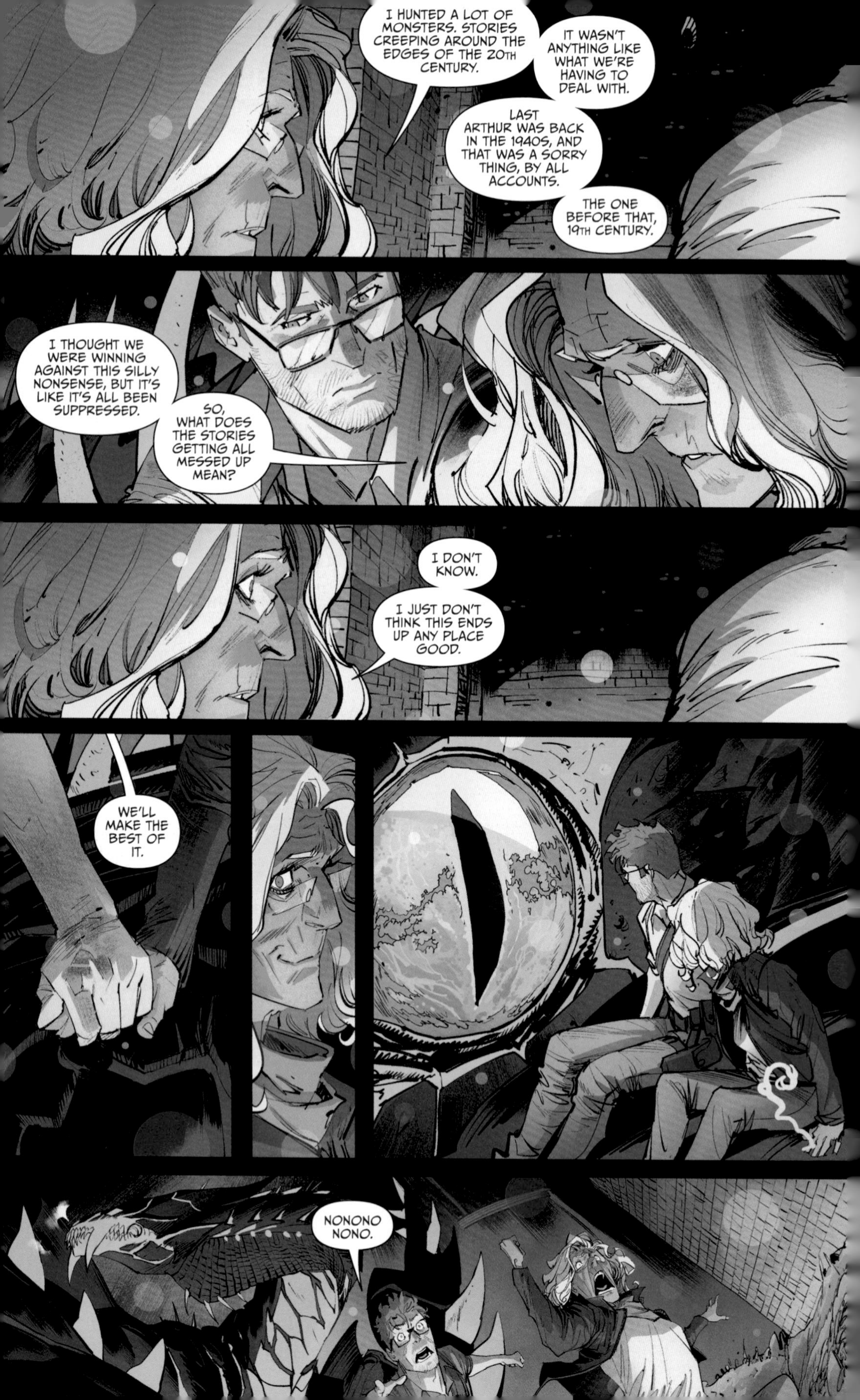
I HUNTED A LOT OF MONSTERS. STORIES CREEPING AROUND THE EDGES OF THE 20TH CENTURY.
IT WASN'T ANYTHING LIKE WHAT WE'RE HAVING TO DEAL WITH.
LAST ARTHUR WAS BACK IN THE 1940S, AND THAT WAS A SORRY THING, BY ALL ACCOUNTS.
THE ONE BEFORE THAT, 19TH CENTURY.
I THOUGHT WE WERE WINNING AGAINST THIS SILLY NONSENSE, BUT IT'S LIKE IT'S ALL BEEN SUPPRESSED.
SO, WHAT DOES THE STORIES GETTING ALL MESSED UP MEAN?
I DON'T KNOW.
I JUST DON'T THINK THIS ENDS UP ANY PLACE GOOD.
WE'LL MAKE THE BEST OF IT.
NONONO NONO.

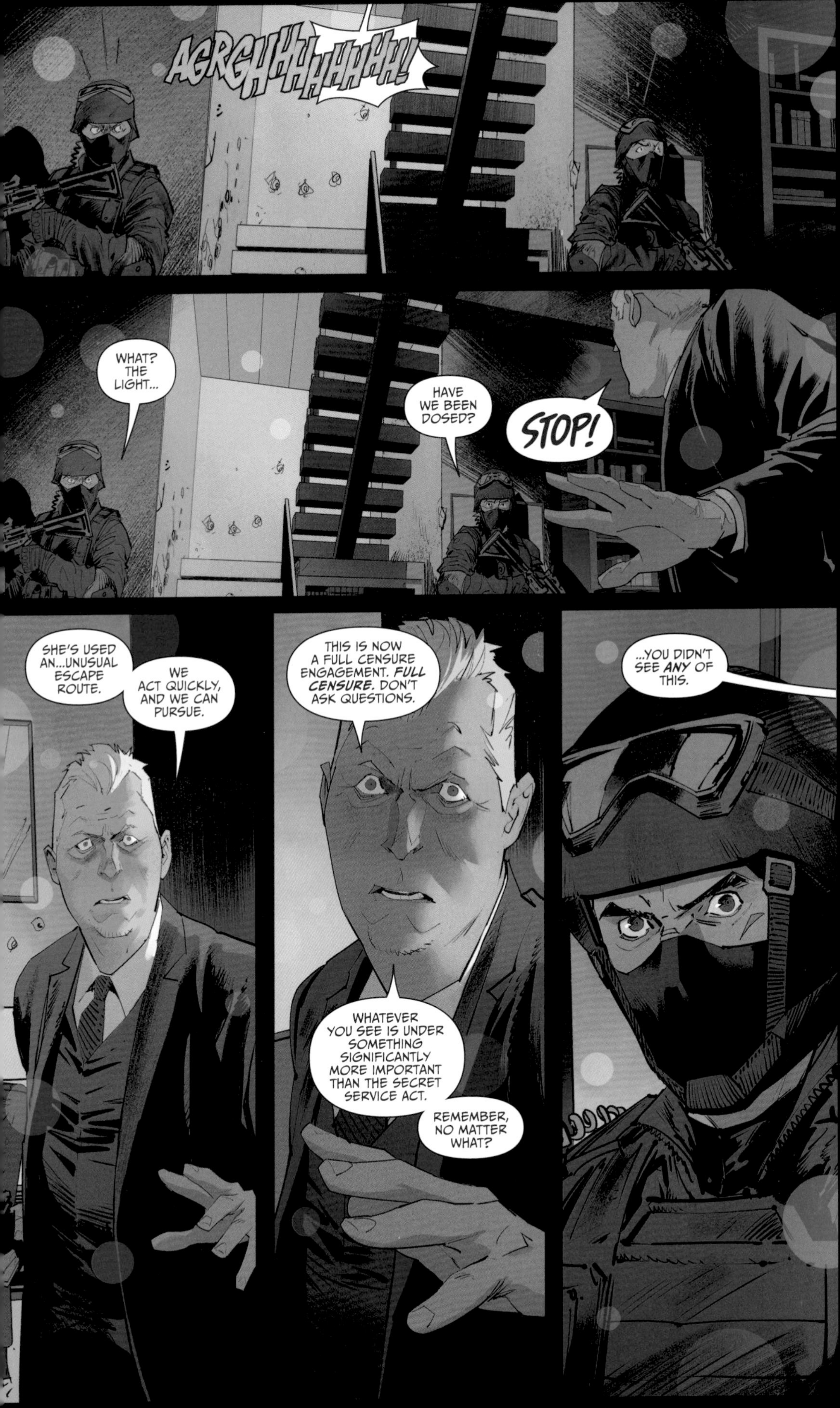
AGRGHHHHHHH!
WHAT? THE LIGHT...
HAVE WE BEEN DOSED?
STOP!
SHE'S USED AN...UNUSUAL ESCAPE ROUTE.
WE ACT QUICKLY, AND WE CAN PURSUE.
THIS IS NOW A FULL CENSURE ENGAGEMENT. FULL CENSURE. DON'T ASK QUESTIONS.
WHATEVER YOU SEE IS UNDER SOMETHING SIGNIFICANTLY MORE IMPORTANT THAN THE SECRET SERVICE ACT.
REMEMBER, NO MATTER WHAT?
...YOU DIDN'T SEE ANY OF THIS.

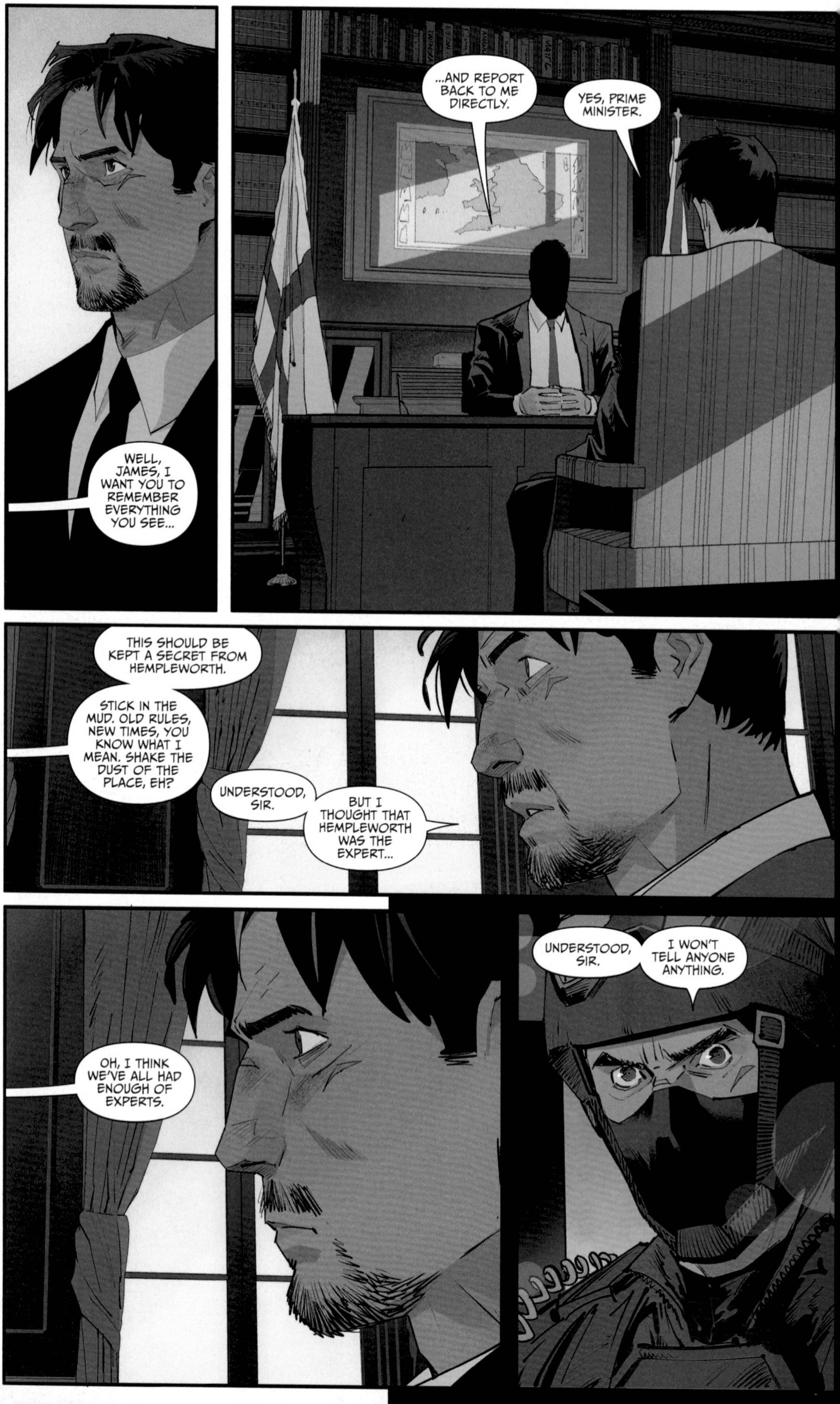

...AND REPORT BACK TO ME DIRECTLY.
YES, PRIME MINISTER.
WELL, JAMES, I WANT YOU TO REMEMBER EVERYTHING YOU SEE...
THIS SHOULD BE KEPT A SECRET FROM HEMPLEWORTH.
STICK IN THE MUD. OLD RULES, NEW TIMES, YOU KNOW WHAT I MEAN. SHAKE THE DUST OF THE PLACE, EH?
UNDERSTOOD, SIR.
BUT I THOUGHT THAT HEMPLEWORTH WAS THE EXPERT...
OH, I THINK WE'VE ALL HAD ENOUGH OF EXPERTS.
UNDERSTOOD, SIR.
I WON'T TELL ANYONE ANYTHING.

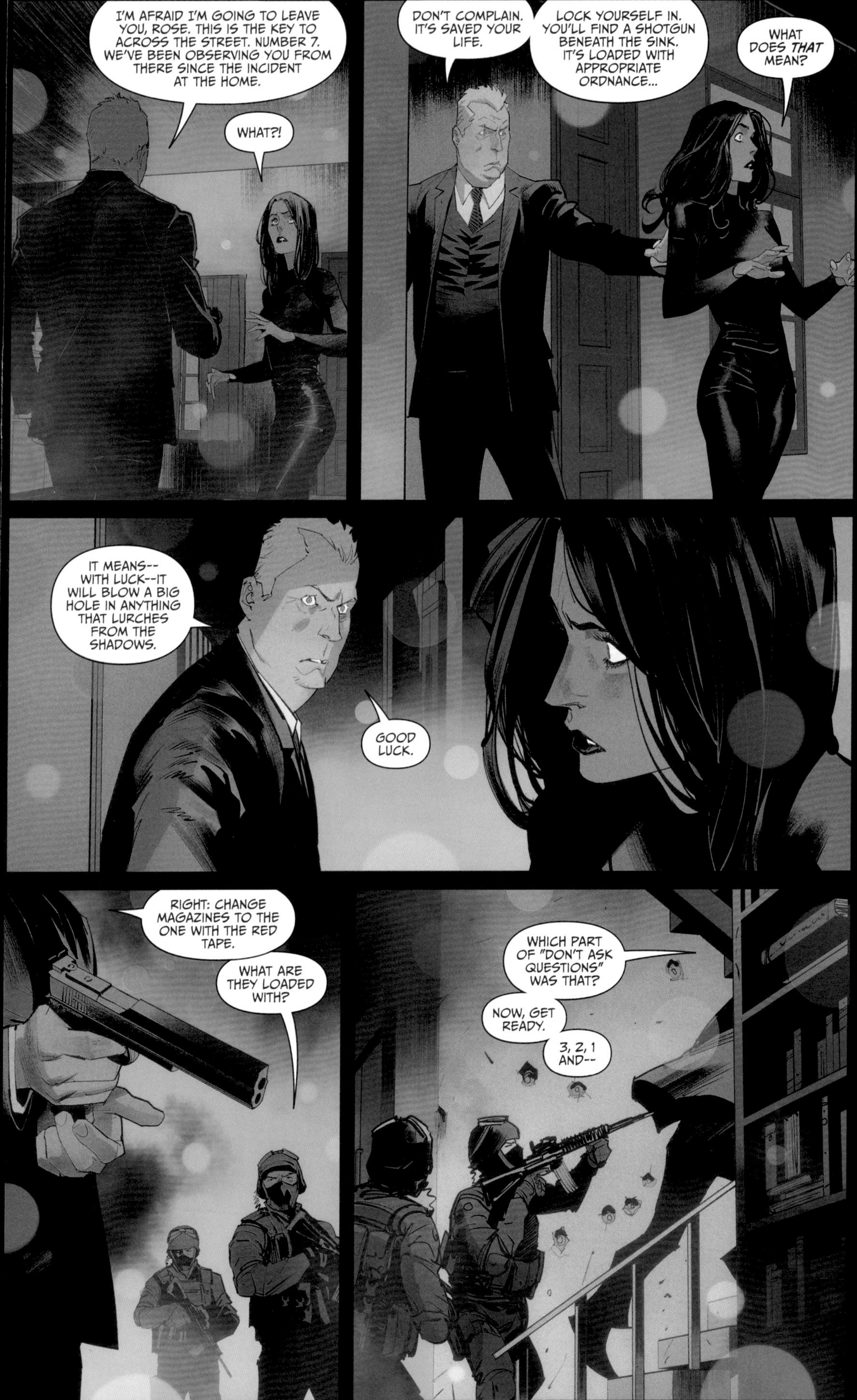
I'M AFRAID I'M GOING TO LEAVE YOU, ROSE. THIS IS THE KEY TO ACROSS THE STREET. NUMBER 7. WE'VE BEEN OBSERVING YOU FROM THERE SINCE THE INCIDENT AT THE HOME.
WHAT?!
DON'T COMPLAIN. IT'S SAVED YOUR LIFE.
LOCK YOURSELF IN. YOU'LL FIND A SHOTGUN BENEATH THE SINK. IT'S LOADED WITH APPROPRIATE ORDNANCE...
WHAT DOES *THAT* MEAN?
IT MEANS-- WITH LUCK--IT WILL BLOW A BIG HOLE IN ANYTHING THAT LURCHES FROM THE SHADOWS.
GOOD LUCK.
RIGHT: CHANGE MAGAZINES TO THE ONE WITH THE RED TAPE.
WHAT ARE THEY LOADED WITH?
WHICH PART OF "DON'T ASK QUESTIONS" WAS THAT?
NOW, GET READY.
3, 2, 1 AND--

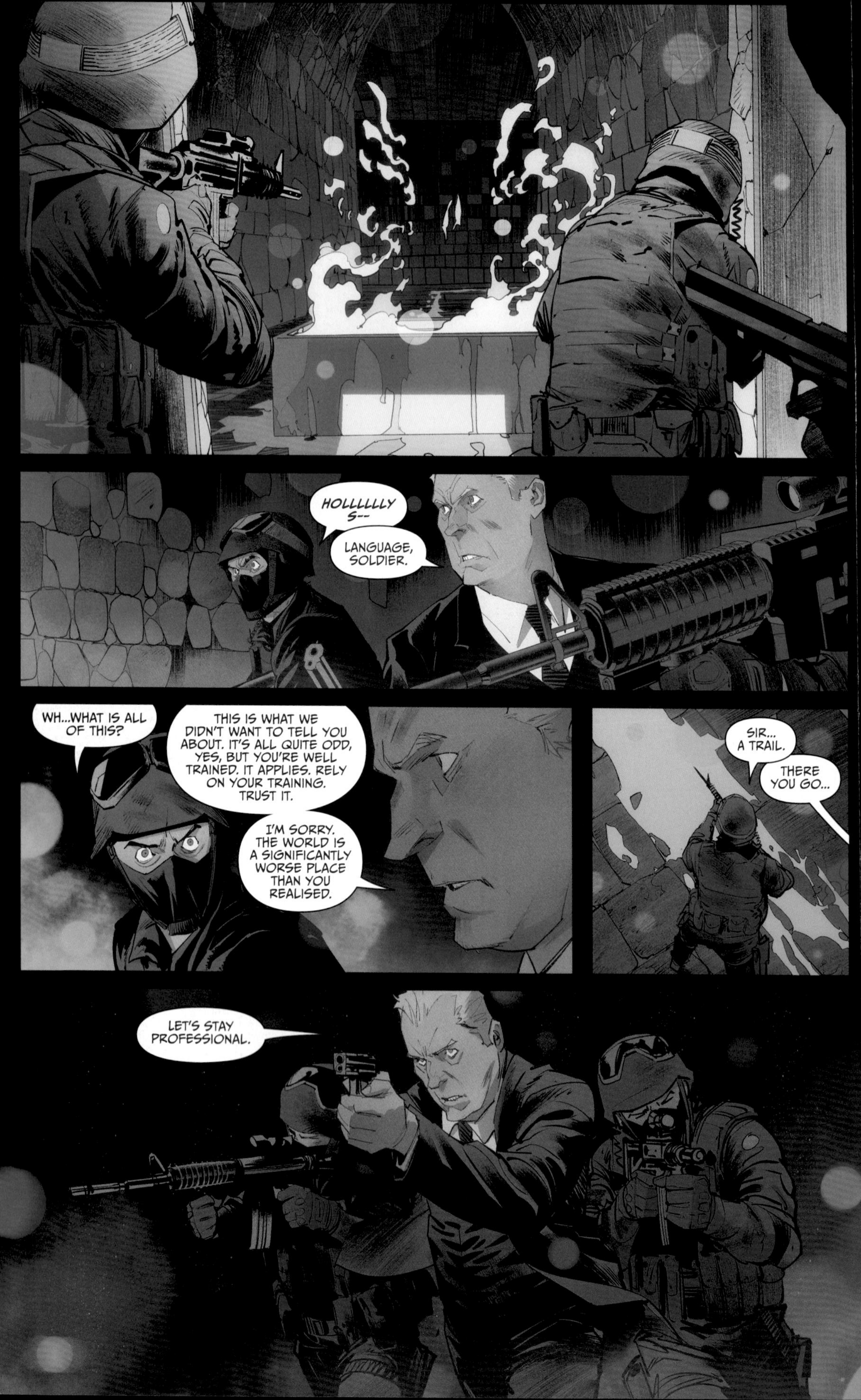

HOLLLLLLY S--
LANGUAGE, SOLDIER.
WH...WHAT IS ALL OF THIS?
THIS IS WHAT WE DIDN'T WANT TO TELL YOU ABOUT. IT'S ALL QUITE ODD, YES, BUT YOU'RE WELL TRAINED. IT APPLIES. RELY ON YOUR TRAINING. TRUST IT.
I'M SORRY. THE WORLD IS A SIGNIFICANTLY WORSE PLACE THAN YOU REALISED.
SIR... A TRAIL.
THERE YOU GO...
LET'S STAY PROFESSIONAL.

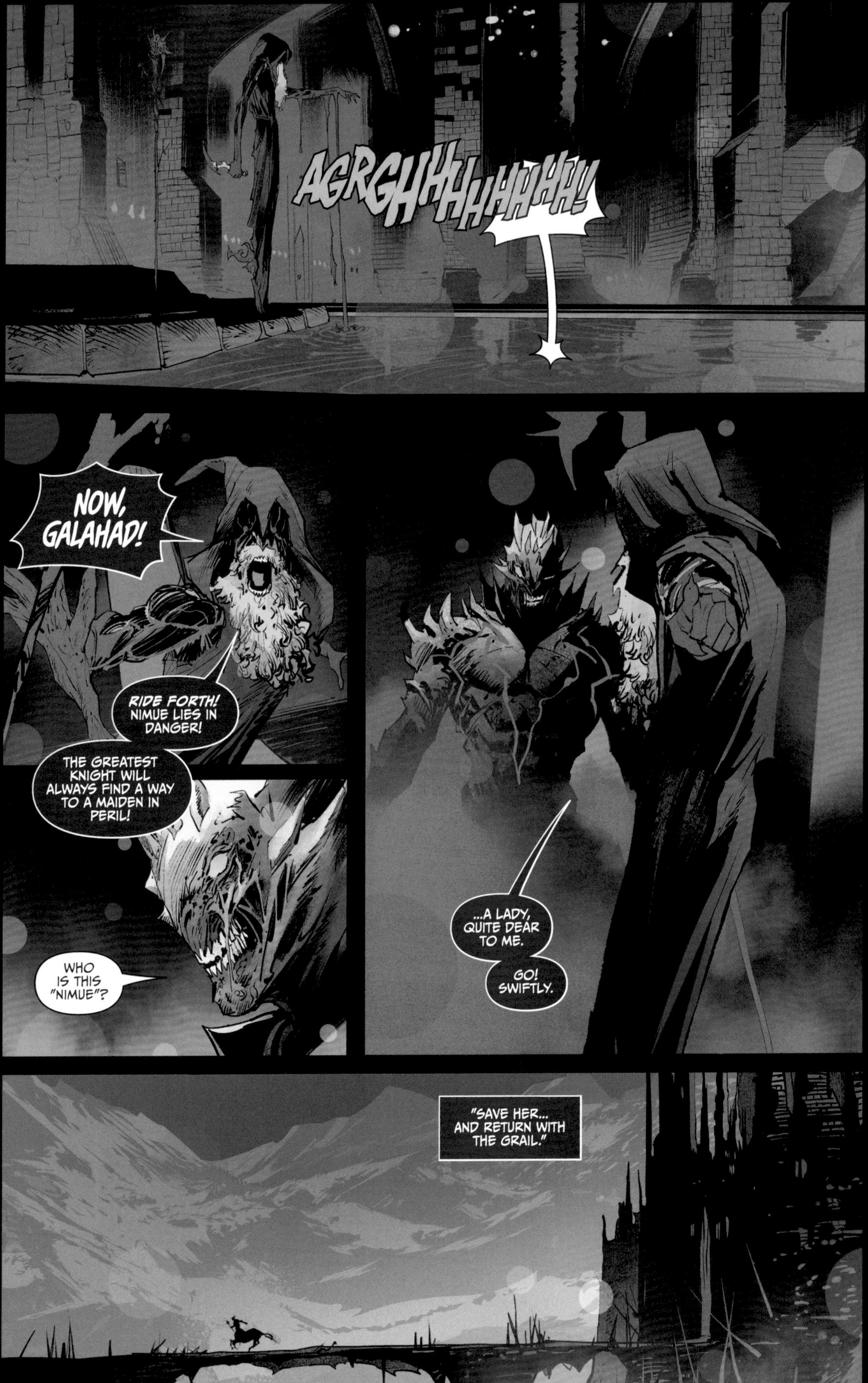
AGRGHHHHHHH!
NOW, GALAHAD!
RIDE FORTH! NIMUE LIES IN DANGER!
THE GREATEST KNIGHT WILL ALWAYS FIND A WAY TO A MAIDEN IN PERIL!
WHO IS THIS "NIMUE"?
...A LADY, QUITE DEAR TO ME.
GO! SWIFTLY.
"SAVE HER... AND RETURN WITH THE GRAIL."

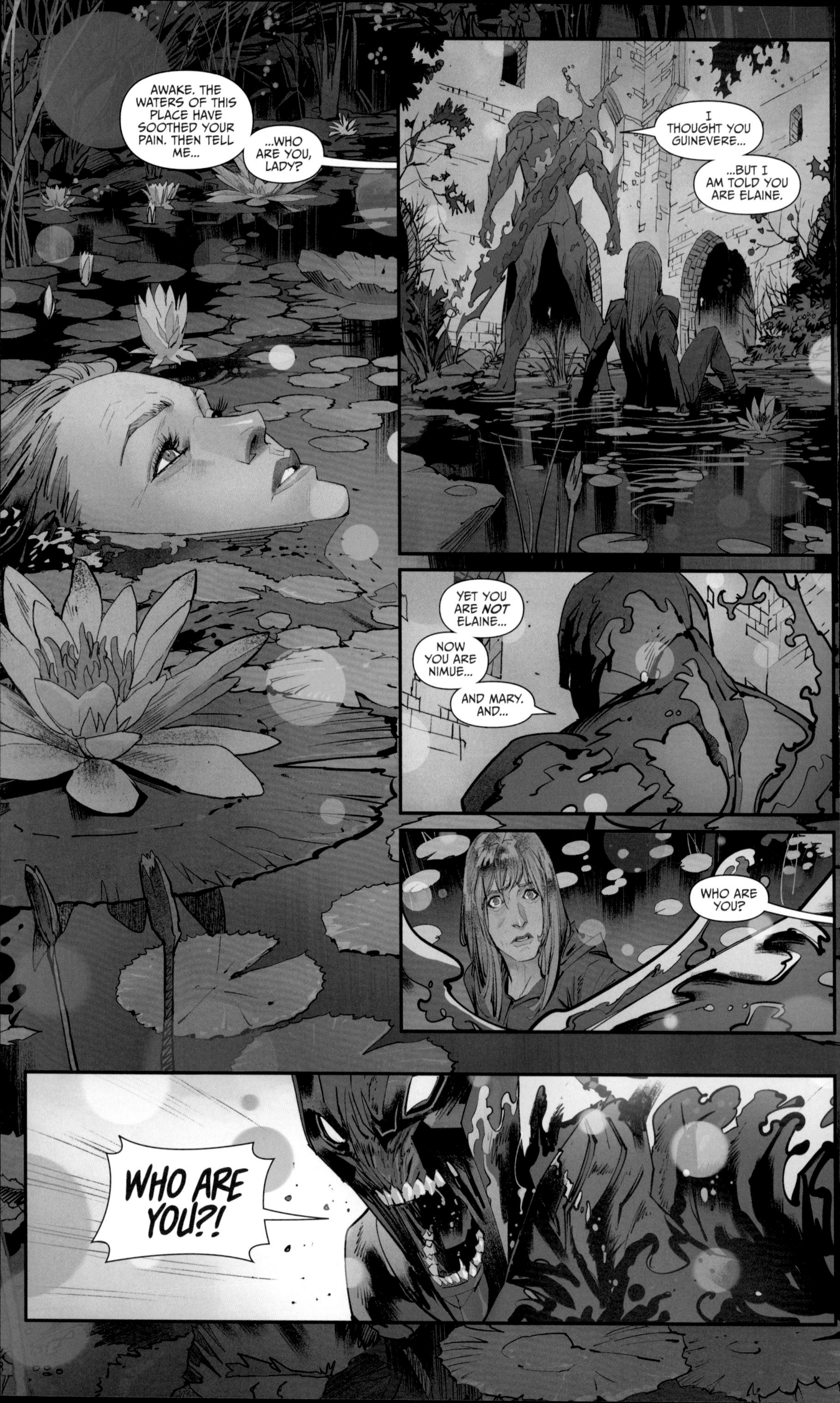
AWAKE. THE WATERS OF THIS PLACE HAVE SOOTHED YOUR PAIN. THEN TELL ME...
...WHO ARE YOU, LADY?
I THOUGHT YOU GUINEVERE...
...BUT I AM TOLD YOU ARE ELAINE.
YET YOU ARE NOT ELAINE...
NOW YOU ARE NIMUE...
AND MARY. AND...
WHO ARE YOU?
WHO ARE YOU?!

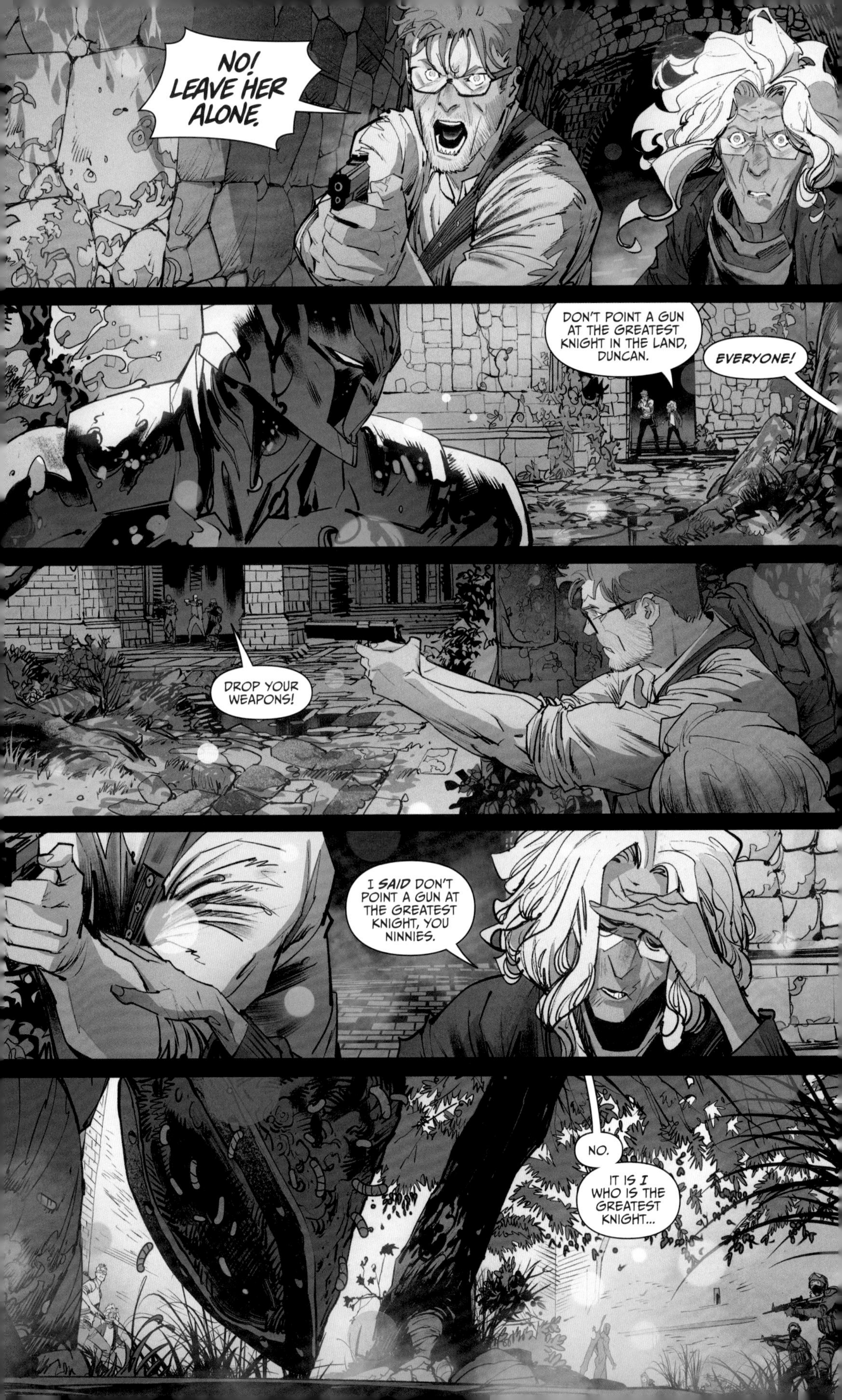
NO! LEAVE HER ALONE.
DON'T POINT A GUN AT THE GREATEST KNIGHT IN THE LAND, DUNCAN.
EVERYONE!
DROP YOUR WEAPONS!
I SAID DON'T POINT A GUN AT THE GREATEST KNIGHT, YOU NINNIES.
NO.
IT IS I WHO IS THE GREATEST KNIGHT...

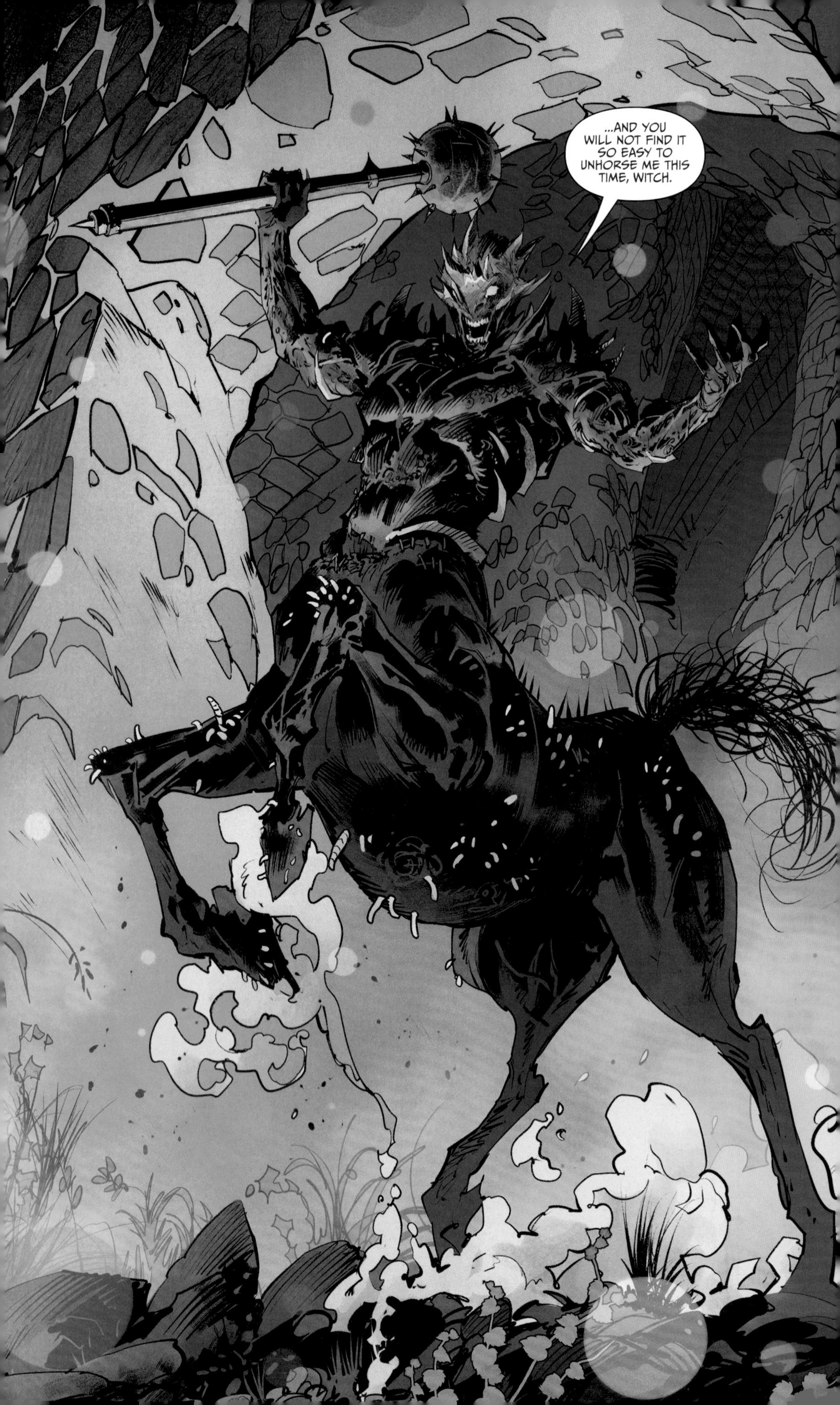
...AND YOU WILL NOT FIND IT SO EASY TO UNHORSE ME THIS TIME, WITCH.

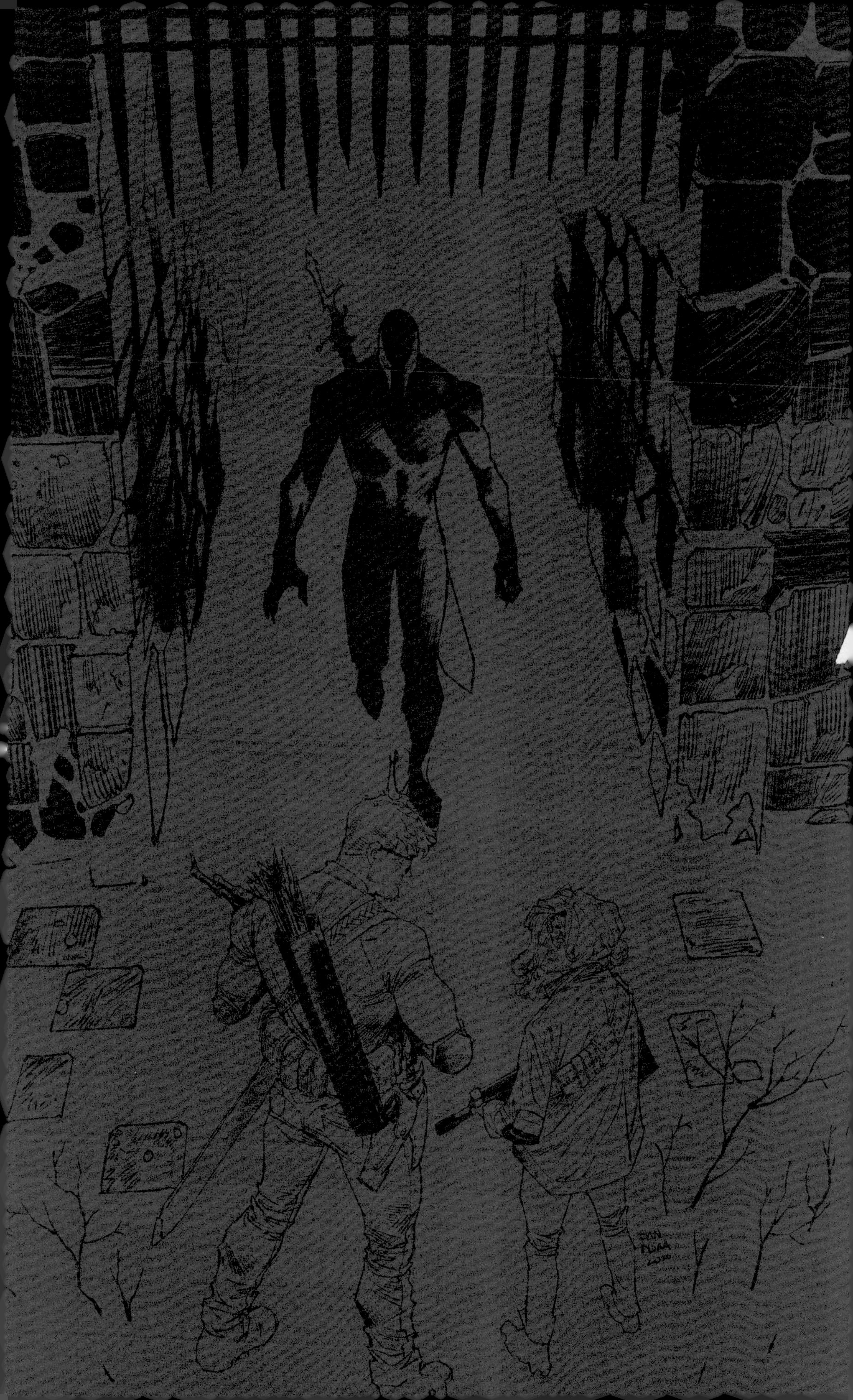

CHAPTER SEVENTEEN

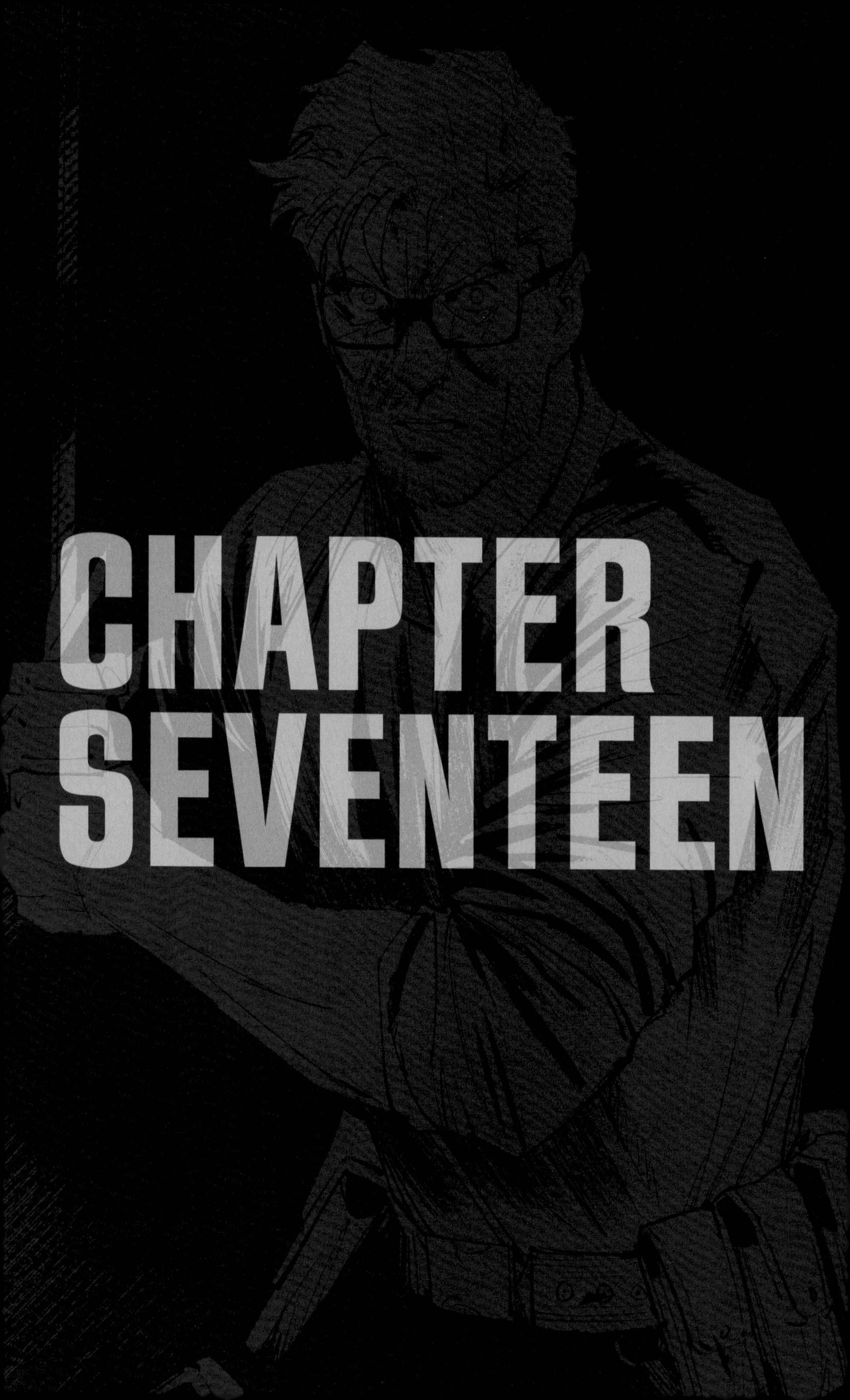

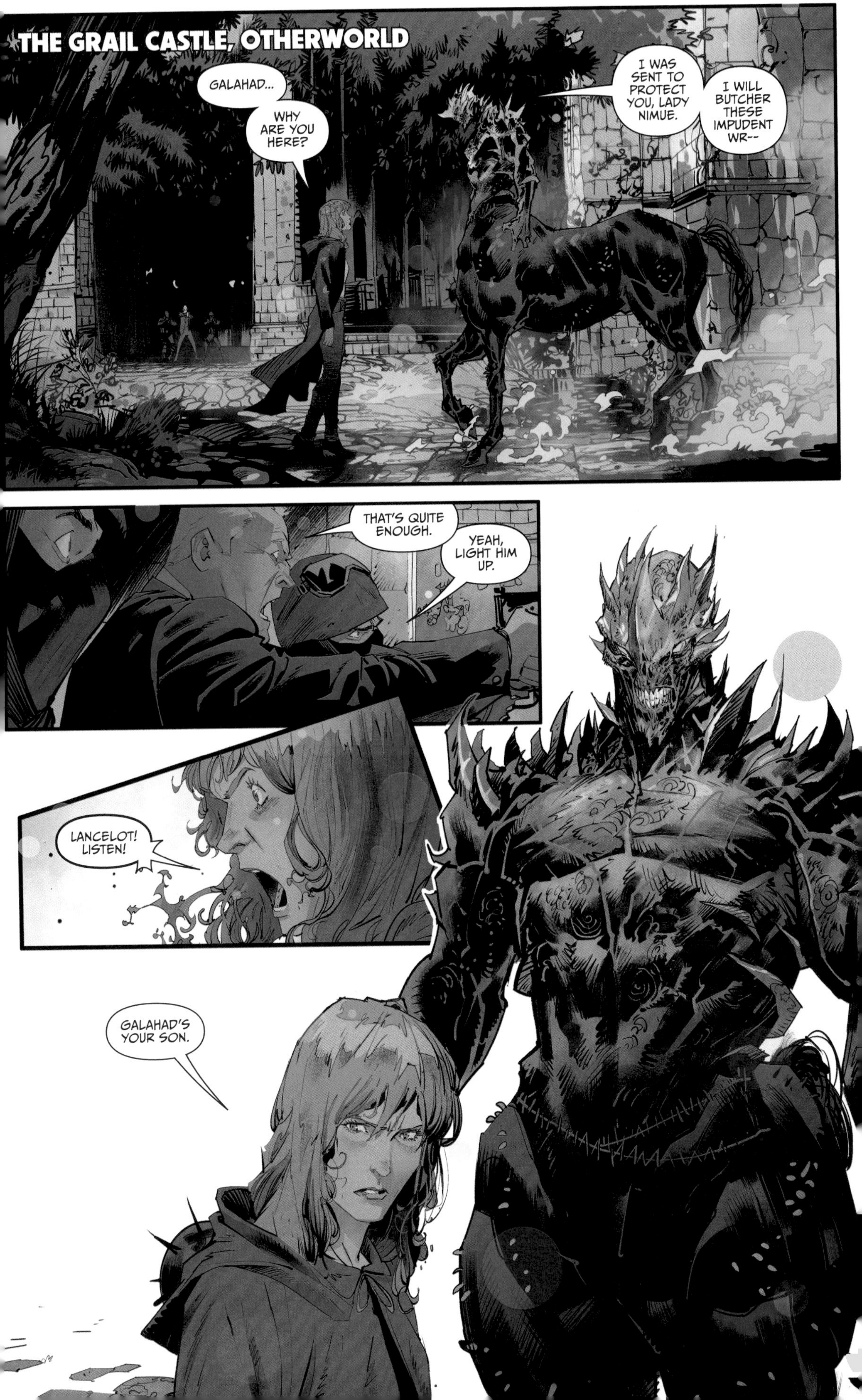
THE GRAIL CASTLE, OTHERWORLD
GALAHAD...
WHY ARE YOU HERE?
I WAS SENT TO PROTECT YOU, LADY NIMUE.
I WILL BUTCHER THESE IMPUDENT WR--
THAT'S QUITE ENOUGH.
YEAH, LIGHT HIM UP.
LANCELOT! LISTEN!
GALAHAD'S YOUR SON.

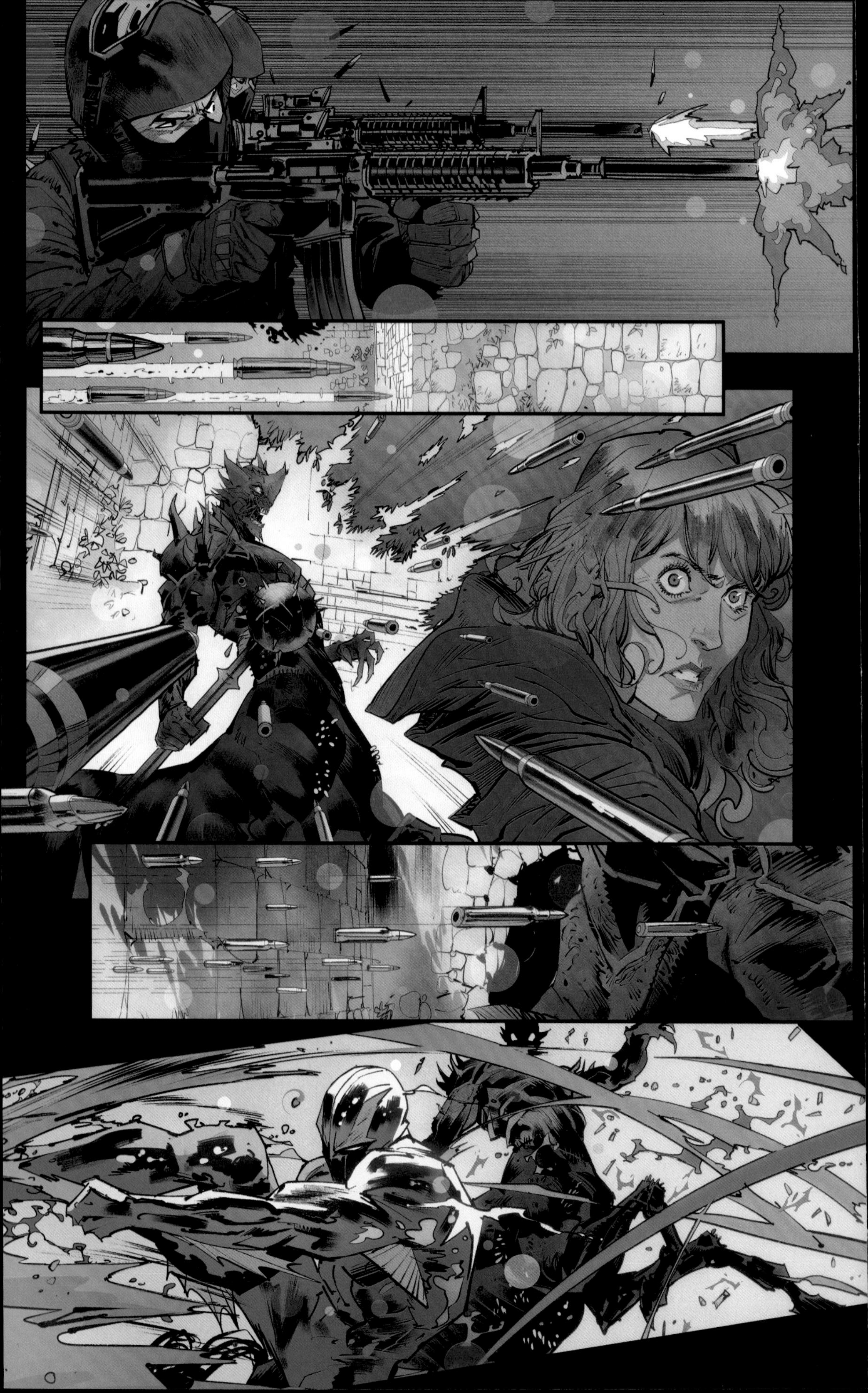

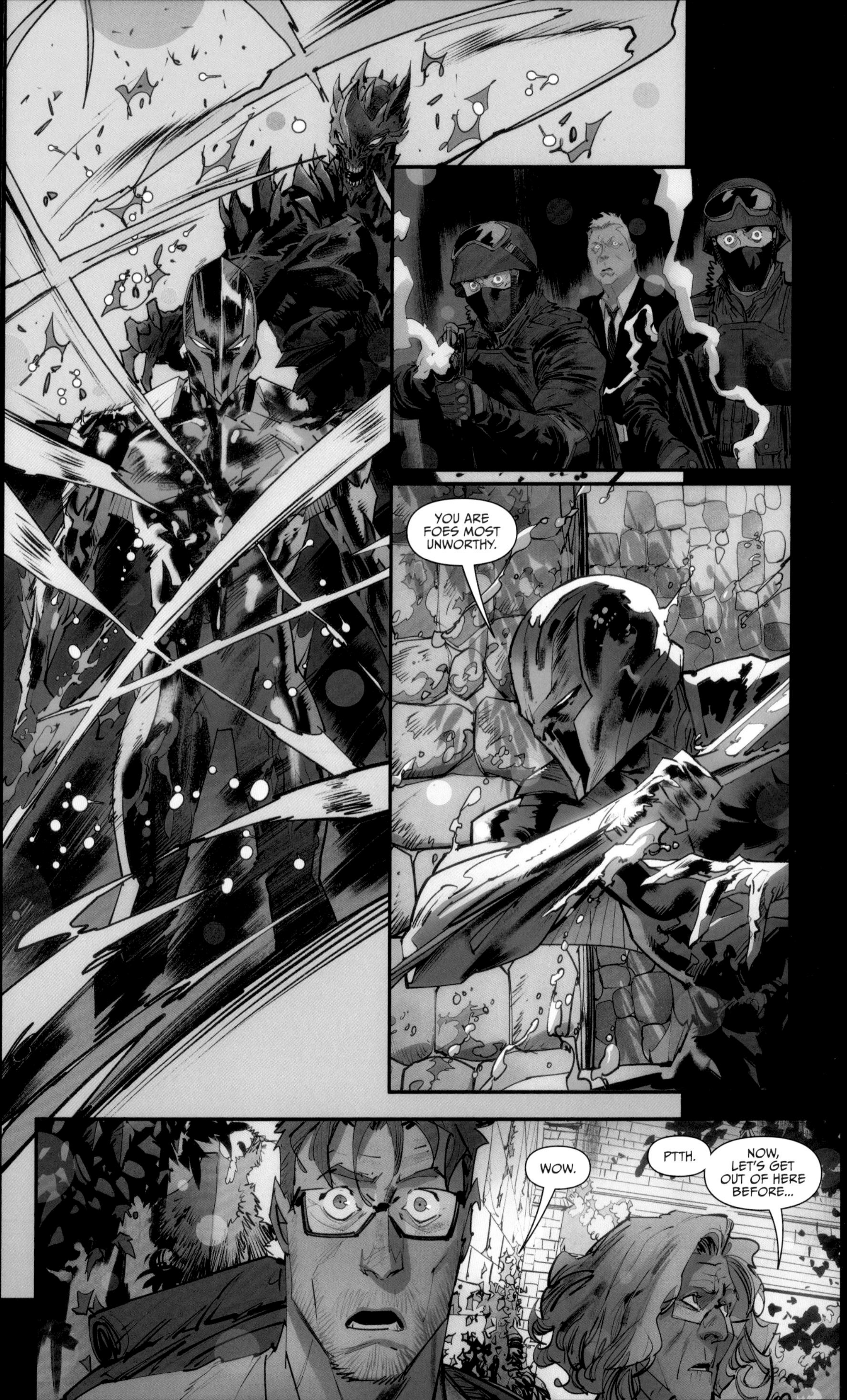
YOU ARE FOES MOST UNWORTHY.
WOW.
PTTH.
NOW, LET'S GET OUT OF HERE BEFORE...

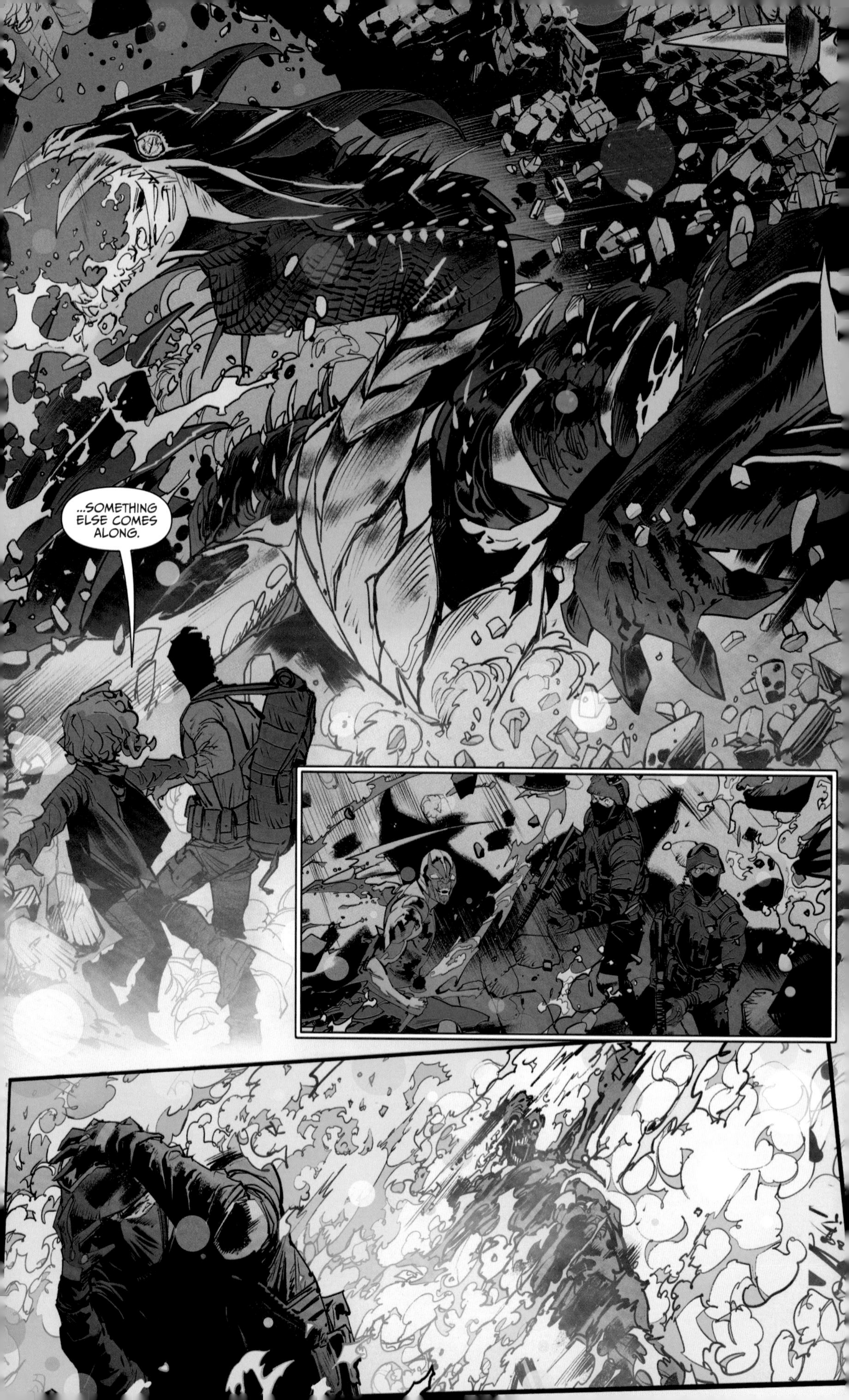
...SOMETHING ELSE COMES ALONG.

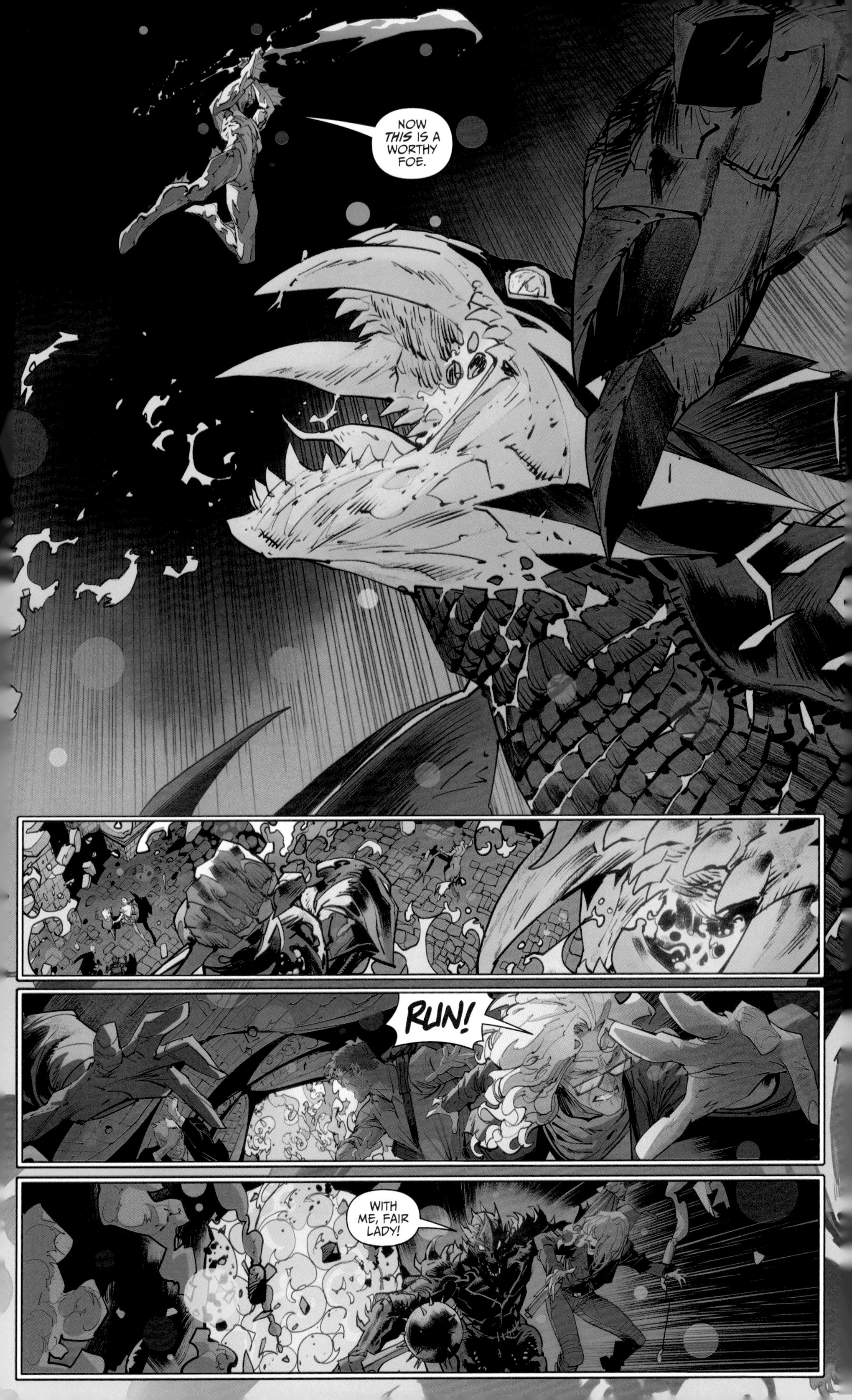
NOW *THIS* IS A WORTHY FOE.
RUN!
WITH ME, FAIR LADY!

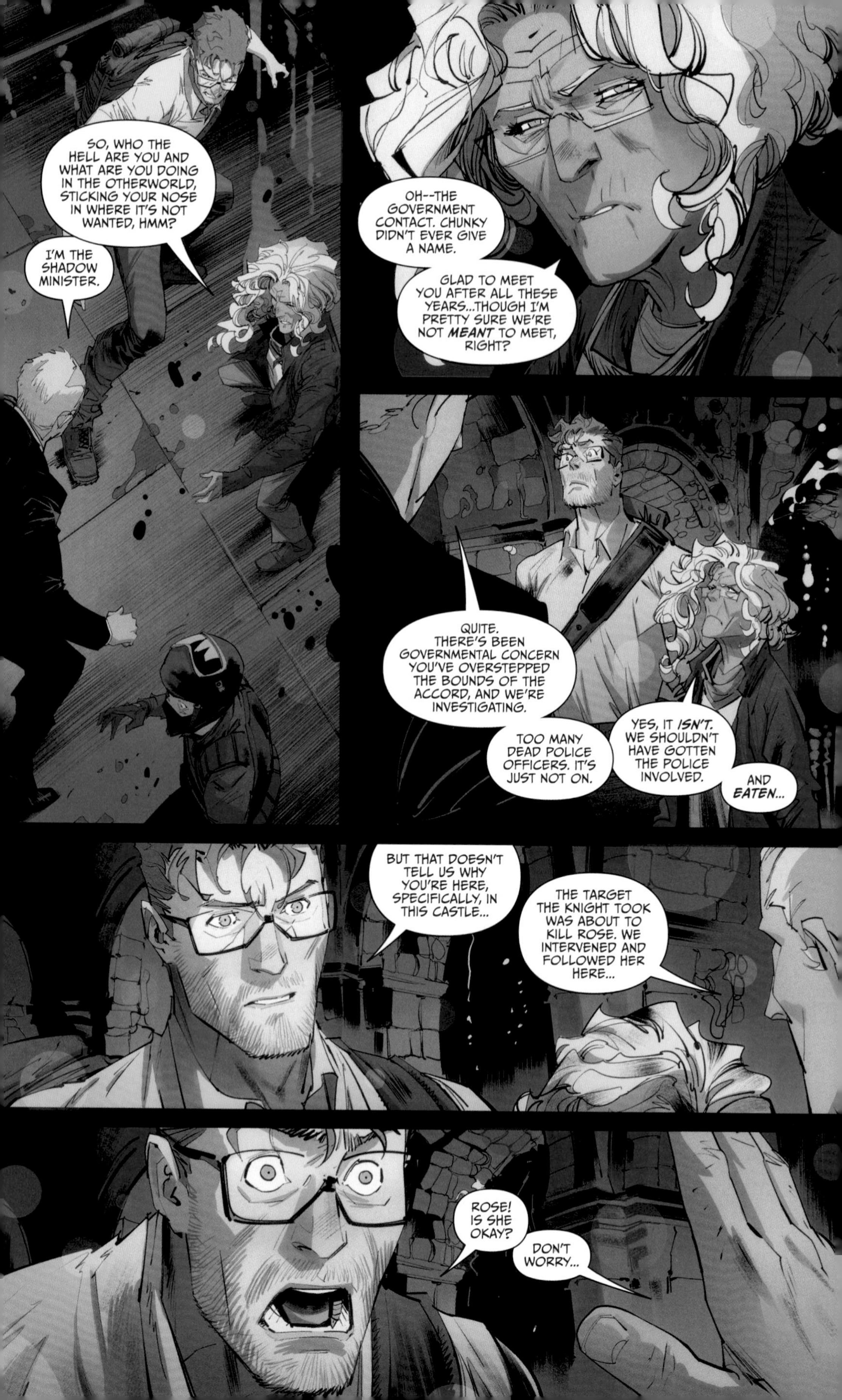
SO, WHO THE HELL ARE YOU AND WHAT ARE YOU DOING IN THE OTHERWORLD, STICKING YOUR NOSE IN WHERE IT'S NOT WANTED, HMM?
I'M THE SHADOW MINISTER.
OH--THE GOVERNMENT CONTACT. CHUNKY DIDN'T EVER GIVE A NAME.
GLAD TO MEET YOU AFTER ALL THESE YEARS...THOUGH I'M PRETTY SURE WE'RE NOT *MEANT* TO MEET, RIGHT?
QUITE. THERE'S BEEN GOVERNMENTAL CONCERN YOU'VE OVERSTEPPED THE BOUNDS OF THE ACCORD, AND WE'RE INVESTIGATING.
TOO MANY DEAD POLICE OFFICERS. IT'S JUST NOT ON.
YES, IT *ISN'T.* WE SHOULDN'T HAVE GOTTEN THE POLICE INVOLVED.
AND *EATEN*...
BUT THAT DOESN'T TELL US WHY YOU'RE HERE, SPECIFICALLY, IN THIS CASTLE...
THE TARGET THE KNIGHT TOOK WAS ABOUT TO KILL ROSE. WE INTERVENED AND FOLLOWED HER HERE...
ROSE! IS SHE OKAY?
DON'T WORRY...

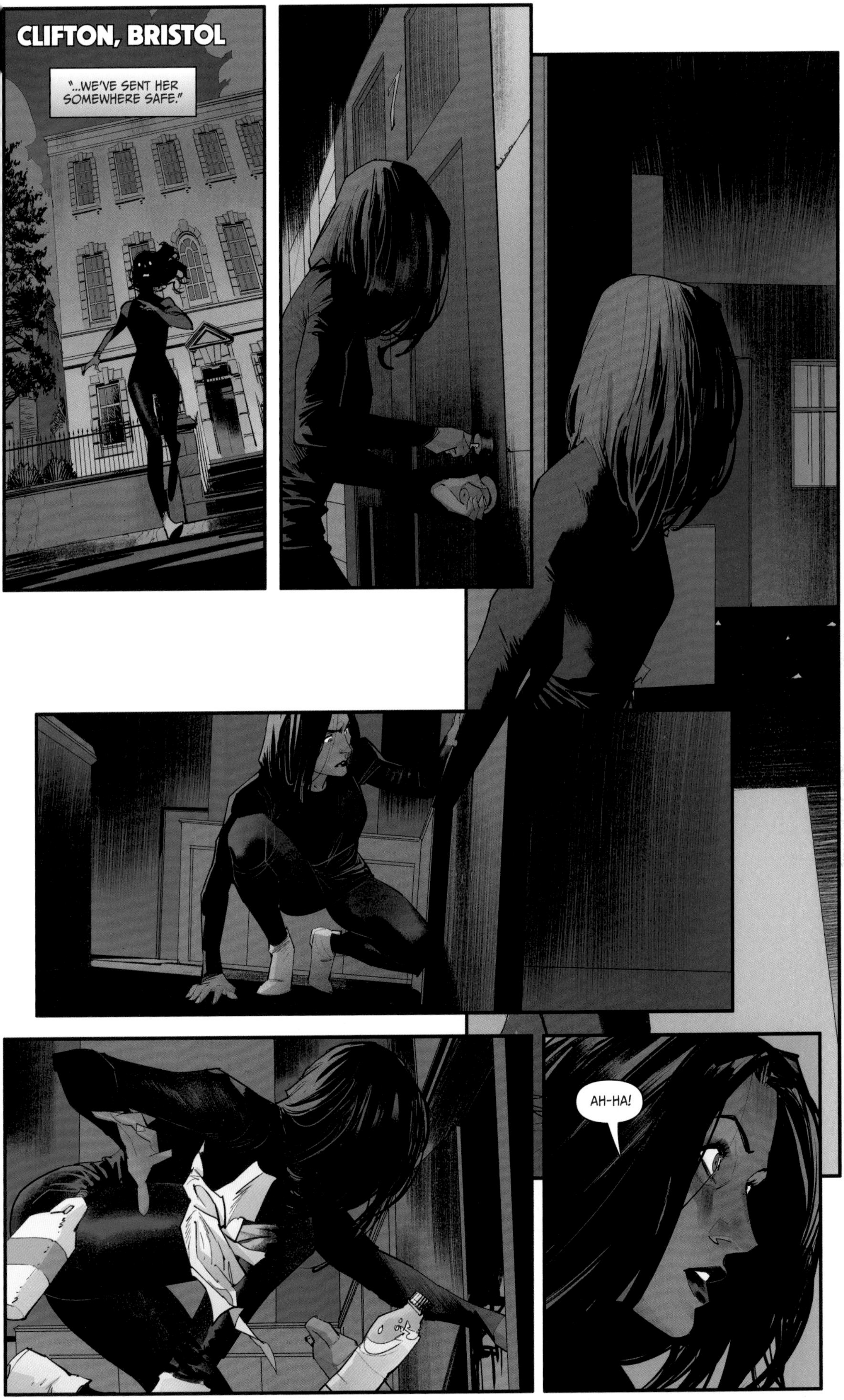
CLIFTON, BRISTOL
"...WE'VE SENT HER SOMEWHERE SAFE."
AH-HA!

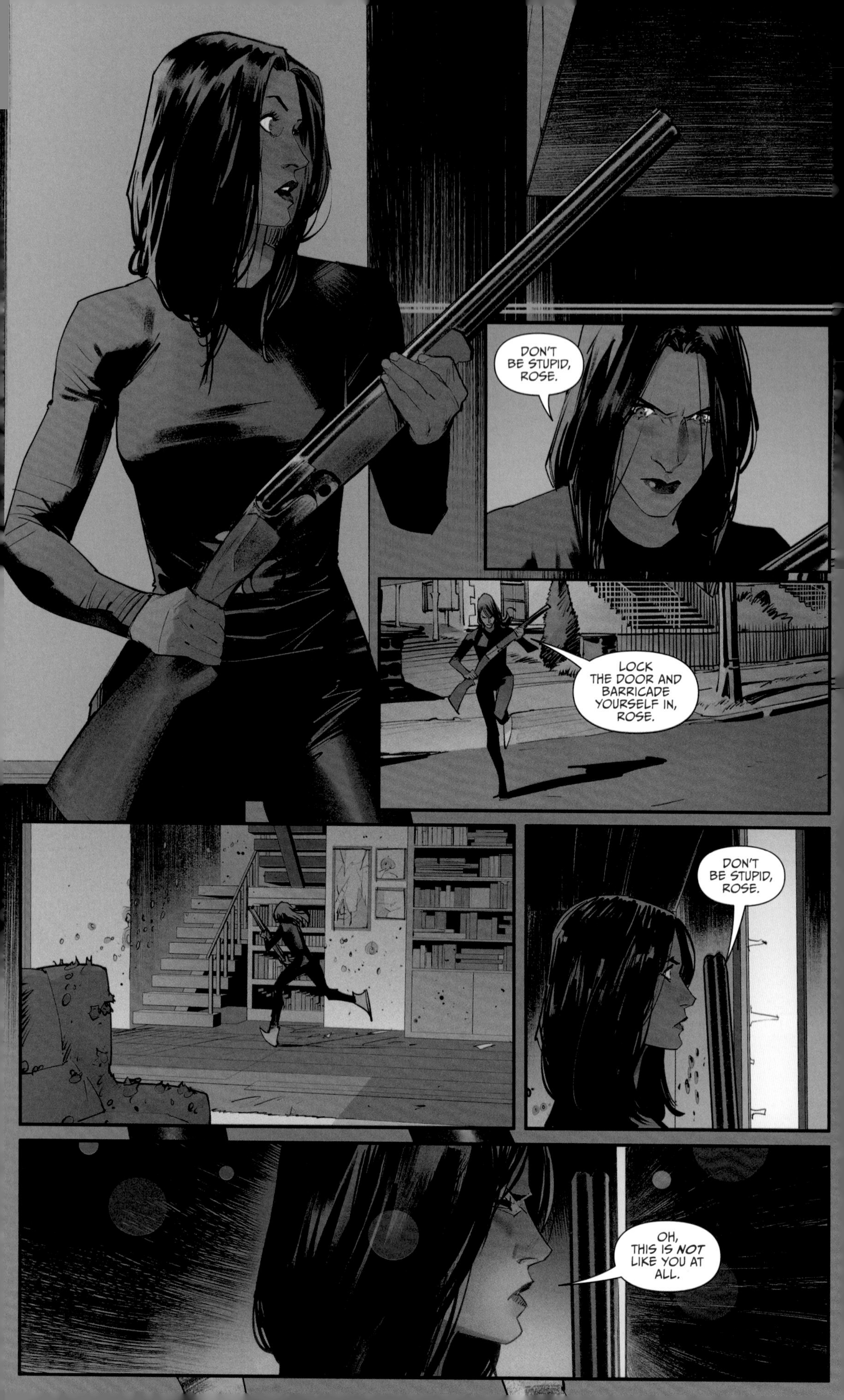
DON'T BE STUPID, ROSE.
LOCK THE DOOR AND BARRICADE YOURSELF IN, ROSE.
DON'T BE STUPID, ROSE.
OH, THIS IS *NOT* LIKE YOU AT ALL.

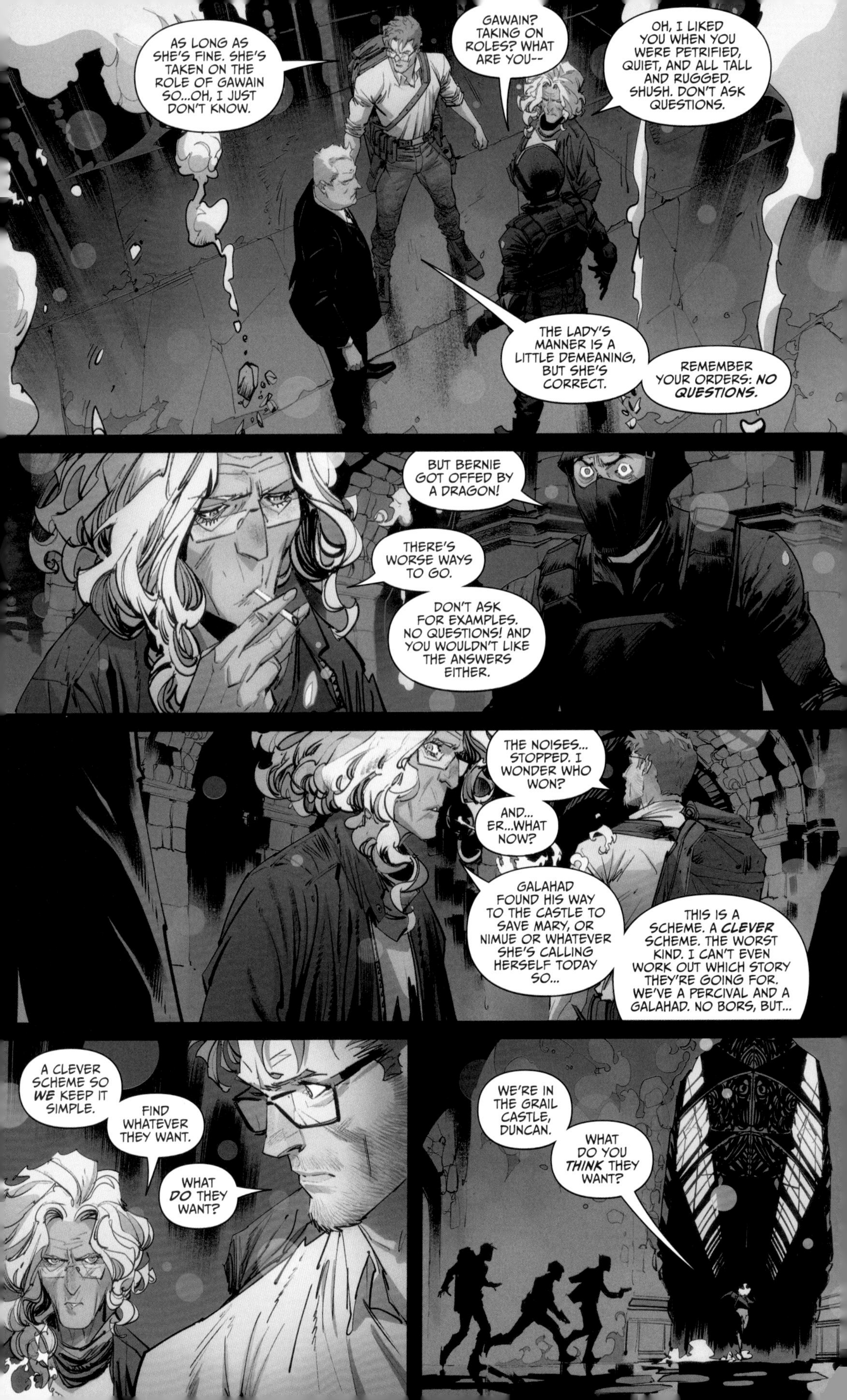
AS LONG AS SHE'S FINE. SHE'S TAKEN ON THE ROLE OF GAWAIN SO...OH, I JUST DON'T KNOW.
GAWAIN? TAKING ON ROLES? WHAT ARE YOU--
OH, I LIKED YOU WHEN YOU WERE PETRIFIED, QUIET, AND ALL TALL AND RUGGED. SHUSH. DON'T ASK QUESTIONS.
THE LADY'S MANNER IS A LITTLE DEMEANING, BUT SHE'S CORRECT.
REMEMBER YOUR ORDERS: ***NO QUESTIONS.***
BUT BERNIE GOT OFFED BY A DRAGON!
THERE'S WORSE WAYS TO GO.
DON'T ASK FOR EXAMPLES. NO QUESTIONS! AND YOU WOULDN'T LIKE THE ANSWERS EITHER.
THE NOISES... STOPPED. I WONDER WHO WON?
AND... ER...WHAT NOW?
GALAHAD FOUND HIS WAY TO THE CASTLE TO SAVE MARY, OR NIMUE OR WHATEVER SHE'S CALLING HERSELF TODAY SO...
THIS IS A SCHEME. A ***CLEVER*** SCHEME. THE WORST KIND. I CAN'T EVEN WORK OUT WHICH STORY THEY'RE GOING FOR. WE'VE A PERCIVAL AND A GALAHAD. NO BORS, BUT...
A CLEVER SCHEME SO ***WE*** KEEP IT SIMPLE.
FIND WHATEVER THEY WANT.
WHAT ***DO*** THEY WANT?
WE'RE IN THE GRAIL CASTLE, DUNCAN.
WHAT DO YOU ***THINK*** THEY WANT?

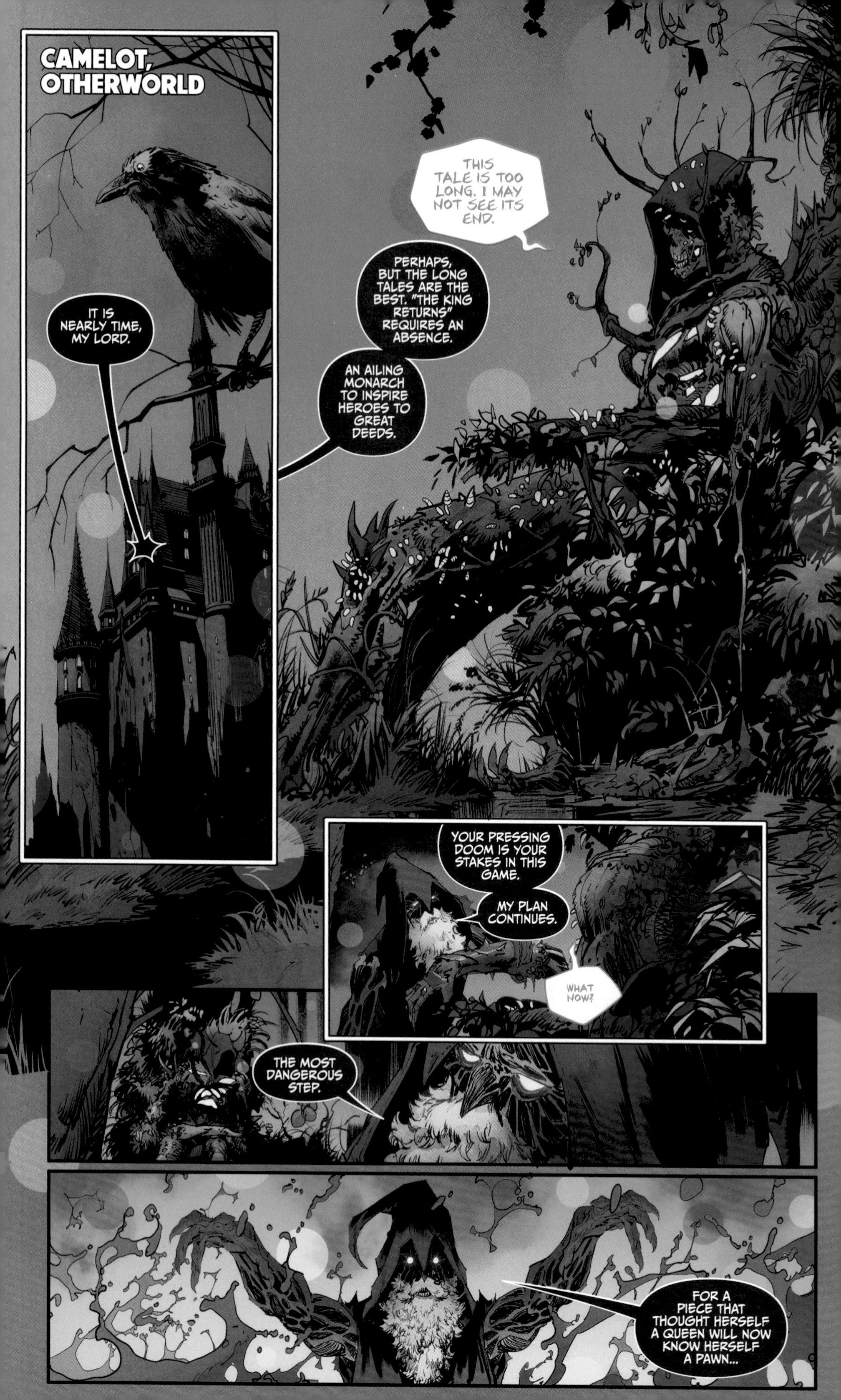

CAMELOT, OTHERWORLD
IT IS NEARLY TIME, MY LORD.
THIS TALE IS TOO LONG. I MAY NOT SEE ITS END.
PERHAPS, BUT THE LONG TALES ARE THE BEST. "THE KING RETURNS" REQUIRES AN ABSENCE.
AN AILING MONARCH TO INSPIRE HEROES TO GREAT DEEDS.
YOUR PRESSING DOOM IS YOUR STAKES IN THIS GAME.
MY PLAN CONTINUES.
WHAT NOW?
THE MOST DANGEROUS STEP.
FOR A PIECE THAT THOUGHT HERSELF A QUEEN WILL NOW KNOW HERSELF A PAWN...

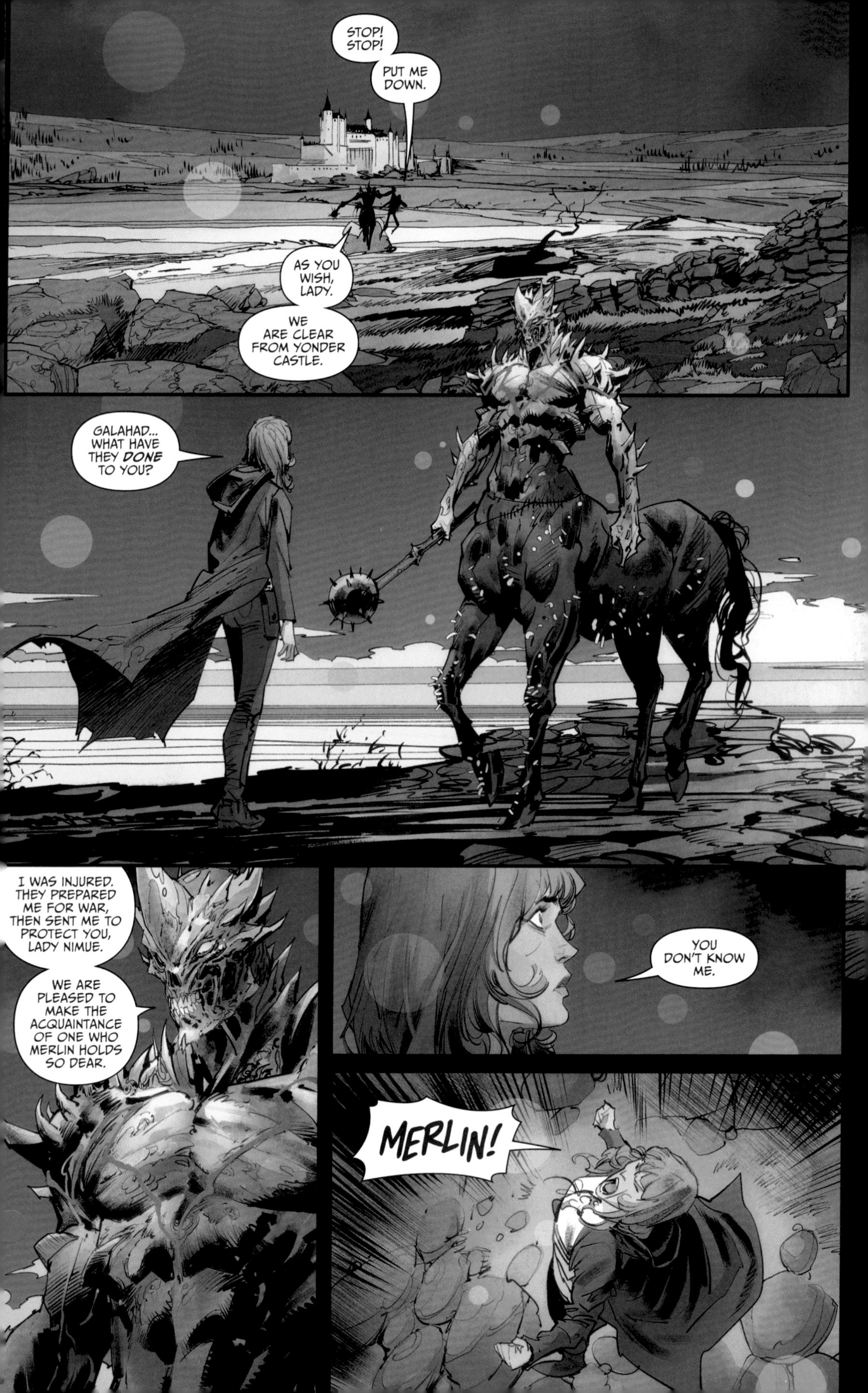
STOP! STOP!
PUT ME DOWN.
AS YOU WISH, LADY.
WE ARE CLEAR FROM YONDER CASTLE.
GALAHAD... WHAT HAVE THEY *DONE* TO YOU?
I WAS INJURED. THEY PREPARED ME FOR WAR, THEN SENT ME TO PROTECT YOU, LADY NIMUE.
WE ARE PLEASED TO MAKE THE ACQUAINTANCE OF ONE WHO MERLIN HOLDS SO DEAR.
YOU DON'T KNOW ME.
MERLIN!

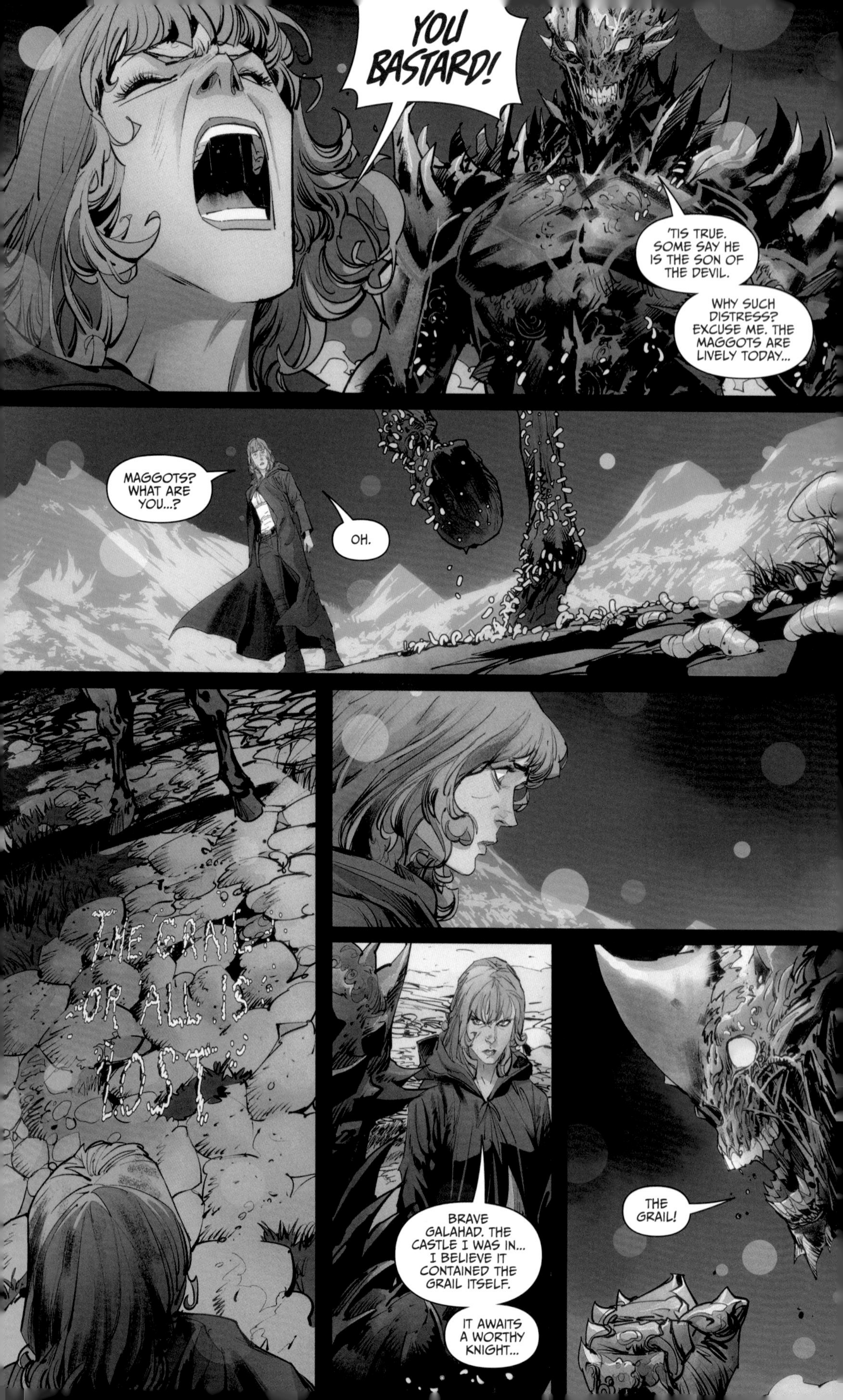
YOU BASTARD!
'TIS TRUE. SOME SAY HE IS THE SON OF THE DEVIL.
WHY SUCH DISTRESS? EXCUSE ME. THE MAGGOTS ARE LIVELY TODAY...
MAGGOTS? WHAT ARE YOU...?
OH.
THE GRAIL OR ALL IS LOST
BRAVE GALAHAD. THE CASTLE I WAS IN... I BELIEVE IT CONTAINED THE GRAIL ITSELF.
IT AWAITS A WORTHY KNIGHT...
THE GRAIL!

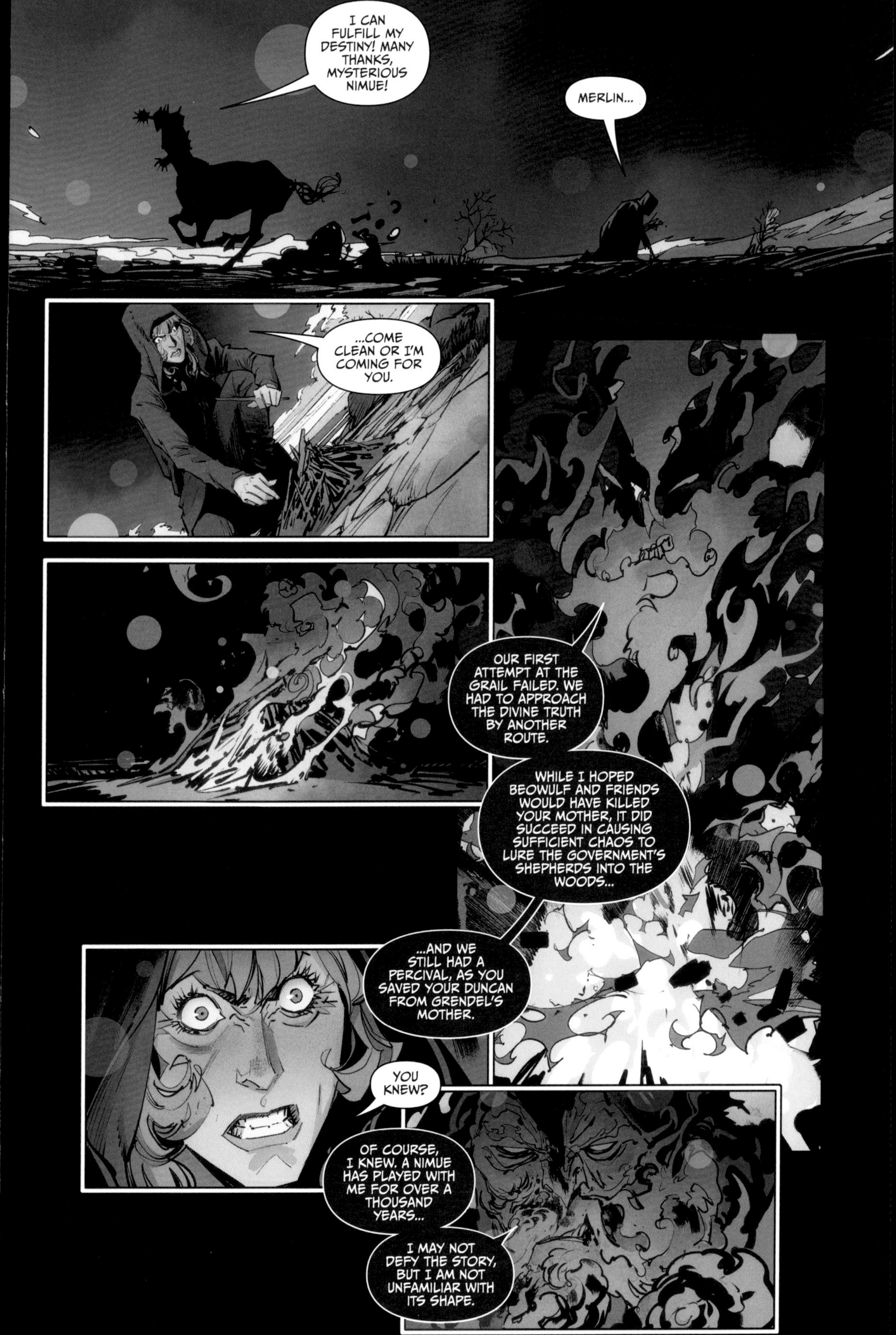
I CAN FULFILL MY DESTINY! MANY THANKS, MYSTERIOUS NIMUE!
MERLIN...
...COME CLEAN OR I'M COMING FOR YOU.
OUR FIRST ATTEMPT AT THE GRAIL FAILED. WE HAD TO APPROACH THE DIVINE TRUTH BY ANOTHER ROUTE.
WHILE I HOPED BEOWULF AND FRIENDS WOULD HAVE KILLED YOUR MOTHER, IT DID SUCCEED IN CAUSING SUFFICIENT CHAOS TO LURE THE GOVERNMENT'S SHEPHERDS INTO THE WOODS...
...AND WE STILL HAD A PERCIVAL, AS YOU SAVED YOUR DUNCAN FROM GRENDEL'S MOTHER.
YOU KNEW?
OF COURSE, I KNEW. A NIMUE HAS PLAYED WITH ME FOR OVER A THOUSAND YEARS...
I MAY NOT DEFY THE STORY, BUT I AM NOT UNFAMILIAR WITH ITS SHAPE.

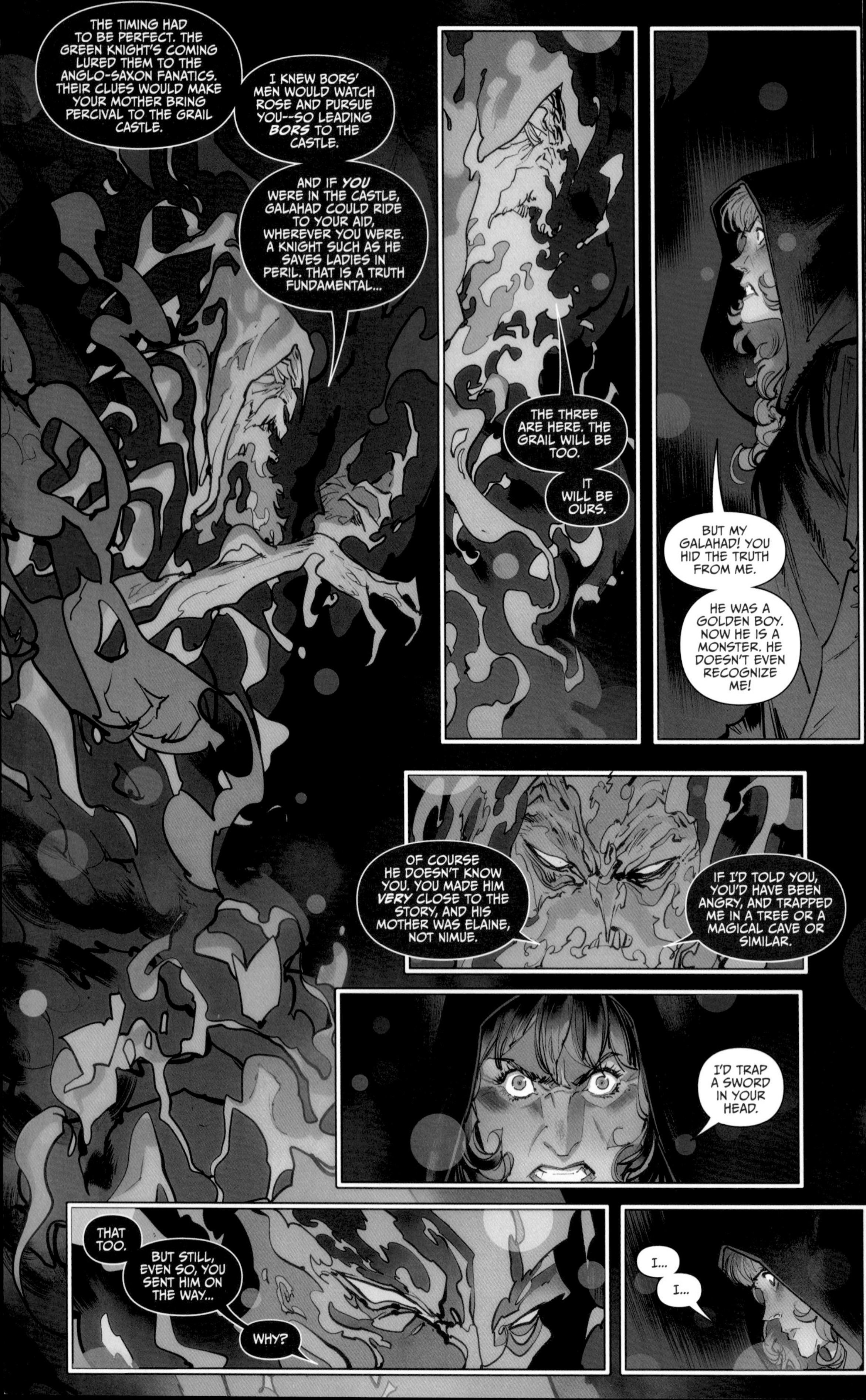
THE TIMING HAD TO BE PERFECT. THE GREEN KNIGHT'S COMING LURED THEM TO THE ANGLO-SAXON FANATICS. THEIR CLUES WOULD MAKE YOUR MOTHER BRING PERCIVAL TO THE GRAIL CASTLE.
I KNEW BORS' MEN WOULD WATCH ROSE AND PURSUE YOU--SO LEADING BORS TO THE CASTLE.
AND IF YOU WERE IN THE CASTLE, GALAHAD COULD RIDE TO YOUR AID, WHEREVER YOU WERE. A KNIGHT SUCH AS HE SAVES LADIES IN PERIL. THAT IS A TRUTH FUNDAMENTAL...
THE THREE ARE HERE. THE GRAIL WILL BE TOO.
IT WILL BE OURS.
BUT MY GALAHAD! YOU HID THE TRUTH FROM ME.
HE WAS A GOLDEN BOY. NOW HE IS A MONSTER. HE DOESN'T EVEN RECOGNIZE ME!
OF COURSE HE DOESN'T KNOW YOU. YOU MADE HIM VERY CLOSE TO THE STORY, AND HIS MOTHER WAS ELAINE, NOT NIMUE.
IF I'D TOLD YOU, YOU'D HAVE BEEN ANGRY, AND TRAPPED ME IN A TREE OR A MAGICAL CAVE OR SIMILAR.
I'D TRAP A SWORD IN YOUR HEAD.
THAT TOO.
BUT STILL, EVEN SO, YOU SENT HIM ON THE WAY...
WHY?
I...
I...

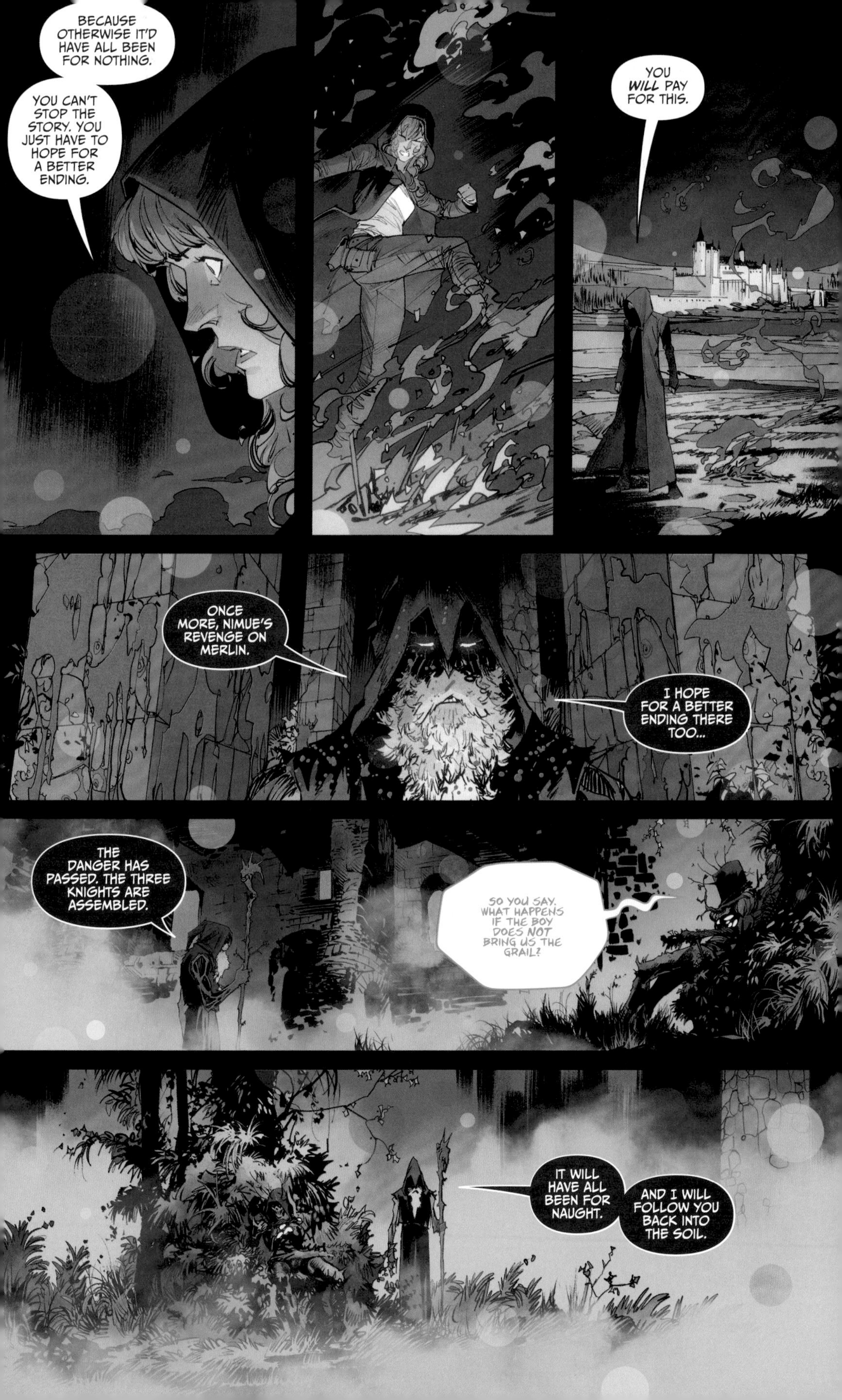

BECAUSE OTHERWISE IT'D HAVE ALL BEEN FOR NOTHING.
YOU CAN'T STOP THE STORY. YOU JUST HAVE TO HOPE FOR A BETTER ENDING.
YOU WILL PAY FOR THIS.
ONCE MORE, NIMUE'S REVENGE ON MERLIN.
I HOPE FOR A BETTER ENDING THERE TOO...
THE DANGER HAS PASSED. THE THREE KNIGHTS ARE ASSEMBLED.
SO YOU SAY. WHAT HAPPENS IF THE BOY DOES NOT BRING US THE GRAIL?
IT WILL HAVE ALL BEEN FOR NAUGHT.
AND I WILL FOLLOW YOU BACK INTO THE SOIL.

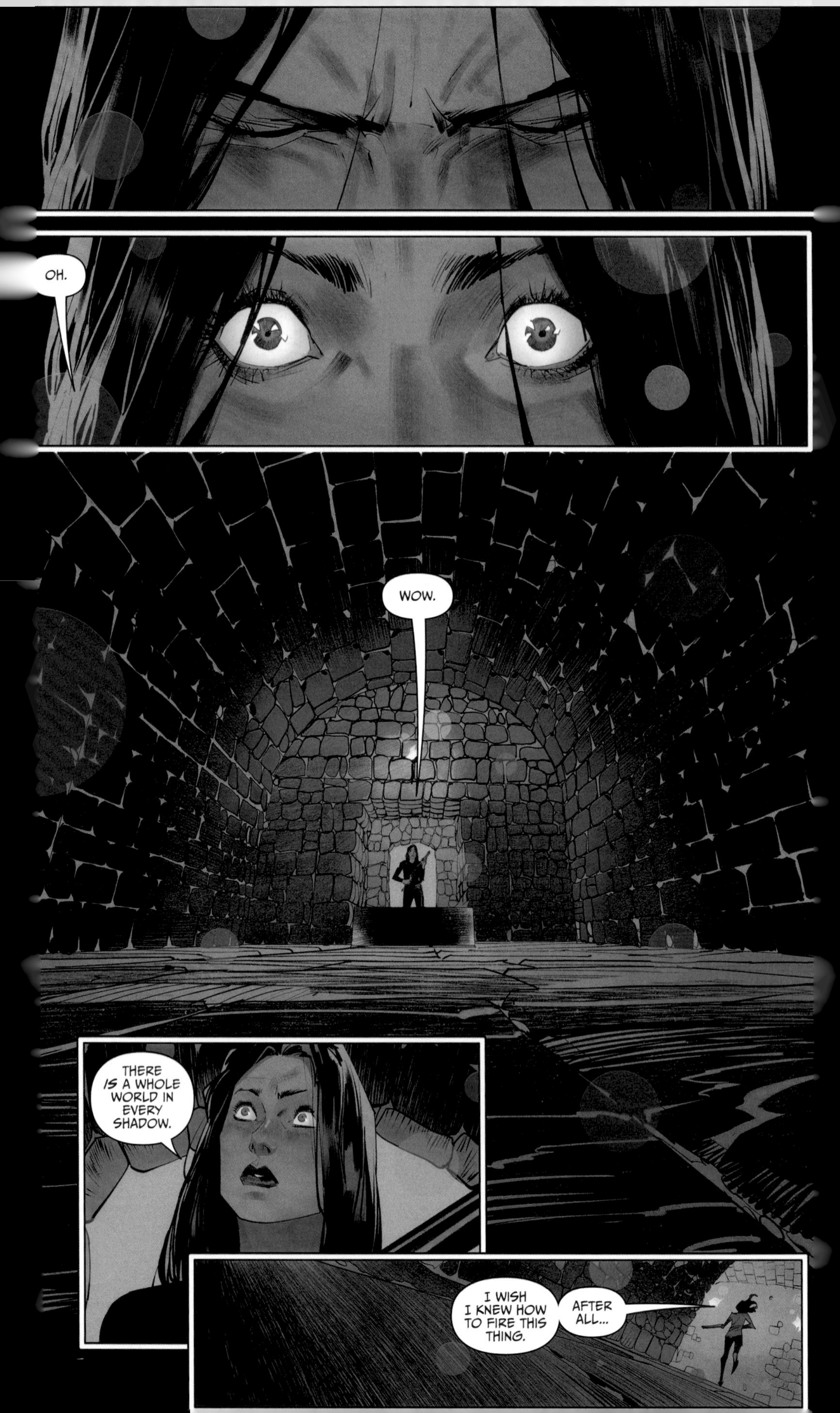
OH.
WOW.
THERE *IS* A WHOLE WORLD IN EVERY SHADOW.
I WISH I KNEW HOW TO FIRE THIS THING.
AFTER ALL...

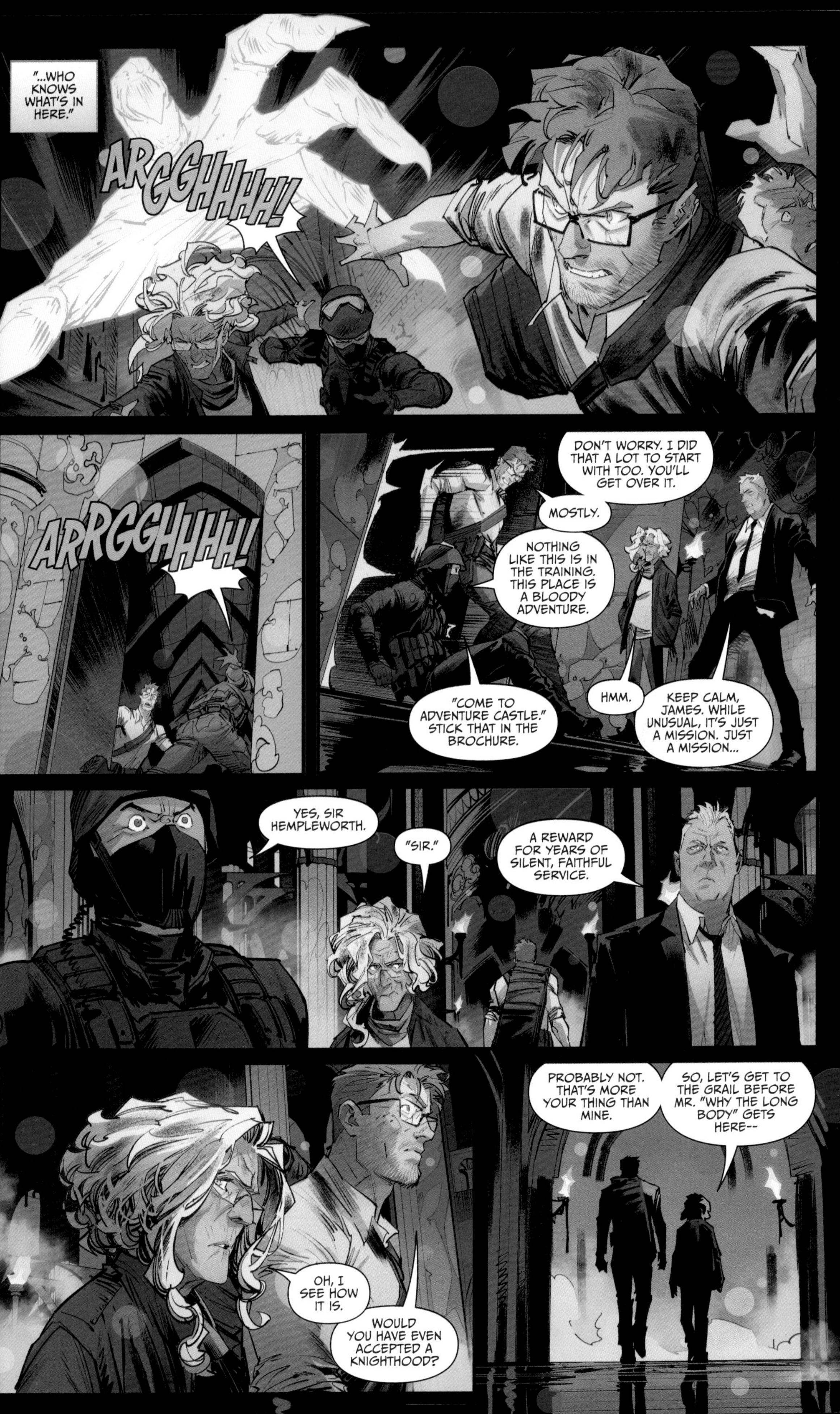
"...WHO KNOWS WHAT'S IN HERE."
ARGGHHHH!
ARRGGHHHH!
DON'T WORRY. I DID THAT A LOT TO START WITH TOO. YOU'LL GET OVER IT.
MOSTLY.
NOTHING LIKE THIS IS IN THE TRAINING. THIS PLACE IS A BLOODY ADVENTURE.
"COME TO ADVENTURE CASTLE." STICK THAT IN THE BROCHURE.
HMM.
KEEP CALM, JAMES. WHILE UNUSUAL, IT'S JUST A MISSION. JUST A MISSION...
YES, SIR HEMPLEWORTH.
"SIR."
A REWARD FOR YEARS OF SILENT, FAITHFUL SERVICE.
OH, I SEE HOW IT IS.
WOULD YOU HAVE EVEN ACCEPTED A KNIGHTHOOD?
PROBABLY NOT. THAT'S MORE YOUR THING THAN MINE.
SO, LET'S GET TO THE GRAIL BEFORE MR. "WHY THE LONG BODY" GETS HERE--

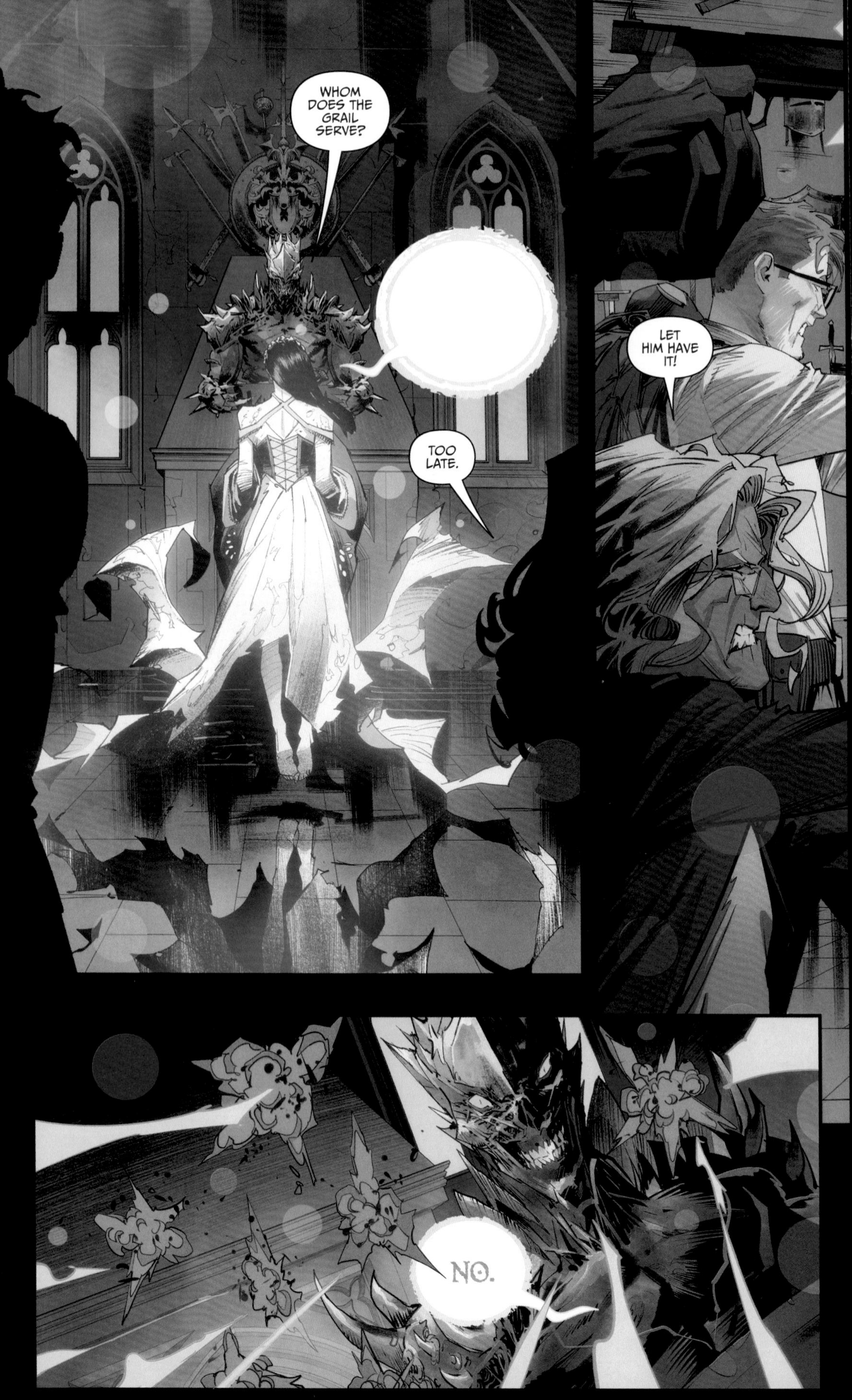
WHOM DOES THE GRAIL SERVE?
TOO LATE.
LET HIM HAVE IT!
NO.

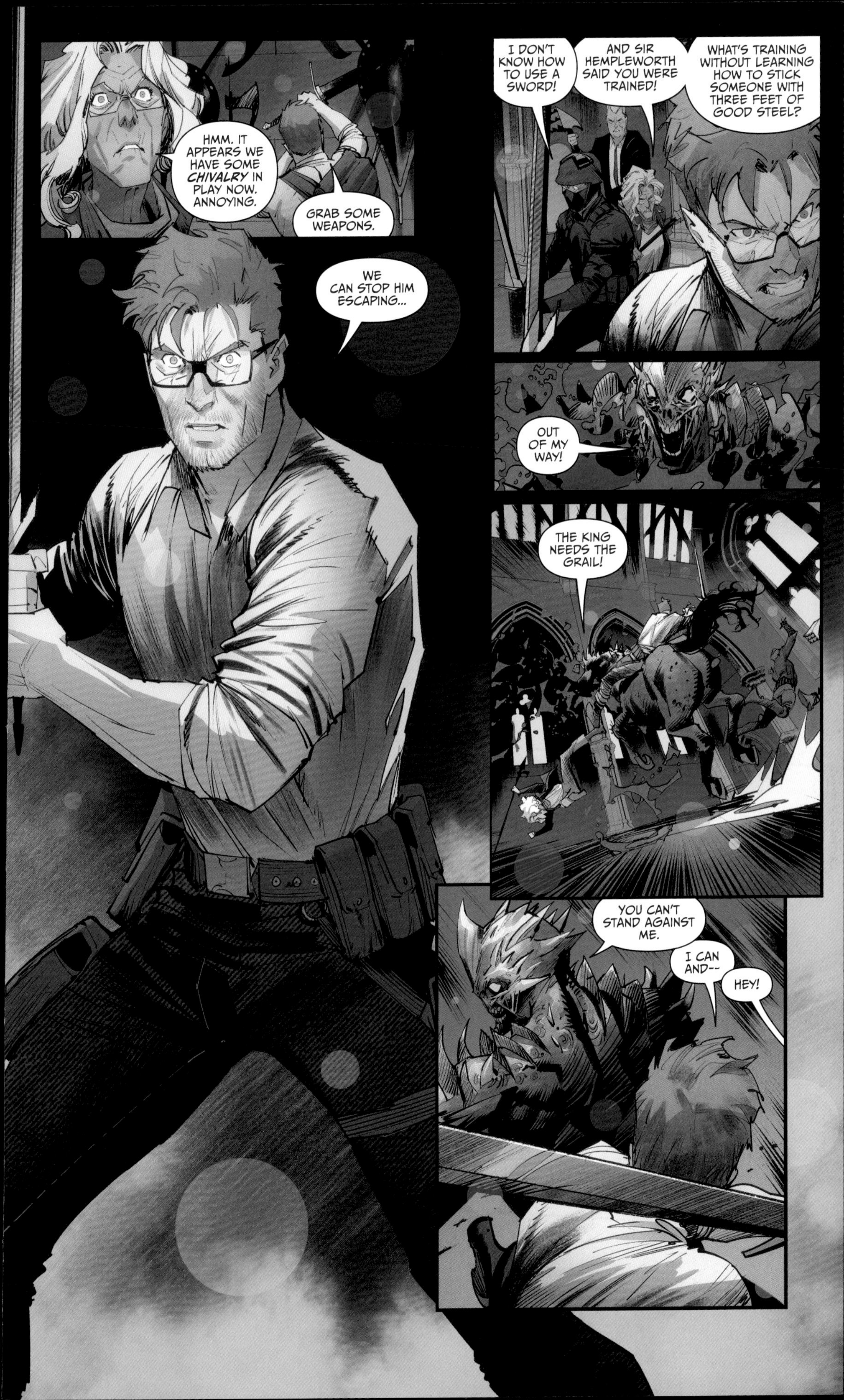

HMM. IT APPEARS WE HAVE SOME *CHIVALRY* IN PLAY NOW. ANNOYING.
GRAB SOME WEAPONS.
WE CAN STOP HIM ESCAPING...
I DON'T KNOW HOW TO USE A SWORD!
AND SIR HEMPLEWORTH SAID YOU WERE TRAINED!
WHAT'S TRAINING WITHOUT LEARNING HOW TO STICK SOMEONE WITH THREE FEET OF GOOD STEEL?
OUT OF MY WAY!
THE KING NEEDS THE GRAIL!
YOU CAN'T STAND AGAINST ME.
I CAN AND--
HEY!

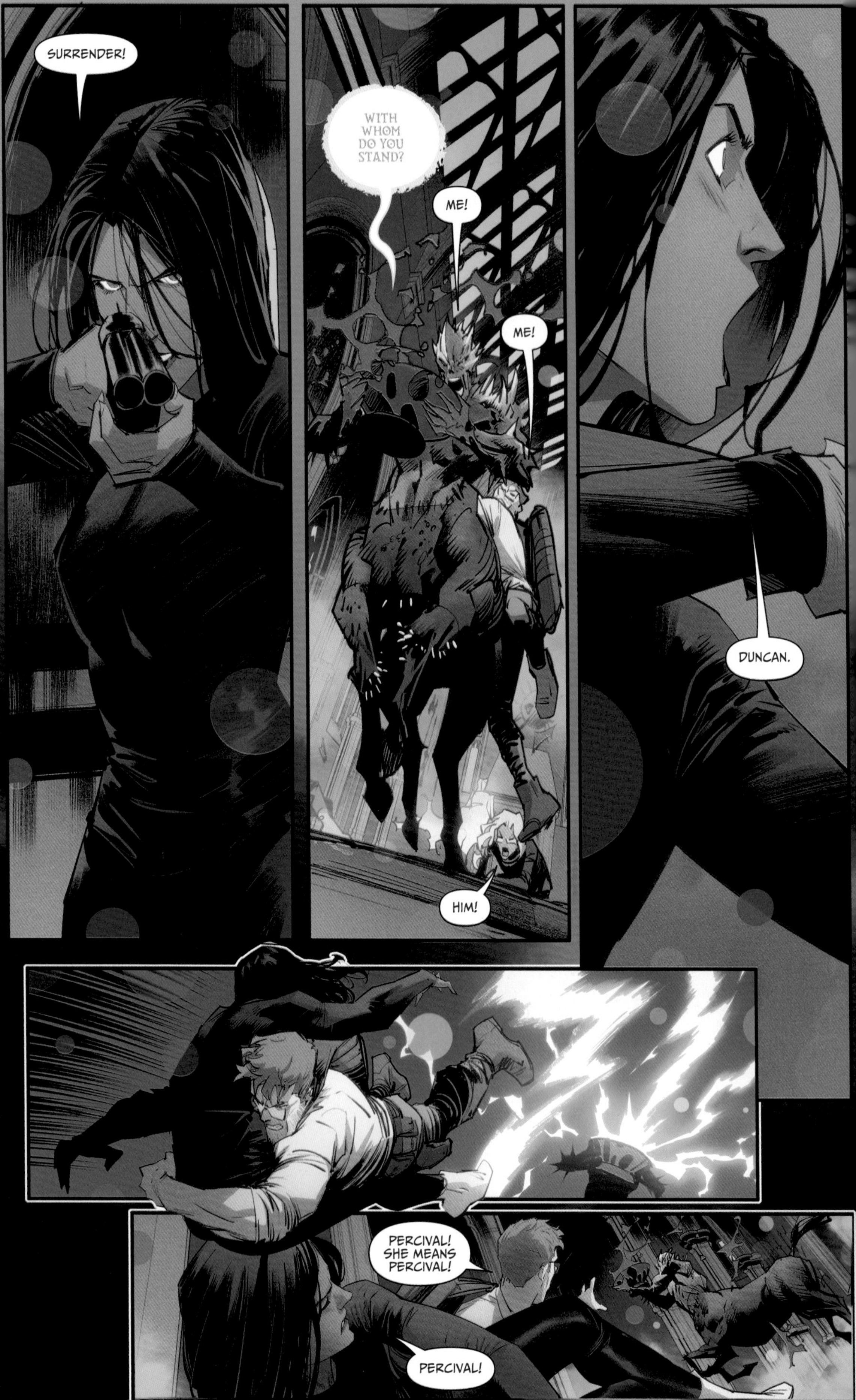
SURRENDER!
WITH WHOM DO YOU STAND?
ME!
ME!
HIM!
DUNCAN.
PERCIVAL! SHE MEANS PERCIVAL!
PERCIVAL!

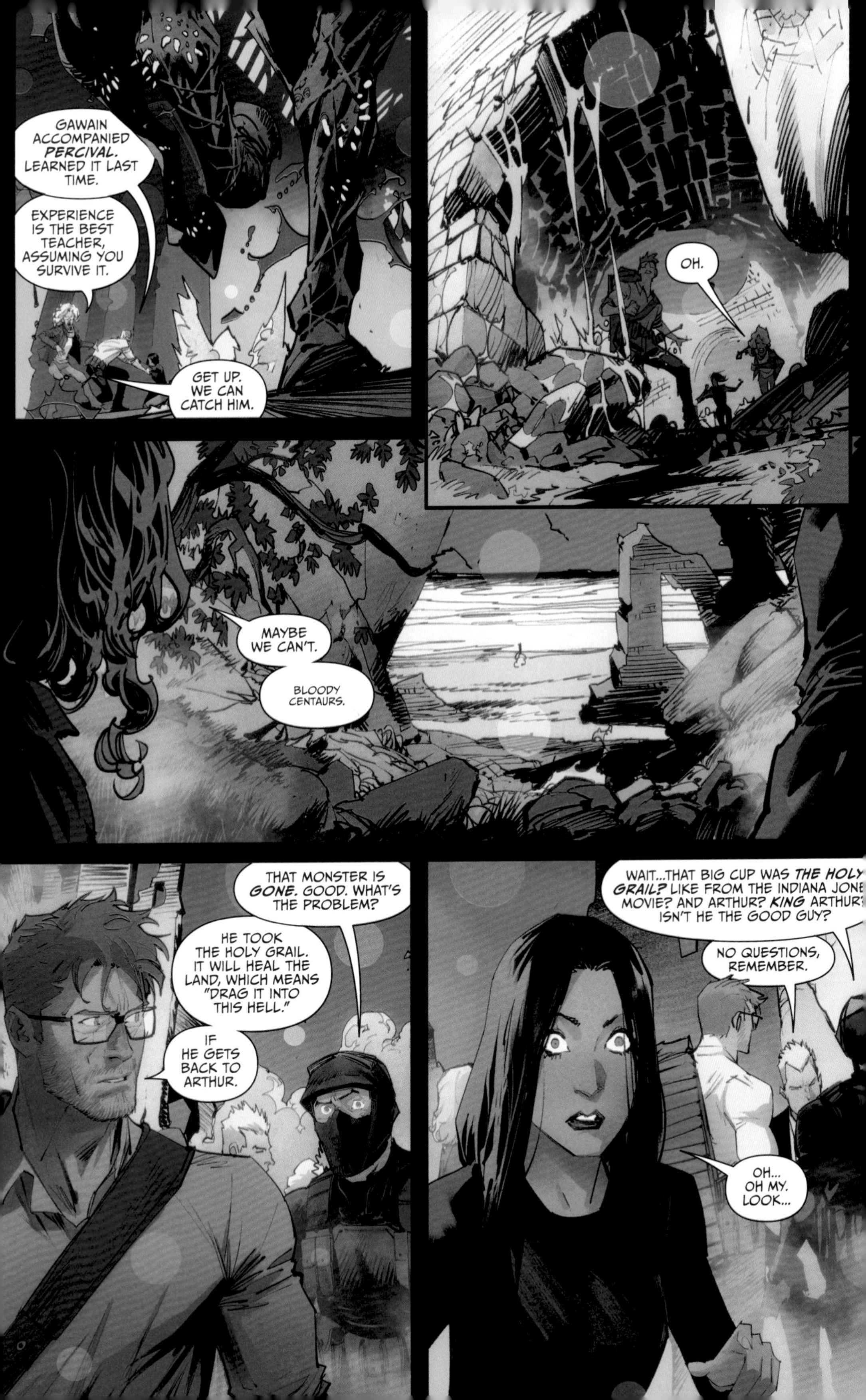
GAWAIN ACCOMPANIED PERCIVAL. LEARNED IT LAST TIME.
EXPERIENCE IS THE BEST TEACHER, ASSUMING YOU SURVIVE IT.
GET UP. WE CAN CATCH HIM.
OH.
MAYBE WE CAN'T.
BLOODY CENTAURS.
THAT MONSTER IS GONE. GOOD. WHAT'S THE PROBLEM?
HE TOOK THE HOLY GRAIL. IT WILL HEAL THE LAND, WHICH MEANS "DRAG IT INTO THIS HELL."
IF HE GETS BACK TO ARTHUR.
WAIT...THAT BIG CUP WAS THE HOLY GRAIL? LIKE FROM THE INDIANA JONE MOVIE? AND ARTHUR? KING ARTHUR ISN'T HE THE GOOD GUY?
NO QUESTIONS, REMEMBER.
OH... OH MY. LOOK...

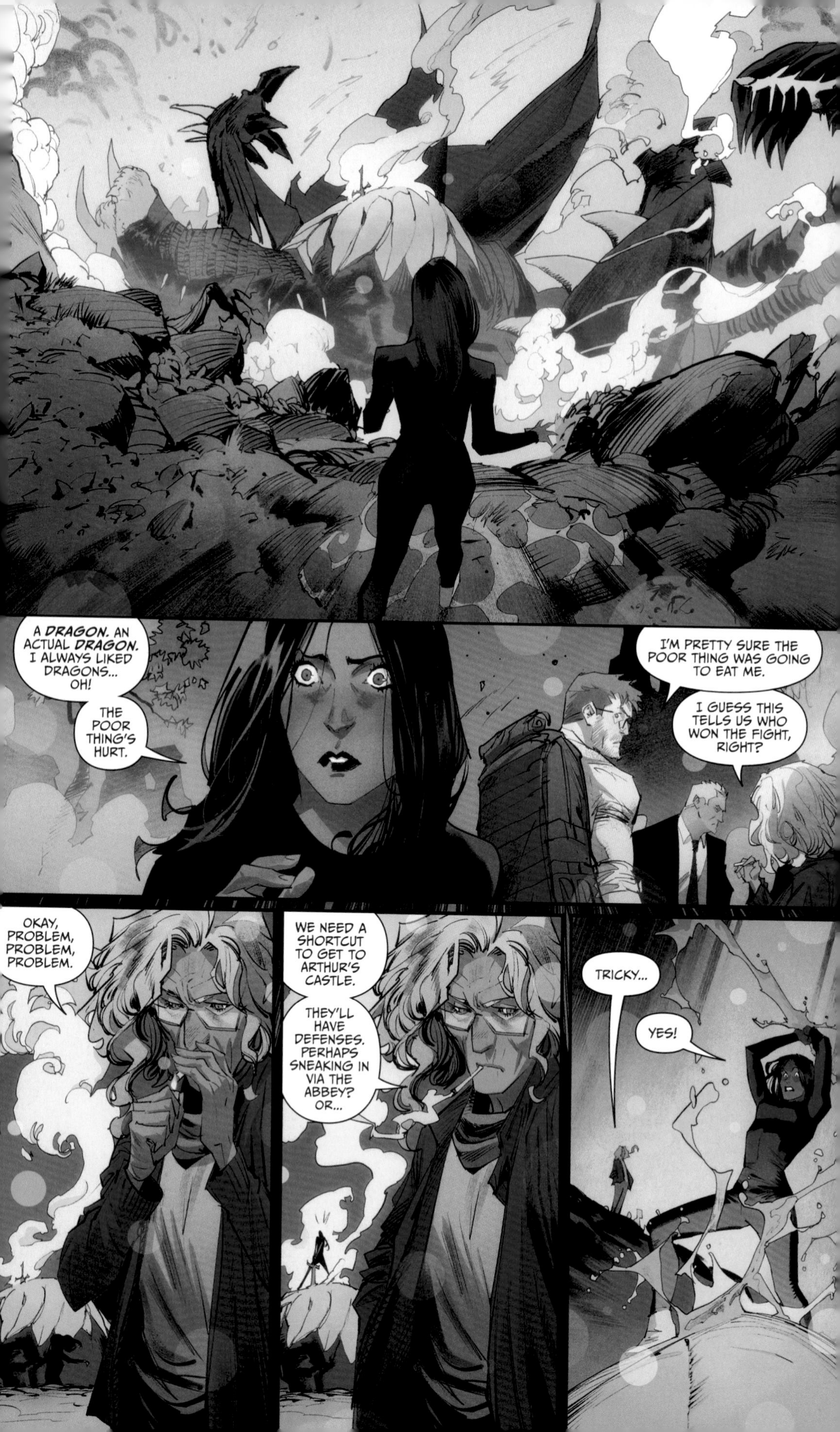
A DRAGON. AN ACTUAL DRAGON. I ALWAYS LIKED DRAGONS... OH!
THE POOR THING'S HURT.
I'M PRETTY SURE THE POOR THING WAS GOING TO EAT ME.
I GUESS THIS TELLS US WHO WON THE FIGHT, RIGHT?
OKAY, PROBLEM, PROBLEM, PROBLEM.
WE NEED A SHORTCUT TO GET TO ARTHUR'S CASTLE.
THEY'LL HAVE DEFENSES. PERHAPS SNEAKING IN VIA THE ABBEY? OR...
TRICKY...
YES!

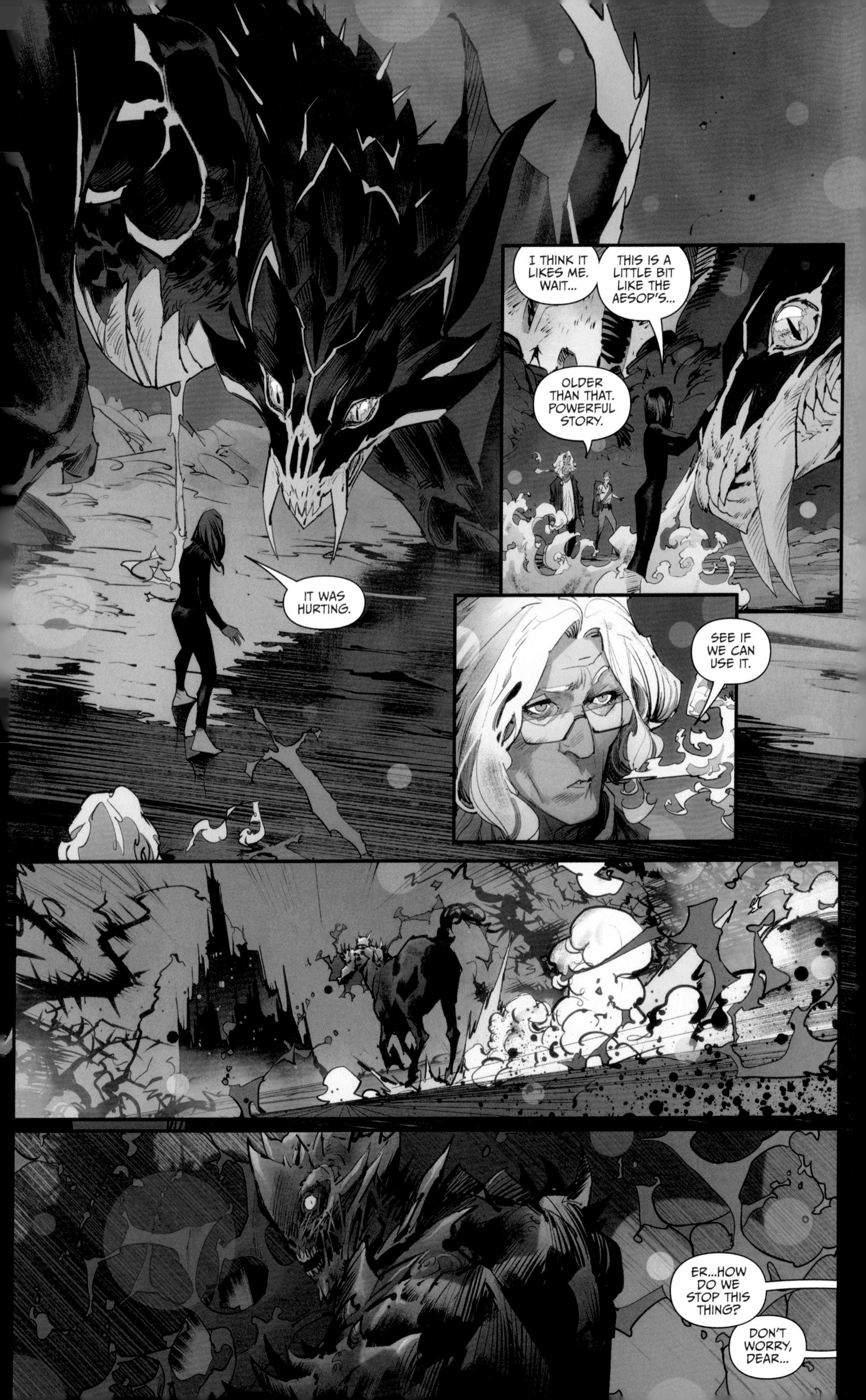
IT WAS HURTING.
I THINK IT LIKES ME. WAIT...
THIS IS A LITTLE BIT LIKE THE AESOP'S...
OLDER THAN THAT. POWERFUL STORY.
SEE IF WE CAN USE IT.
ER...HOW DO WE STOP THIS THING?
DON'T WORRY, DEAR...

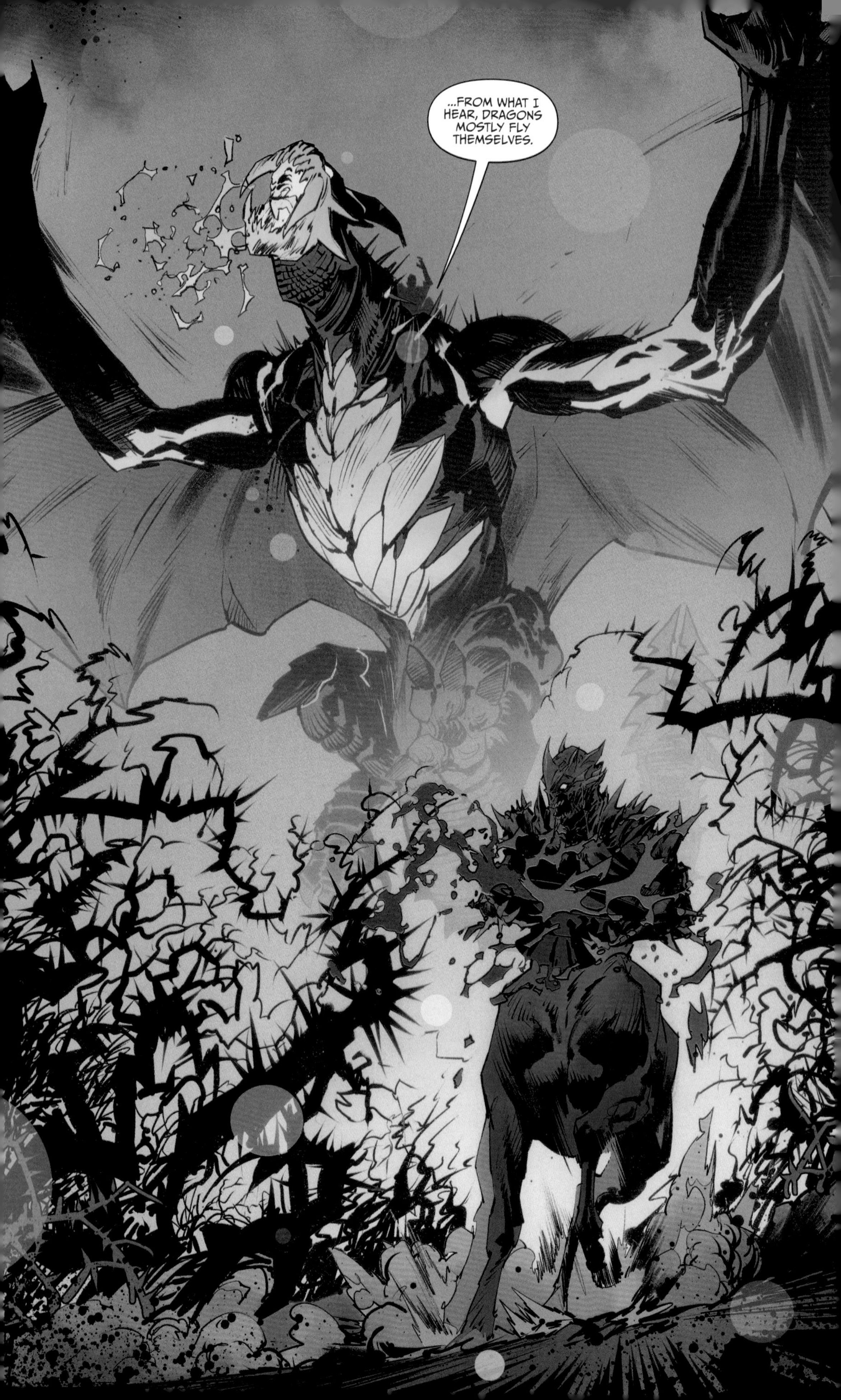
...FROM WHAT I HEAR, DRAGONS MOSTLY FLY THEMSELVES.

CHAPTER EIGHTEEN

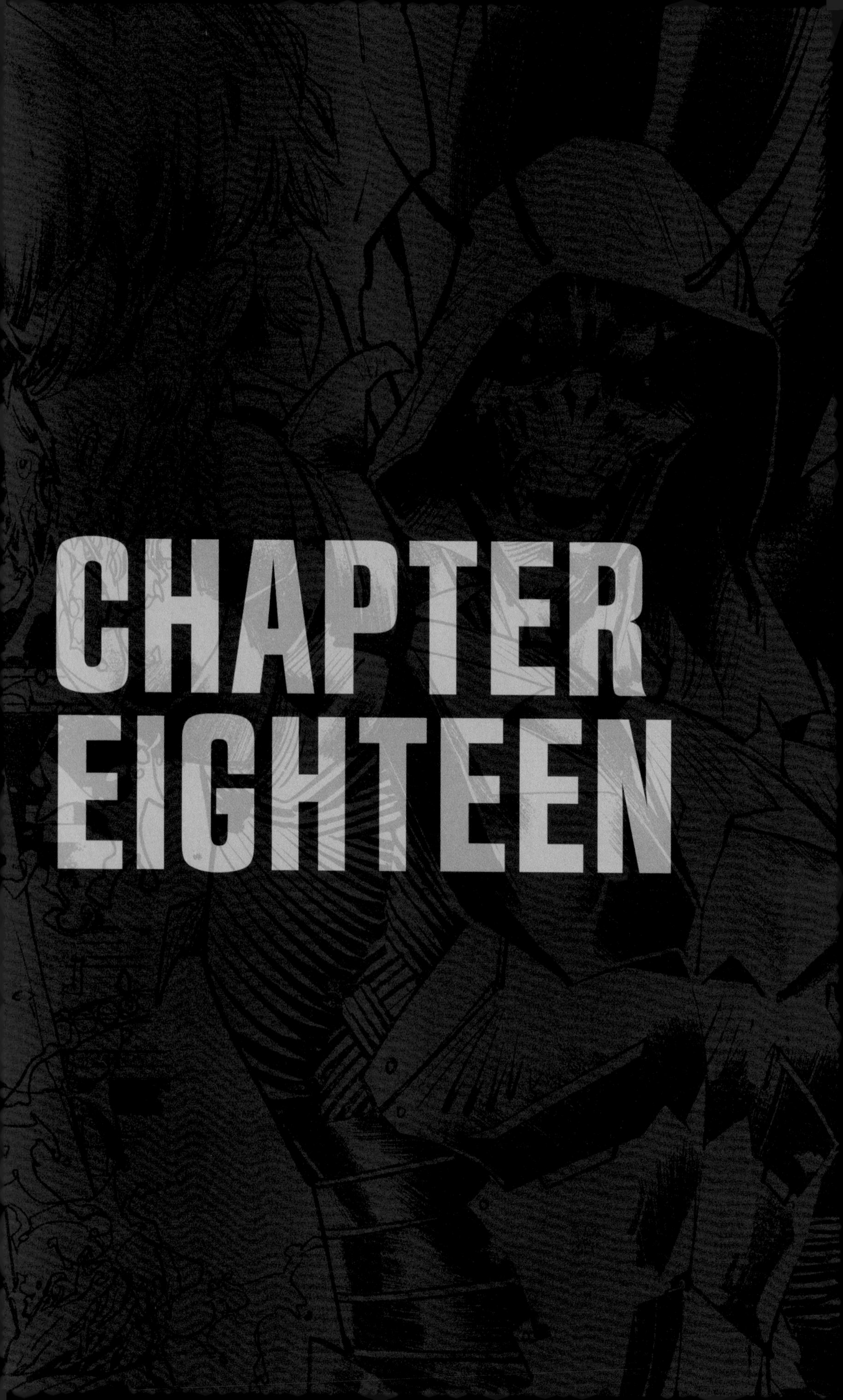

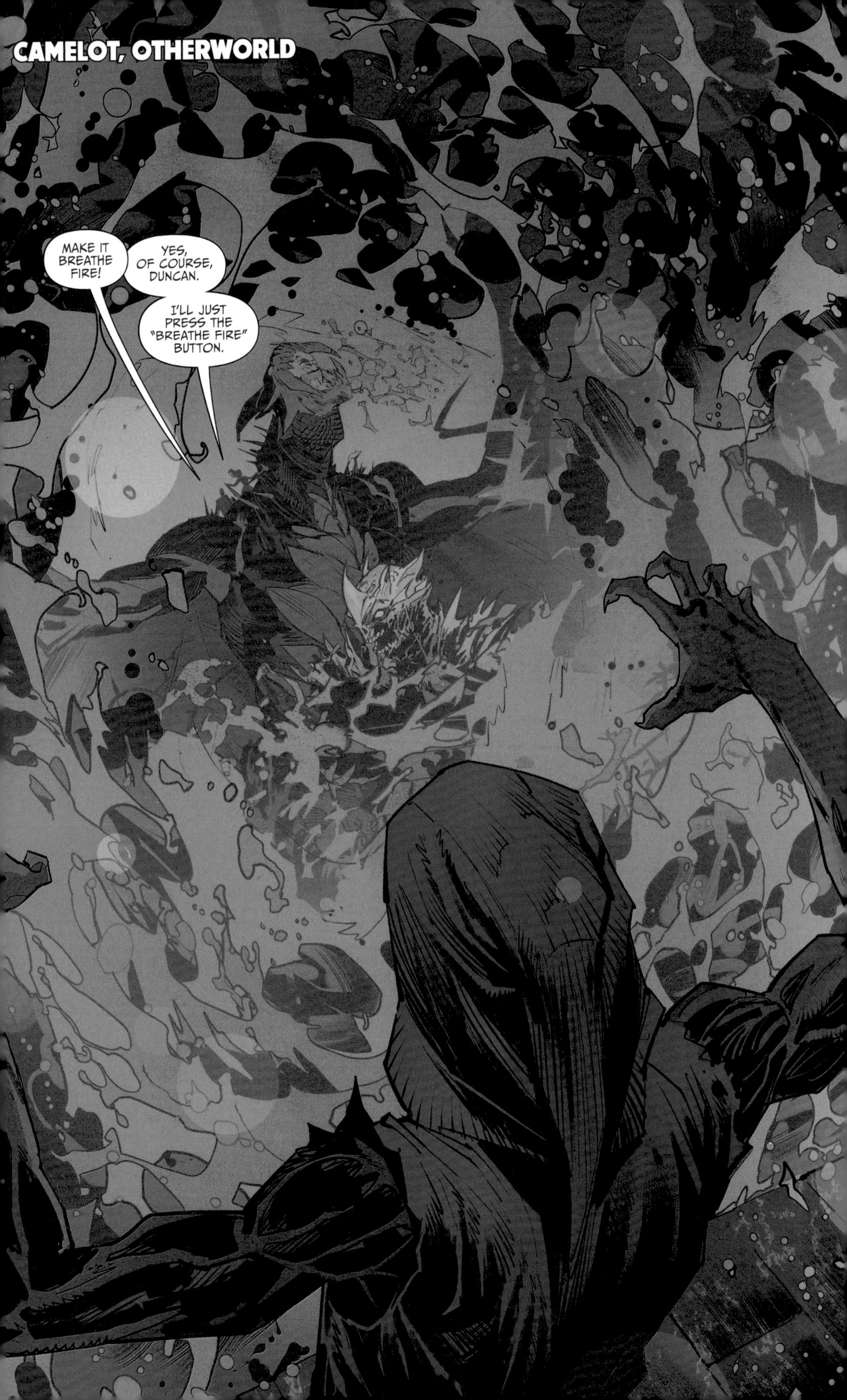
CAMELOT, OTHERWORLD
MAKE IT BREATHE FIRE!
YES, OF COURSE, DUNCAN.
I'LL JUST PRESS THE "BREATHE FIRE" BUTTON.

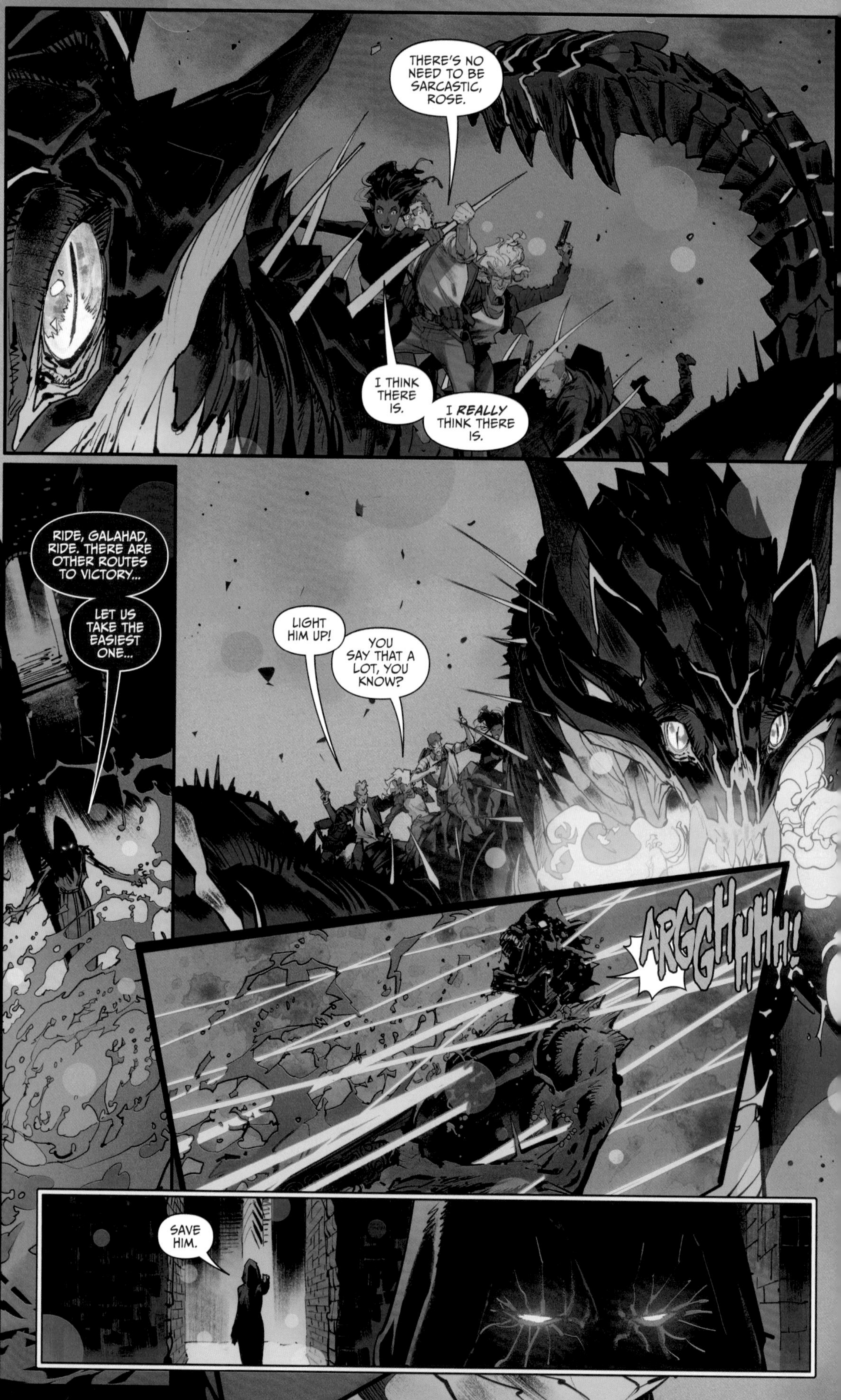
THERE'S NO NEED TO BE SARCASTIC, ROSE.
I THINK THERE IS.
I *REALLY* THINK THERE IS.
RIDE, GALAHAD, RIDE. THERE ARE OTHER ROUTES TO VICTORY...
LET US TAKE THE EASIEST ONE...
LIGHT HIM UP!
YOU SAY THAT A LOT, YOU KNOW?
ARGGHHHH!
SAVE HIM.

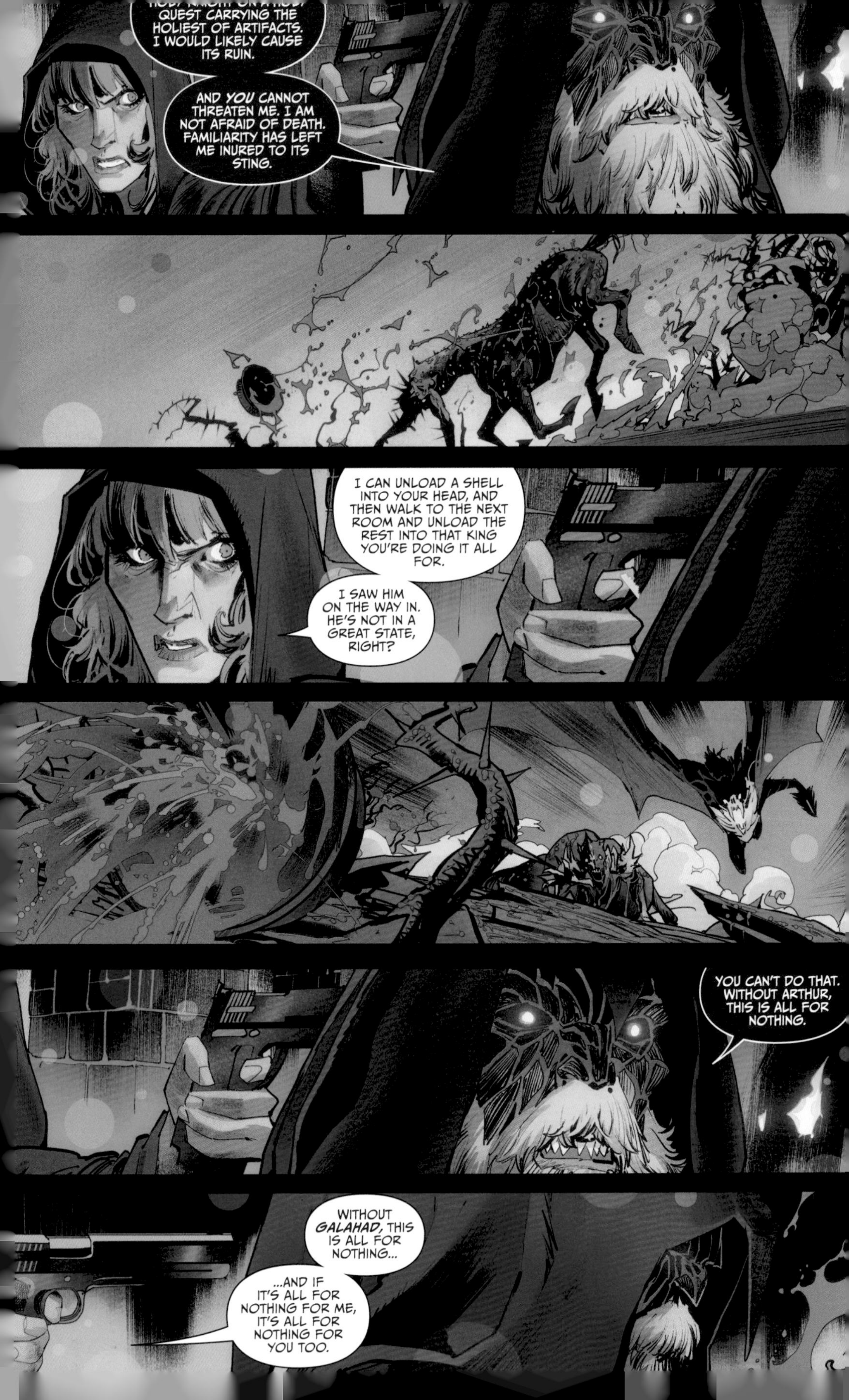
QUEST CARRYING THE HOLIEST OF ARTIFACTS. I WOULD LIKELY CAUSE ITS RUIN.
AND YOU CANNOT THREATEN ME. I AM NOT AFRAID OF DEATH. FAMILIARITY HAS LEFT ME INURED TO ITS STING.
I CAN UNLOAD A SHELL INTO YOUR HEAD, AND THEN WALK TO THE NEXT ROOM AND UNLOAD THE REST INTO THAT KING YOU'RE DOING IT ALL FOR.
I SAW HIM ON THE WAY IN. HE'S NOT IN A GREAT STATE, RIGHT?
YOU CAN'T DO THAT. WITHOUT ARTHUR, THIS IS ALL FOR NOTHING.
WITHOUT GALAHAD, THIS IS ALL FOR NOTHING...
...AND IF IT'S ALL FOR NOTHING FOR ME, IT'S ALL FOR NOTHING FOR YOU TOO.

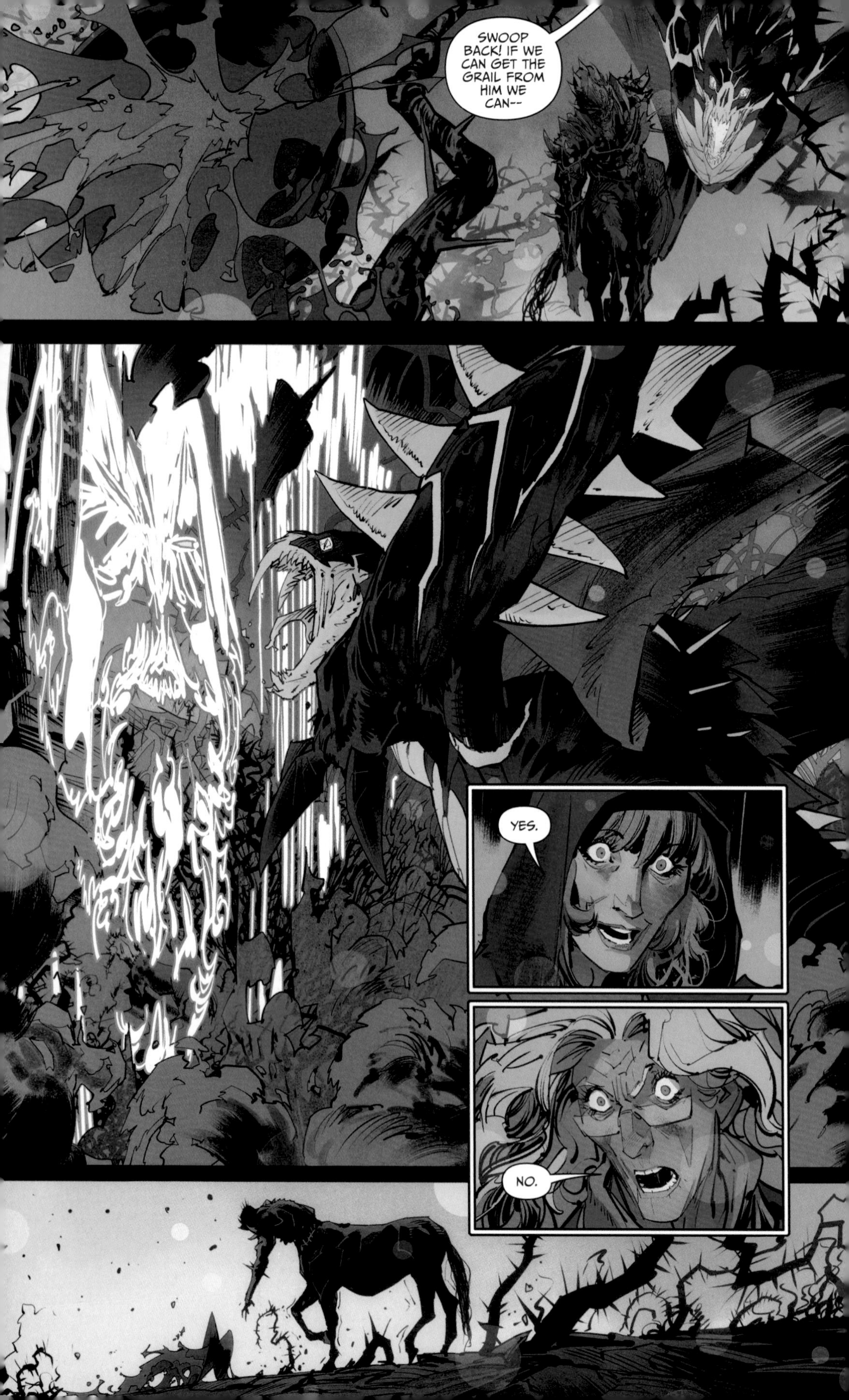
SWOOP BACK! IF WE CAN GET THE GRAIL FROM HIM WE CAN--
YES.
NO.

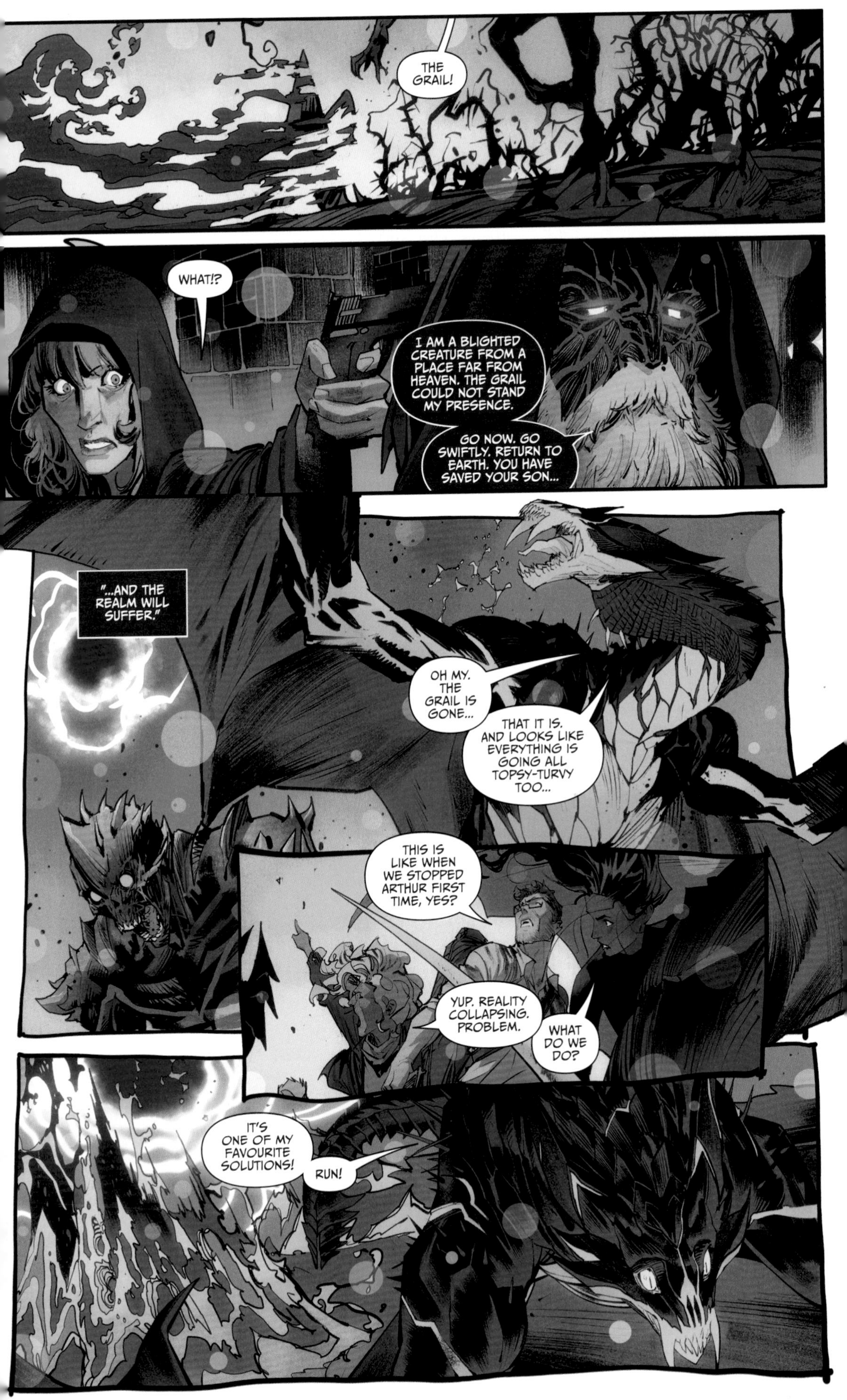
THE GRAIL!
WHAT!?
I AM A BLIGHTED CREATURE FROM A PLACE FAR FROM HEAVEN. THE GRAIL COULD NOT STAND MY PRESENCE.
GO NOW. GO SWIFTLY. RETURN TO EARTH. YOU HAVE SAVED YOUR SON...
"...AND THE REALM WILL SUFFER."
OH MY. THE GRAIL IS GONE...
THAT IT IS. AND LOOKS LIKE EVERYTHING IS GOING ALL TOPSY-TURVY TOO...
THIS IS LIKE WHEN WE STOPPED ARTHUR FIRST TIME, YES?
YUP. REALITY COLLAPSING. PROBLEM.
WHAT DO WE DO?
IT'S ONE OF MY FAVOURITE SOLUTIONS!
RUN!

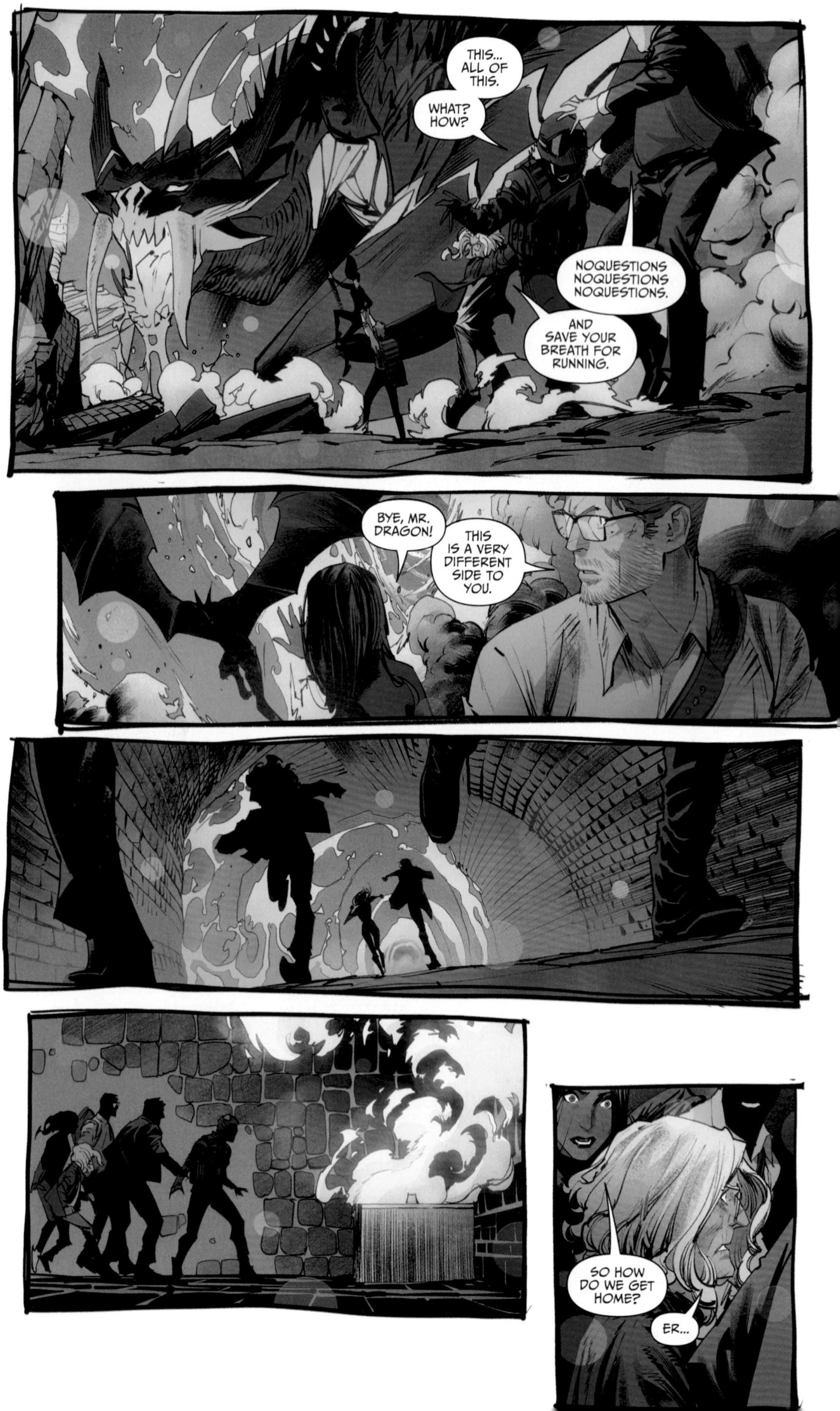
THIS... ALL OF THIS.
WHAT? HOW?
NOQUESTIONS NOQUESTIONS NOQUESTIONS.
AND SAVE YOUR BREATH FOR RUNNING.
BYE, MR. DRAGON!
THIS IS A VERY DIFFERENT SIDE TO YOU.
SO HOW DO WE GET HOME?
ER...

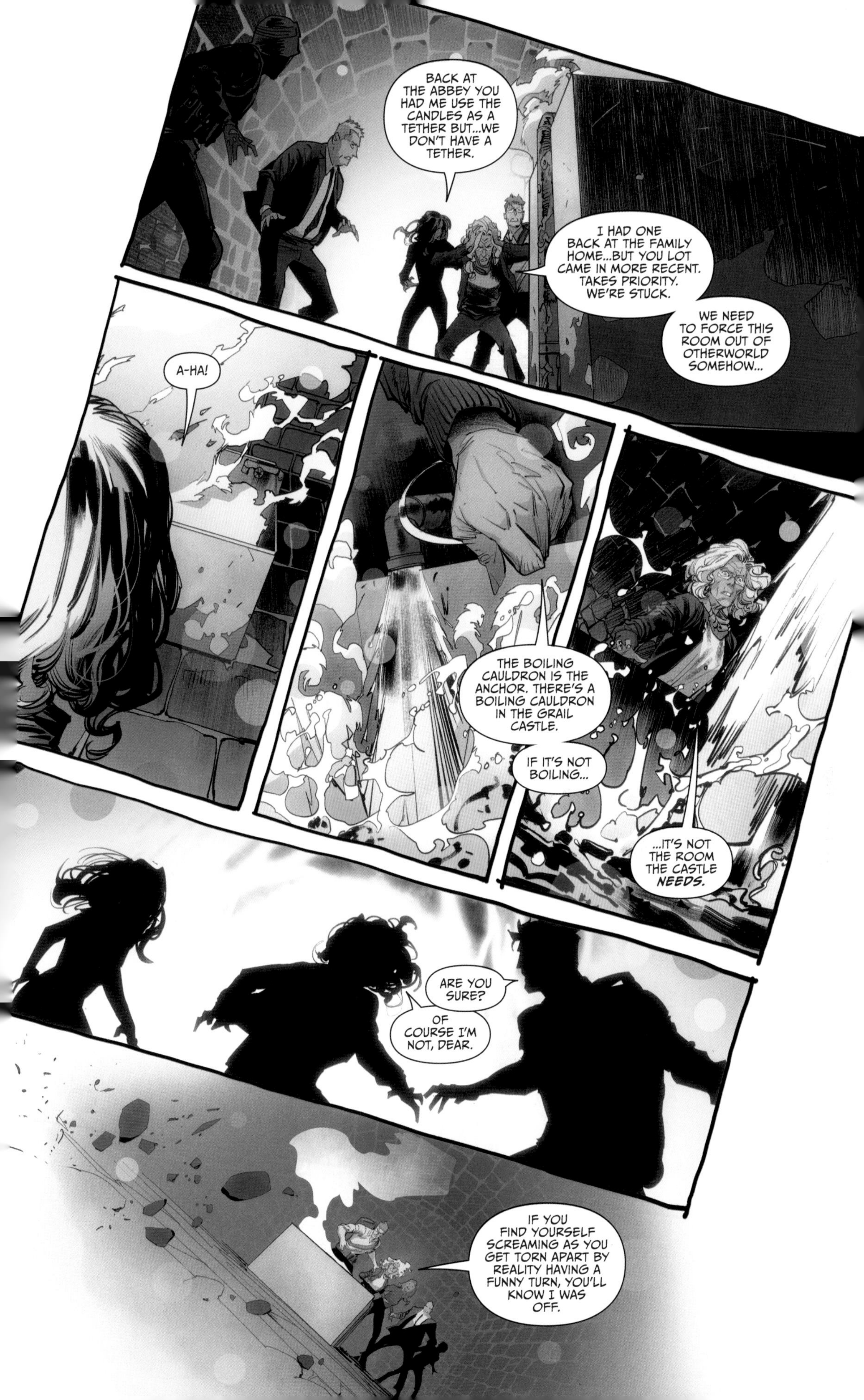
BACK AT THE ABBEY YOU HAD ME USE THE CANDLES AS A TETHER BUT...WE DON'T HAVE A TETHER.
I HAD ONE BACK AT THE FAMILY HOME...BUT YOU LOT CAME IN MORE RECENT. TAKES PRIORITY. WE'RE STUCK.
WE NEED TO FORCE THIS ROOM OUT OF OTHERWORLD SOMEHOW...
A-HA!
THE BOILING CAULDRON IS THE ANCHOR. THERE'S A BOILING CAULDRON IN THE GRAIL CASTLE.
IF IT'S NOT BOILING...
...IT'S NOT THE ROOM THE CASTLE *NEEDS.*
ARE YOU SURE?
OF COURSE I'M NOT, DEAR.
IF YOU FIND YOURSELF SCREAMING AS YOU GET TORN APART BY REALITY HAVING A FUNNY TURN, YOU'LL KNOW I WAS OFF.

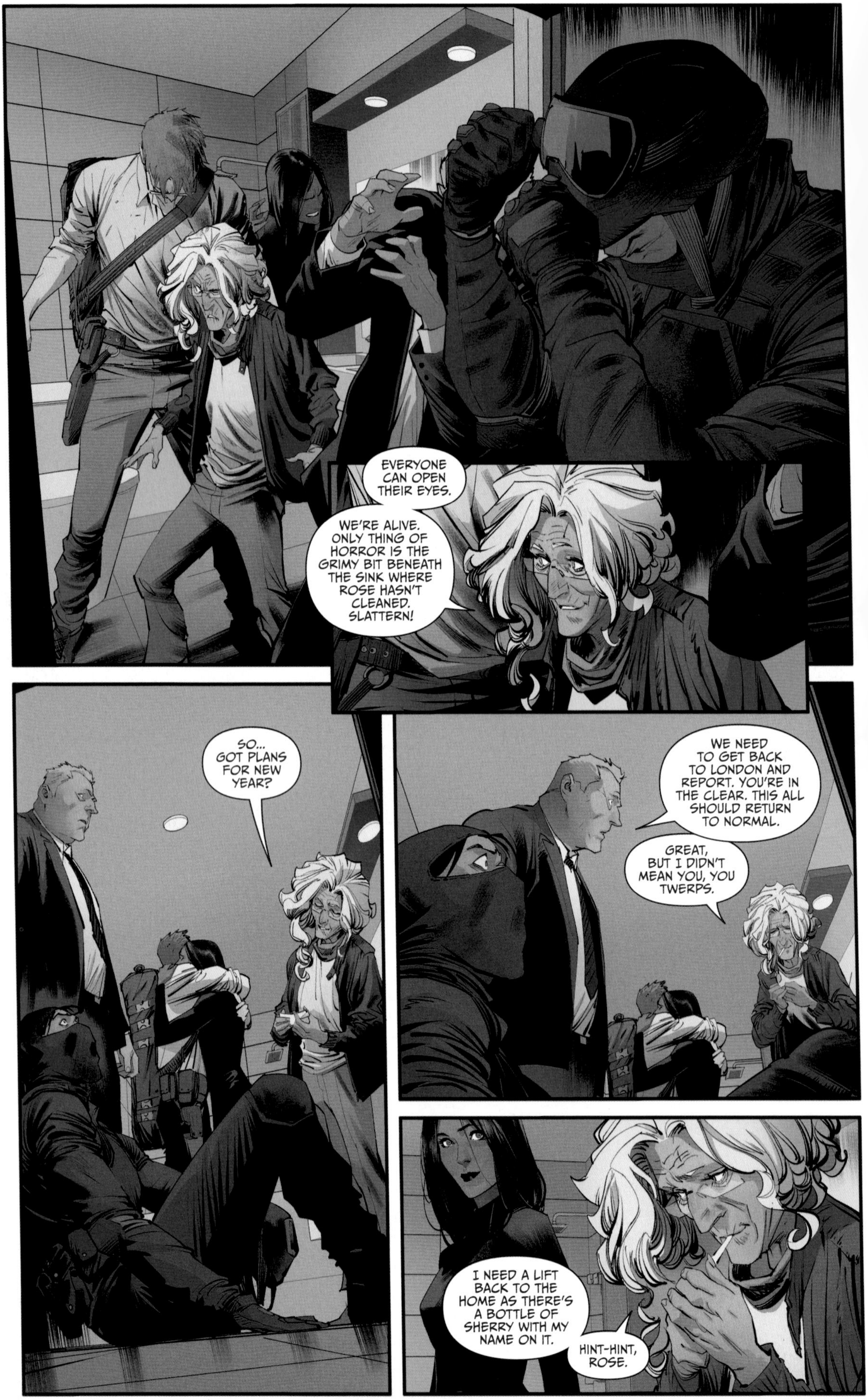
EVERYONE CAN OPEN THEIR EYES.
WE'RE ALIVE. ONLY THING OF HORROR IS THE GRIMY BIT BENEATH THE SINK WHERE ROSE HASN'T CLEANED. SLATTERN!
SO... GOT PLANS FOR NEW YEAR?
WE NEED TO GET BACK TO LONDON AND REPORT. YOU'RE IN THE CLEAR. THIS ALL SHOULD RETURN TO NORMAL.
GREAT, BUT I DIDN'T MEAN YOU, YOU TWERPS.
I NEED A LIFT BACK TO THE HOME AS THERE'S A BOTTLE OF SHERRY WITH MY NAME ON IT.
HINT-HINT, ROSE.

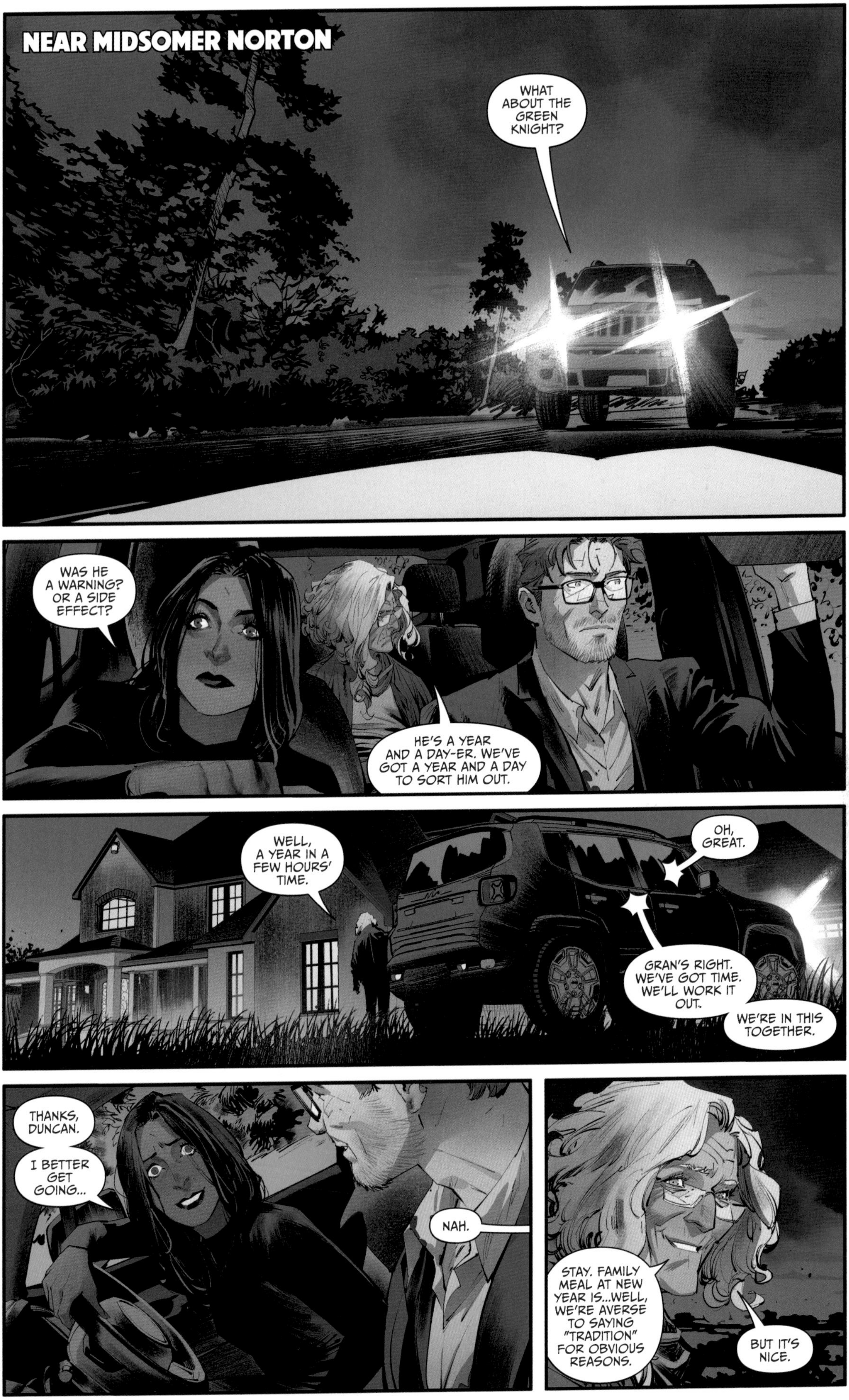
NEAR MIDSOMER NORTON
WHAT ABOUT THE GREEN KNIGHT?
WAS HE A WARNING? OR A SIDE EFFECT?
HE'S A YEAR AND A DAY-ER. WE'VE GOT A YEAR AND A DAY TO SORT HIM OUT.
WELL, A YEAR IN A FEW HOURS' TIME.
OH, GREAT.
GRAN'S RIGHT. WE'VE GOT TIME. WE'LL WORK IT OUT.
WE'RE IN THIS TOGETHER.
THANKS, DUNCAN.
I BETTER GET GOING...
NAH.
STAY. FAMILY MEAL AT NEW YEAR IS...WELL, WE'RE AVERSE TO SAYING "TRADITION" FOR OBVIOUS REASONS.
BUT IT'S NICE.

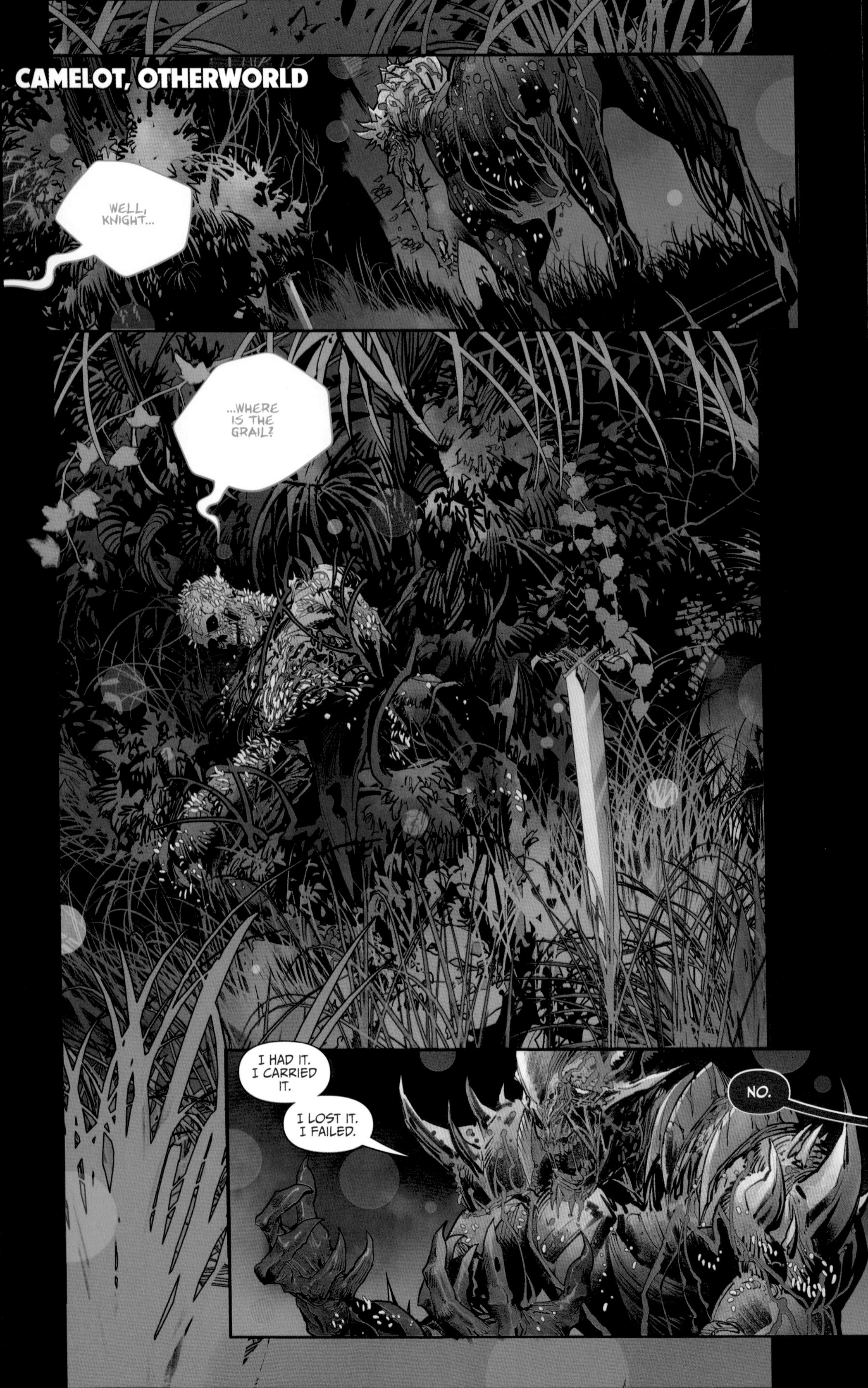
CAMELOT, OTHERWORLD
WELL, KNIGHT...
...WHERE IS THE GRAIL?
I HAD IT. I CARRIED IT.
I LOST IT. I FAILED.
NO.

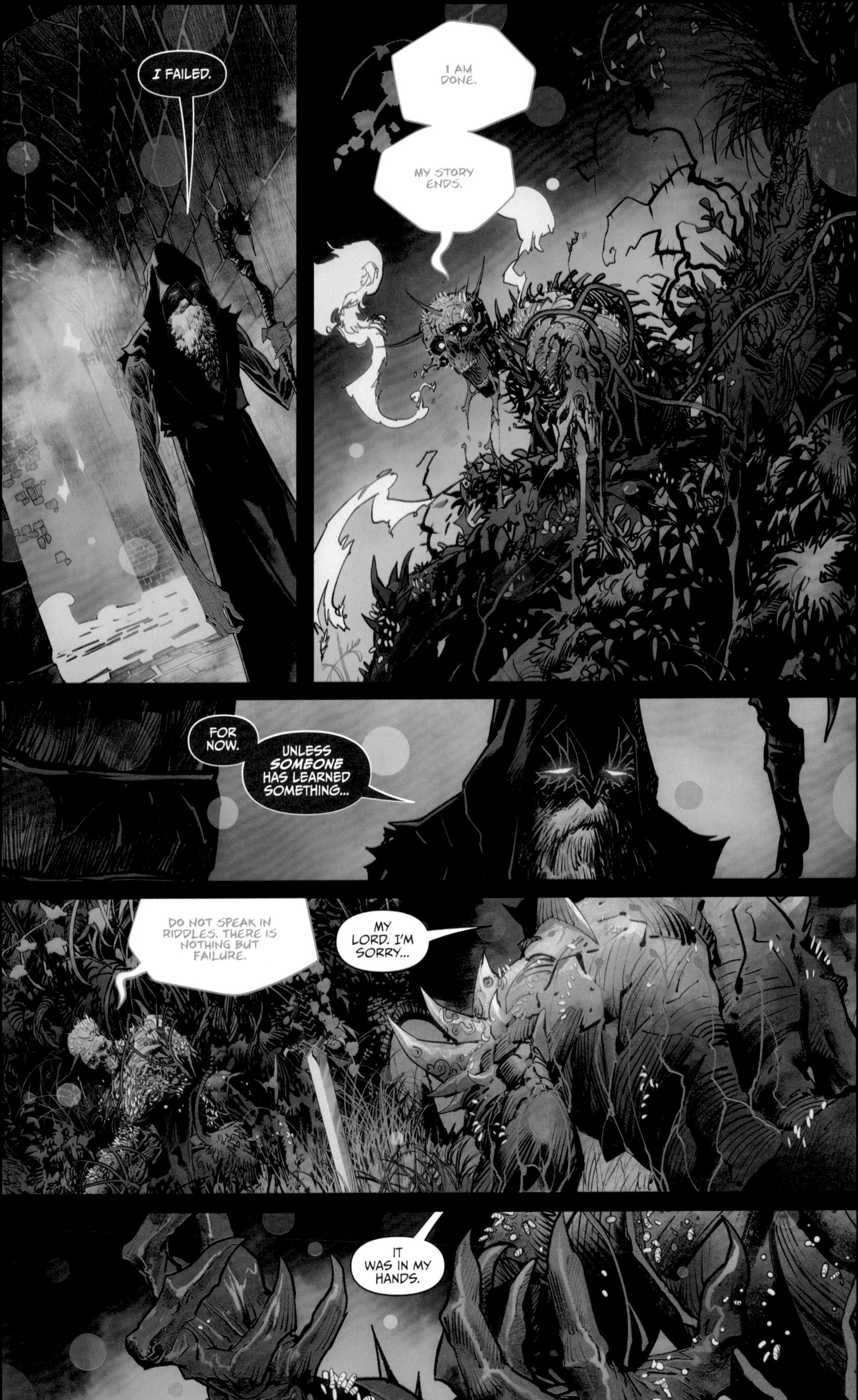
I FAILED.
I AM DONE.
MY STORY ENDS.
FOR NOW.
UNLESS *SOMEONE* HAS LEARNED SOMETHING...
DO NOT SPEAK IN RIDDLES. THERE IS NOTHING BUT FAILURE.
MY LORD. I'M SORRY...
IT WAS IN MY HANDS.

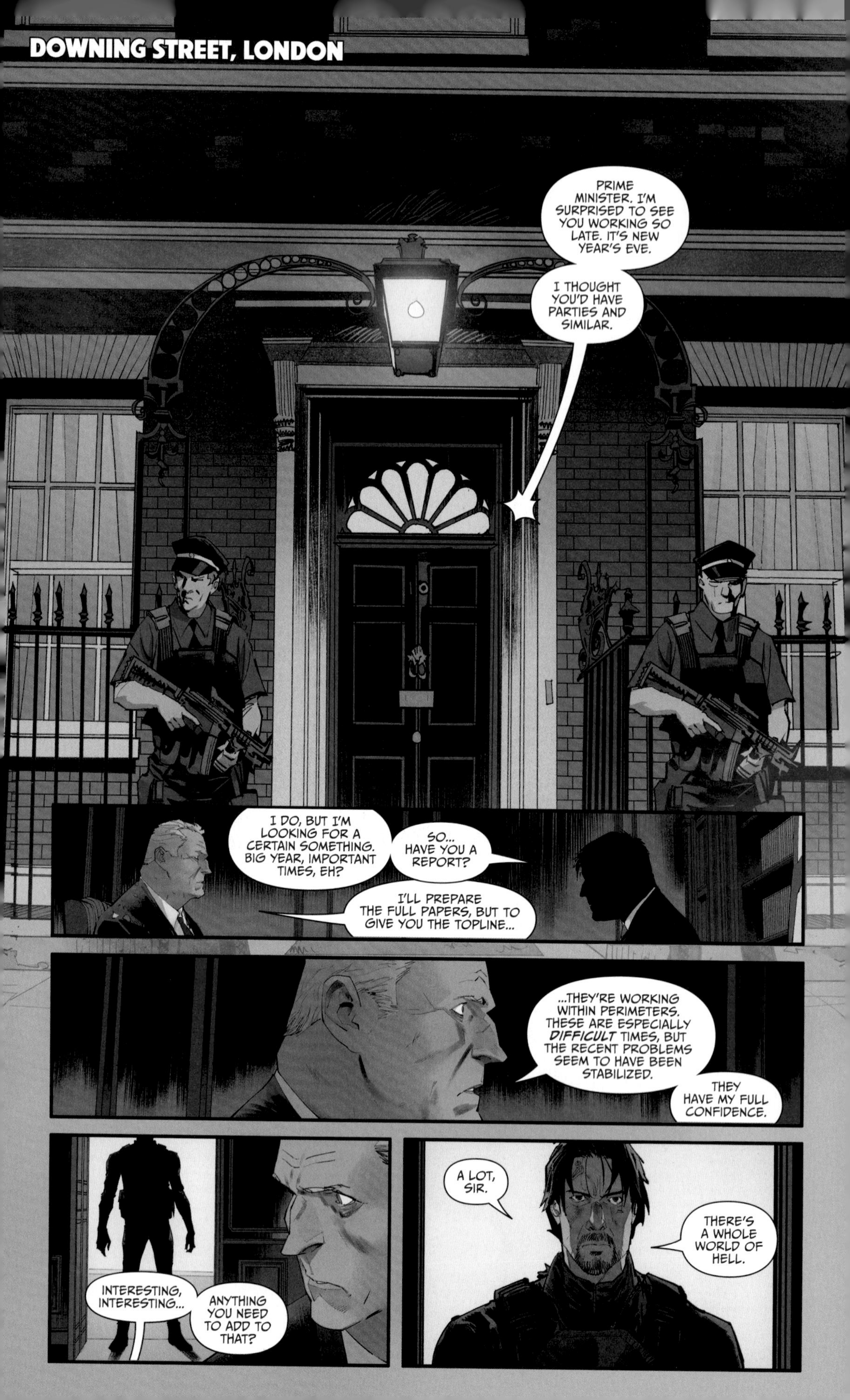
DOWNING STREET, LONDON
PRIME MINISTER. I'M SURPRISED TO SEE YOU WORKING SO LATE. IT'S NEW YEAR'S EVE.
I THOUGHT YOU'D HAVE PARTIES AND SIMILAR.
I DO, BUT I'M LOOKING FOR A CERTAIN SOMETHING. BIG YEAR, IMPORTANT TIMES, EH?
SO... HAVE YOU A REPORT?
I'LL PREPARE THE FULL PAPERS, BUT TO GIVE YOU THE TOPLINE...
...THEY'RE WORKING WITHIN PERIMETERS. THESE ARE ESPECIALLY *DIFFICULT* TIMES, BUT THE RECENT PROBLEMS SEEM TO HAVE BEEN STABILIZED.
THEY HAVE MY FULL CONFIDENCE.
INTERESTING, INTERESTING...
ANYTHING YOU NEED TO ADD TO THAT?
A LOT, SIR.
THERE'S A WHOLE WORLD OF HELL.

JAMES... STOP!

REMEMBER YOUR ORDERS.

I'M AFRAID HE IS, HEMPLEWORTH, OLD CHAP.

YOU. THIS IS YOU.

SIR-- THIS ISN'T RIGHT.

NO, KEEPING SECRETS FROM THE BRITISH PEOPLE IS WHAT ISN'T RIGHT. IN OUR BRAVE NEW LAND SOMETHING HAS TO BRING THE PEOPLE TOGETHER.

ONE CAN ASPIRE TO BE CHURCHILL...BUT WHAT'S CHURCHILL WITHOUT A WAR? THIS WILL BE MINE...

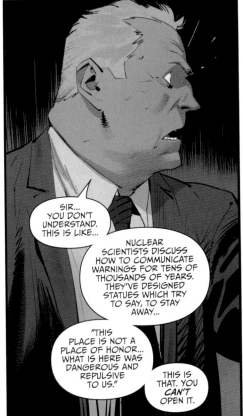

SIR... YOU DON'T UNDERSTAND. THIS IS LIKE...

NUCLEAR SCIENTISTS DISCUSS HOW TO COMMUNICATE WARNINGS FOR TENS OF THOUSANDS OF YEARS. THEY'VE DESIGNED STATUES WHICH TRY TO SAY, TO STAY AWAY...

"THIS PLACE IS NOT A PLACE OF HONOR... WHAT IS HERE WAS DANGEROUS AND REPULSIVE TO US."

THIS IS THAT. YOU CAN'T OPEN IT.

OH, EXPERTS, EXPERTS, EXPERTS. REMEMBER THE "SERVICE" IN "CIVIL SERVICE," HEMPLEWORTH.

COME ON, JAMES. SPEAK UP. TELL ME ABOUT THIS AWFUL THREAT...

THERE'S... MONSTERS. IT'S THE ONLY WORD FOR IT. I'VE GOT FOOTAGE ON MY BODYCAM.

THEY...IT SOUNDS MAD, BUT--

WH--

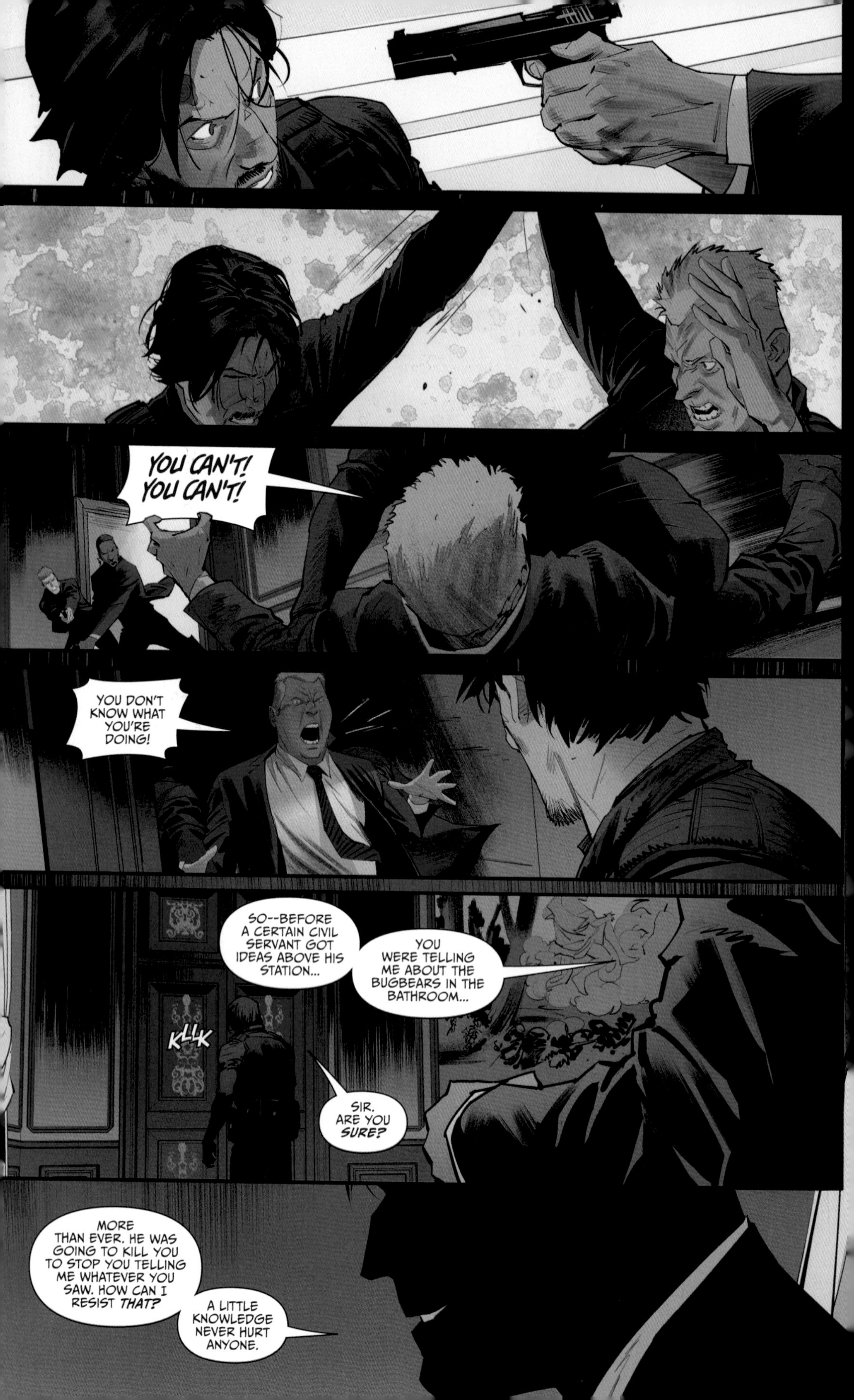
YOU CAN'T! YOU CAN'T!
YOU DON'T KNOW WHAT YOU'RE DOING!
SO--BEFORE A CERTAIN CIVIL SERVANT GOT IDEAS ABOVE HIS STATION...
YOU WERE TELLING ME ABOUT THE BUGBEARS IN THE BATHROOM...
KLLK
SIR. ARE YOU *SURE?*
MORE THAN EVER. HE WAS GOING TO KILL YOU TO STOP YOU TELLING ME WHATEVER YOU SAW. HOW CAN I RESIST *THAT?*
A LITTLE KNOWLEDGE NEVER HURT ANYONE.

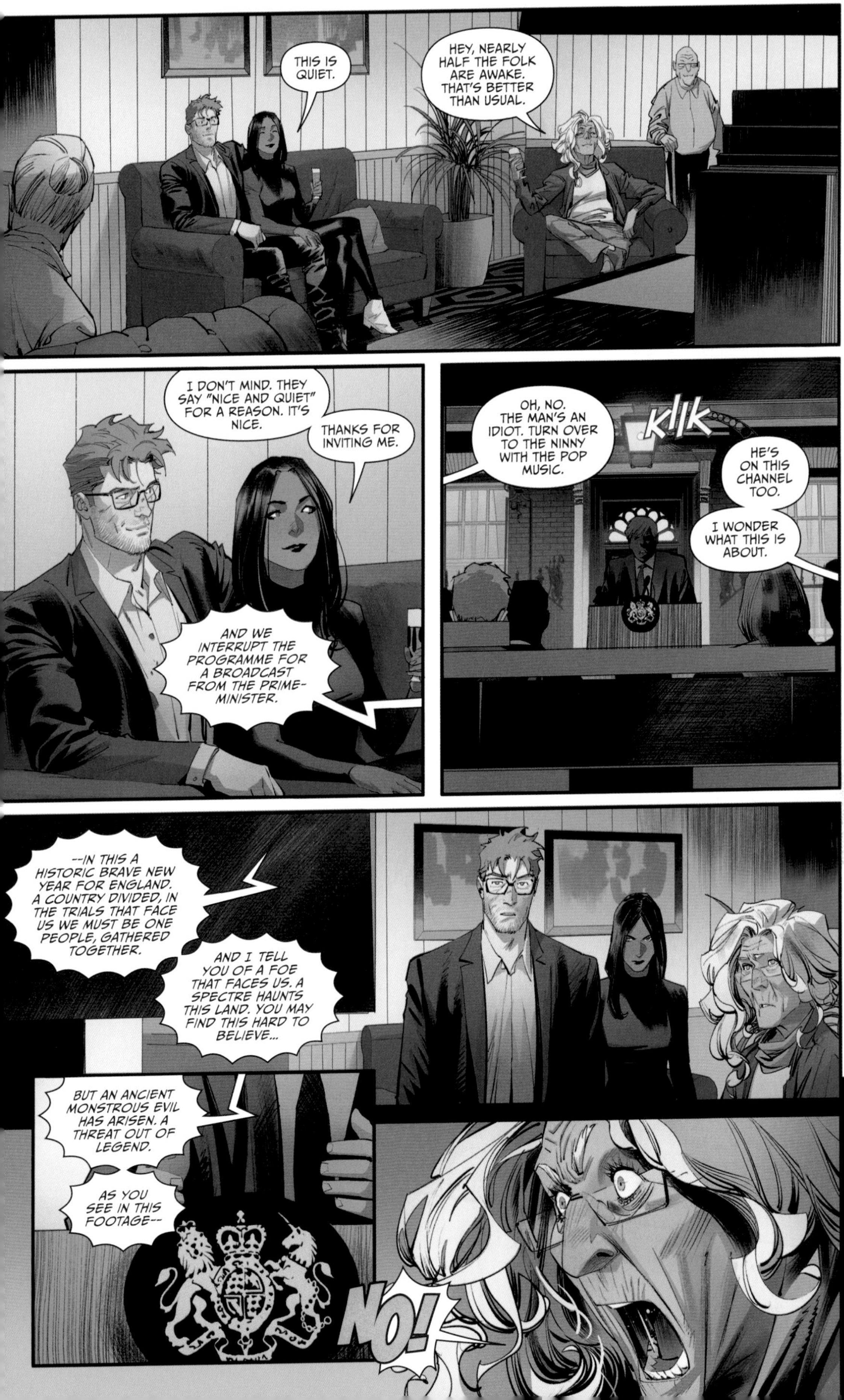
THIS IS QUIET.
HEY, NEARLY HALF THE FOLK ARE AWAKE. THAT'S BETTER THAN USUAL.
I DON'T MIND. THEY SAY "NICE AND QUIET" FOR A REASON. IT'S NICE.
THANKS FOR INVITING ME.
AND WE INTERRUPT THE PROGRAMME FOR A BROADCAST FROM THE PRIME-MINISTER.
OH, NO. THE MAN'S AN IDIOT. TURN OVER TO THE NINNY WITH THE POP MUSIC.
KLIK
HE'S ON THIS CHANNEL TOO.
I WONDER WHAT THIS IS ABOUT.
--IN THIS A HISTORIC BRAVE NEW YEAR FOR ENGLAND. A COUNTRY DIVIDED, IN THE TRIALS THAT FACE US WE MUST BE ONE PEOPLE, GATHERED TOGETHER.
AND I TELL YOU OF A FOE THAT FACES US. A SPECTRE HAUNTS THIS LAND. YOU MAY FIND THIS HARD TO BELIEVE...
BUT AN ANCIENT MONSTROUS EVIL HAS ARISEN. A THREAT OUT OF LEGEND.
AS YOU SEE IN THIS FOOTAGE--
NO!

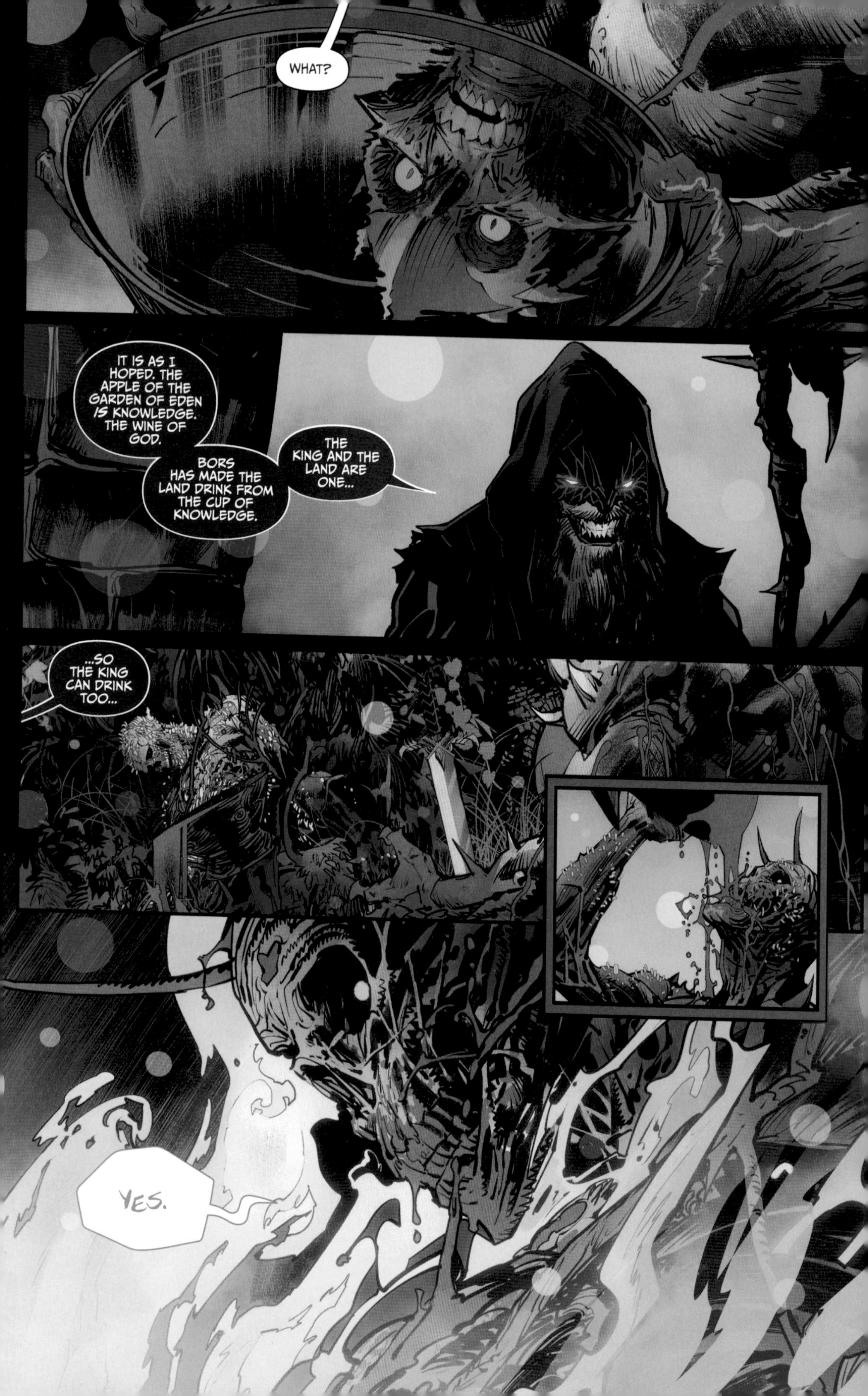
WHAT?
IT IS AS I HOPED. THE APPLE OF THE GARDEN OF EDEN IS KNOWLEDGE. THE WINE OF GOD.
BORS HAS MADE THE LAND DRINK FROM THE CUP OF KNOWLEDGE.
THE KING AND THE LAND ARE ONE...
...SO THE KING CAN DRINK TOO...
YES.

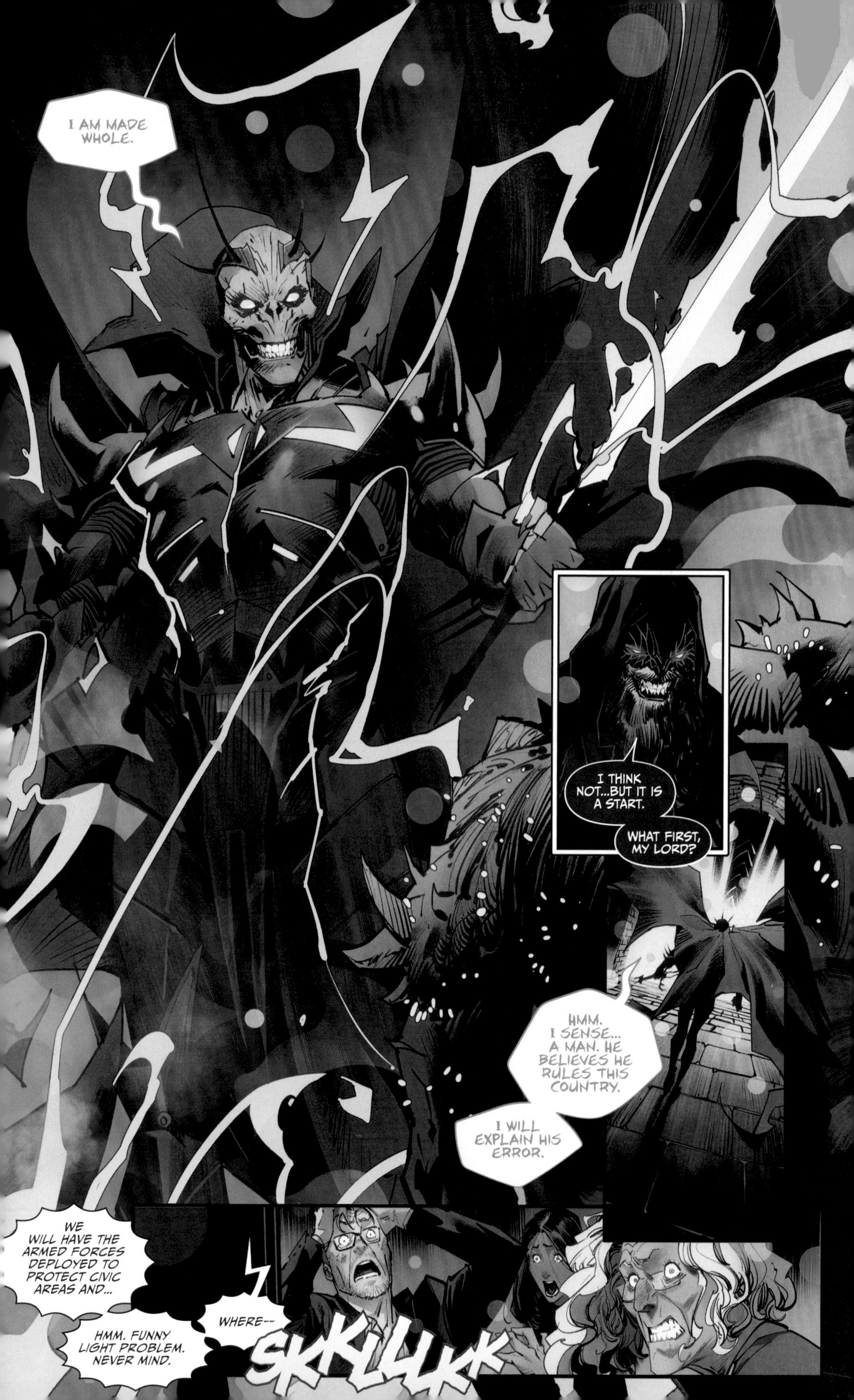
I AM MADE WHOLE.
I THINK NOT...BUT IT IS A START.
WHAT FIRST, MY LORD?
HMM. I SENSE... A MAN. HE BELIEVES HE RULES THIS COUNTRY.
I WILL EXPLAIN HIS ERROR.
WE WILL HAVE THE ARMED FORCES DEPLOYED TO PROTECT CIVIC AREAS AND...
HMM. FUNNY LIGHT PROBLEM. NEVER MIND.
WHERE--
SKKLLKK

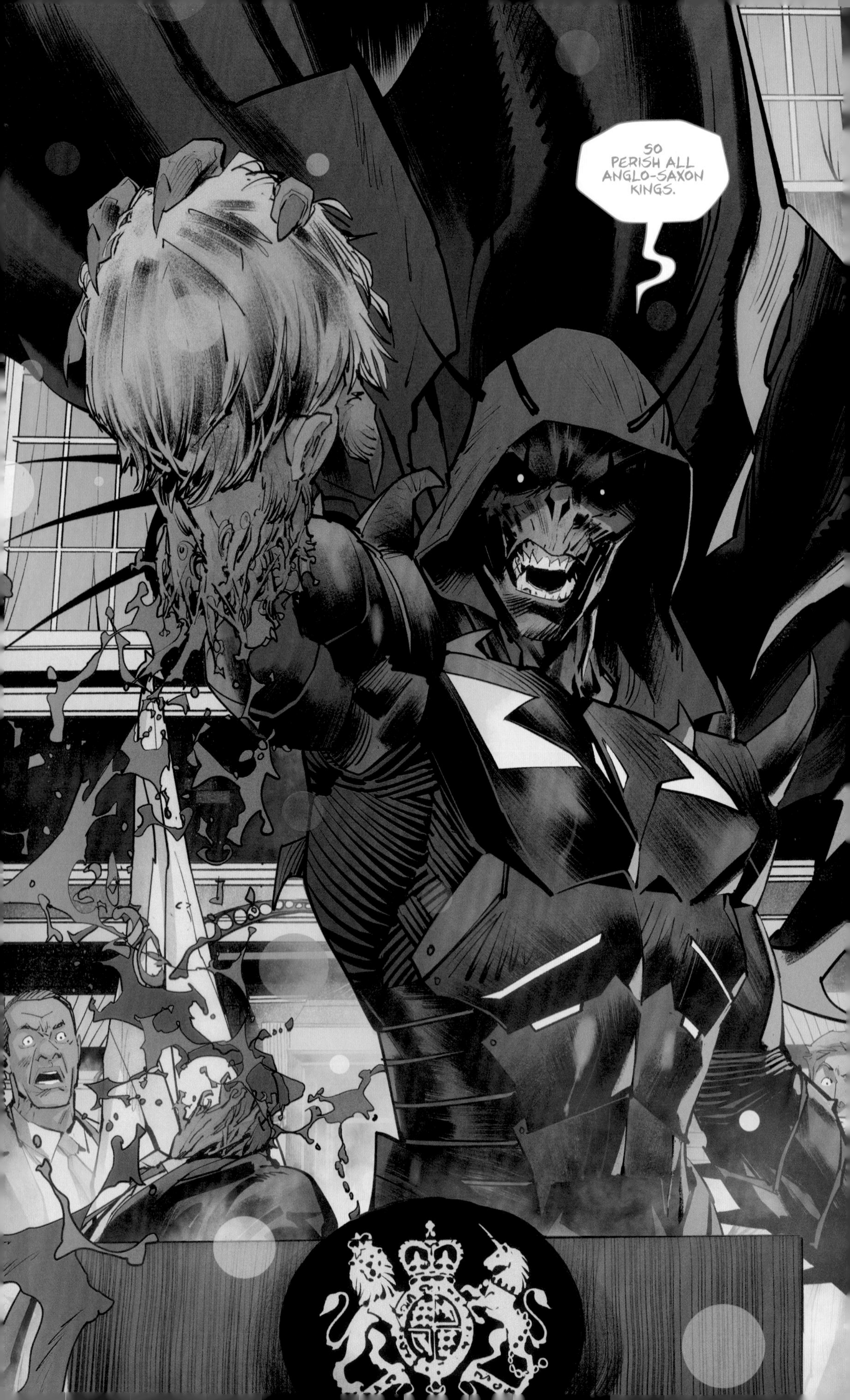
SO PERISH ALL ANGLO-SAXON KINGS.

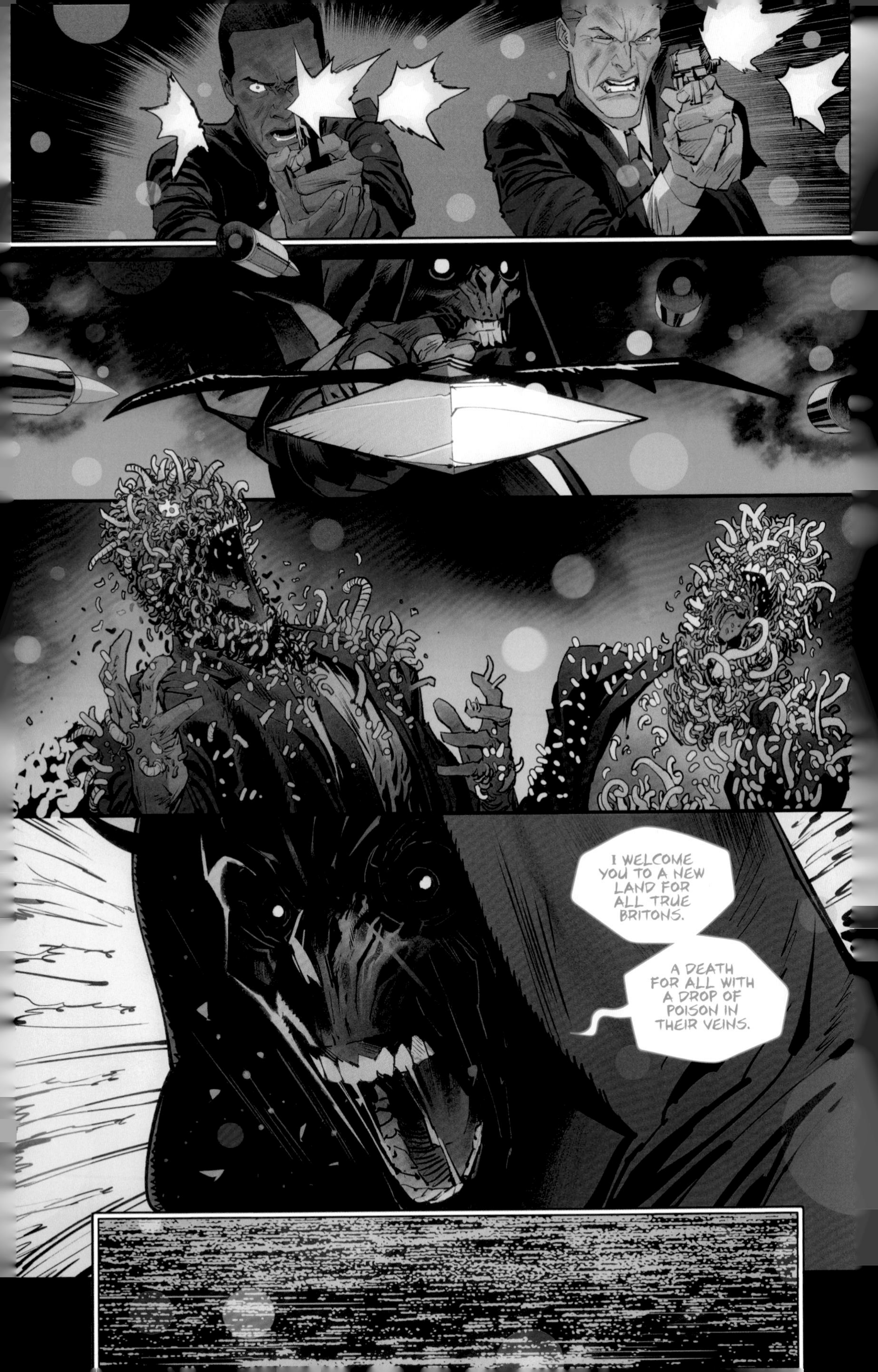
I WELCOME YOU TO A NEW LAND FOR ALL TRUE BRITONS.
A DEATH FOR ALL WITH A DROP OF POISON IN THEIR VEINS.

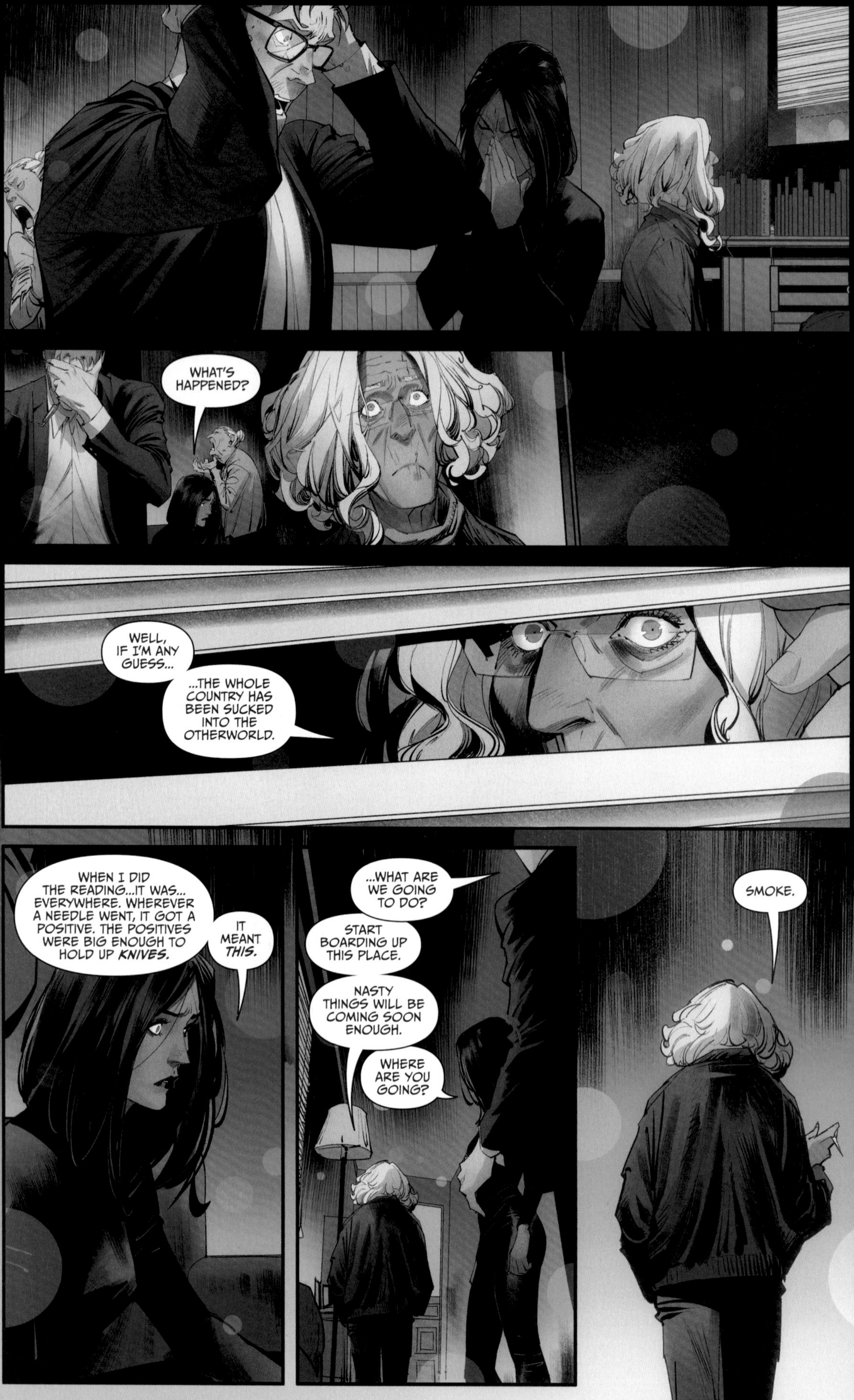
WHAT'S HAPPENED?
WELL, IF I'M ANY GUESS...
...THE WHOLE COUNTRY HAS BEEN SUCKED INTO THE OTHERWORLD.
WHEN I DID THE READING...IT WAS... EVERYWHERE. WHEREVER A NEEDLE WENT, IT GOT A POSITIVE. THE POSITIVES WERE BIG ENOUGH TO HOLD UP KNIVES.
IT MEANT THIS.
...WHAT ARE WE GOING TO DO?
START BOARDING UP THIS PLACE.
NASTY THINGS WILL BE COMING SOON ENOUGH.
WHERE ARE YOU GOING?
SMOKE.

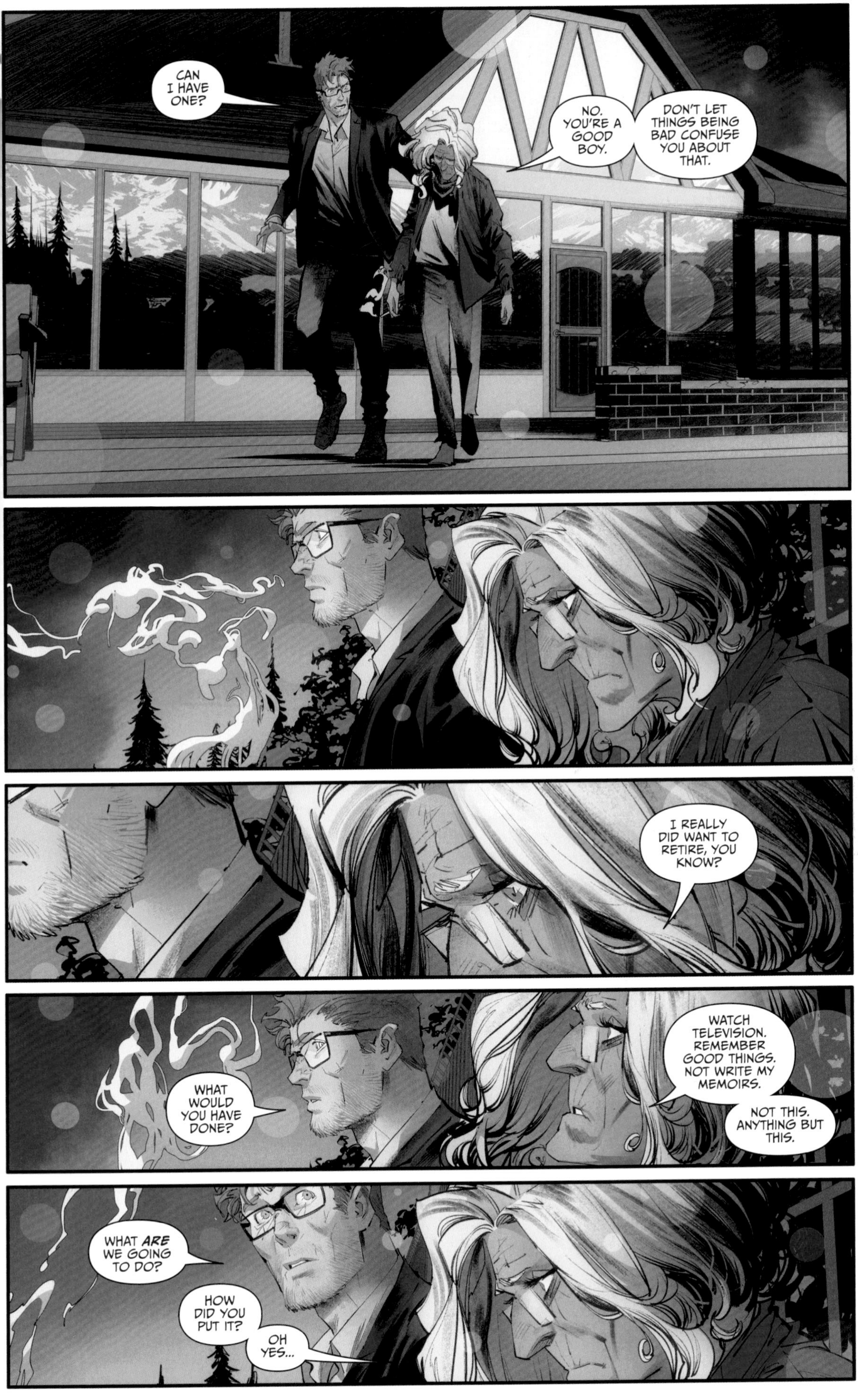
CAN I HAVE ONE?
NO. YOU'RE A GOOD BOY.
DON'T LET THINGS BEING BAD CONFUSE YOU ABOUT THAT.
I REALLY DID WANT TO RETIRE, YOU KNOW?
WATCH TELEVISION. REMEMBER GOOD THINGS. NOT WRITE MY MEMOIRS.
WHAT WOULD YOU HAVE DONE?
NOT THIS. ANYTHING BUT THIS.
WHAT *ARE* WE GOING TO DO?
HOW DID YOU PUT IT?
OH YES...

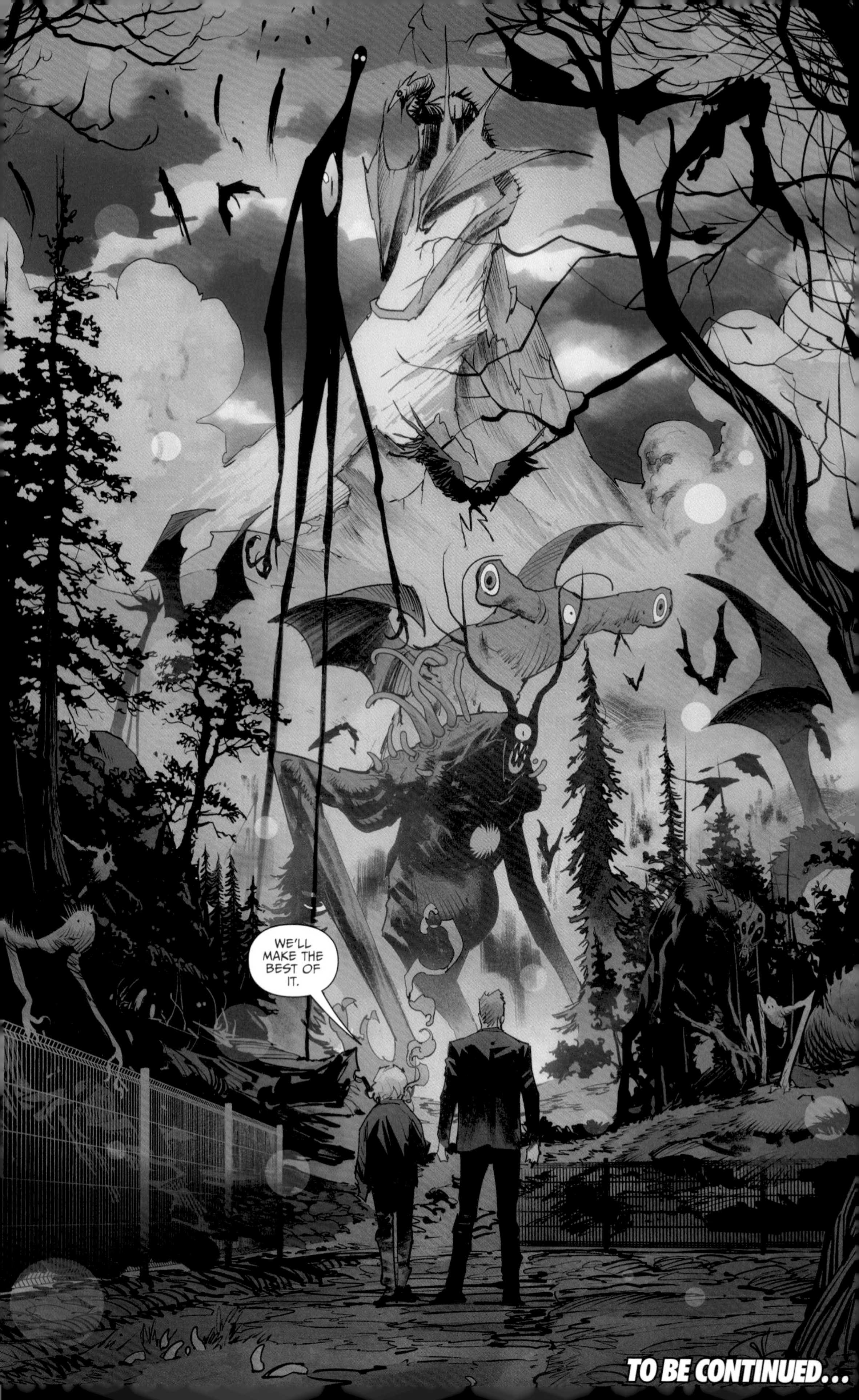
WE'LL MAKE THE BEST OF IT.
TO BE CONTINUED...

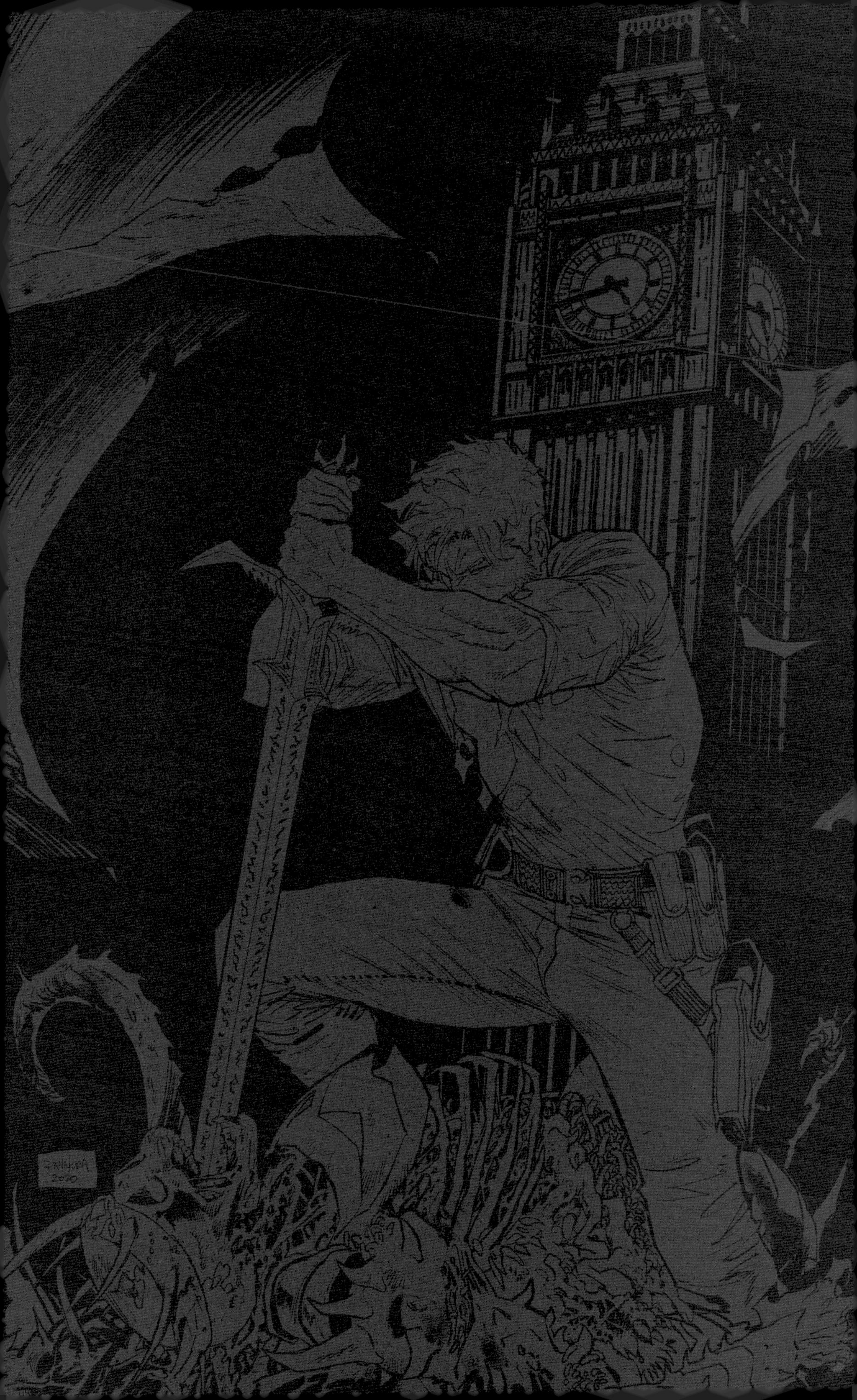

COVER GALLERY

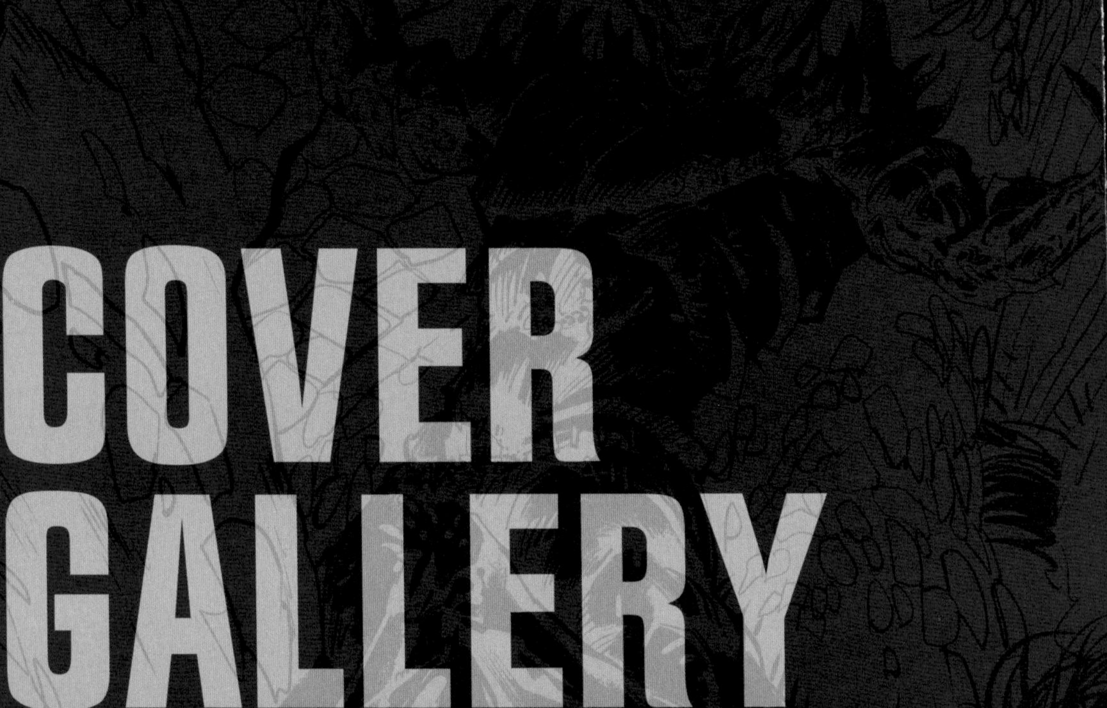

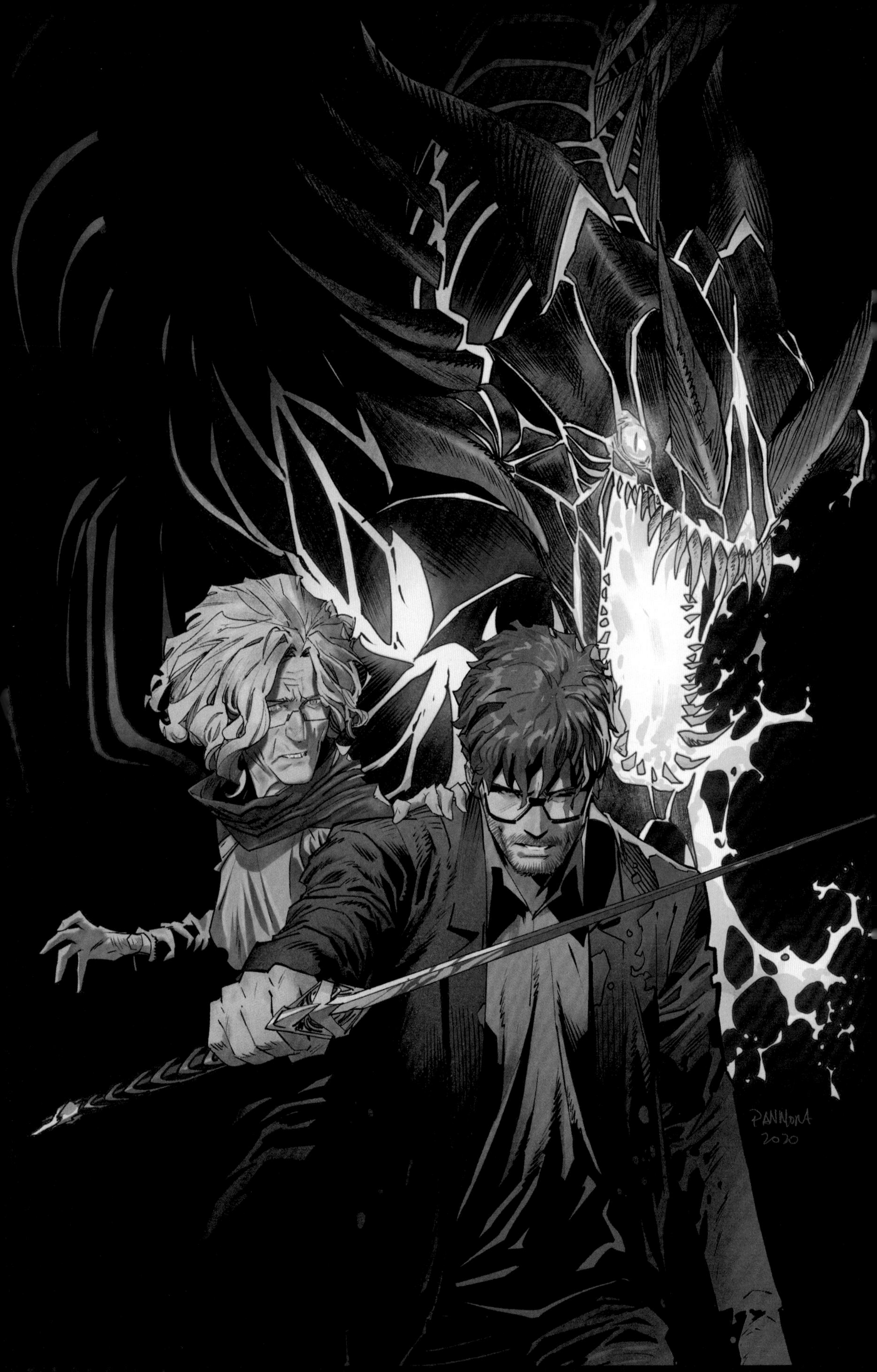
DANMORA
2020

ISSUE THIRTEEN COVER BY **DAN MORA**

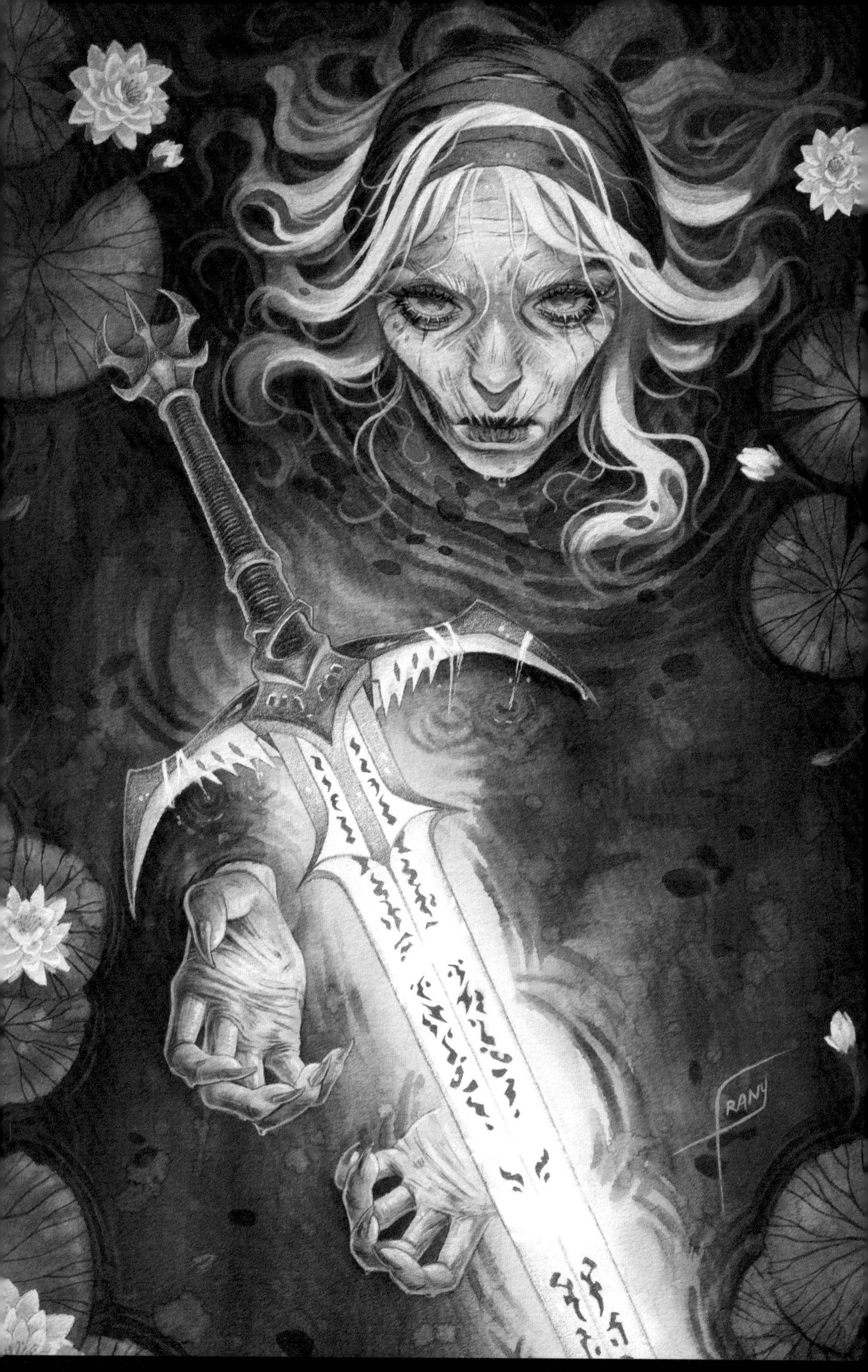
FRANY

ISSUE THIRTEEN VARIANT COVER BY **FRANY**

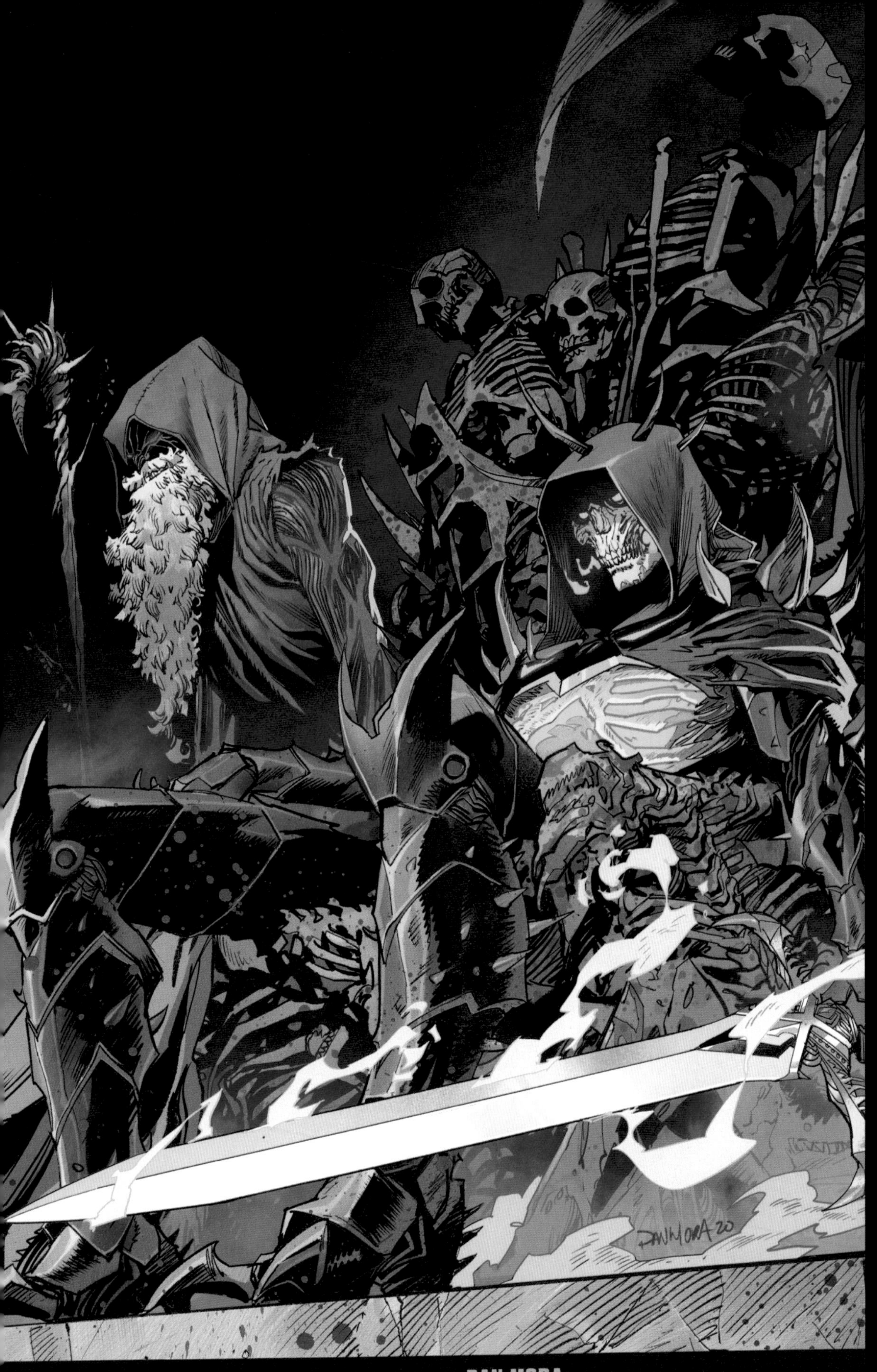
DAN MORA '20

ISSUE FOURTEEN COVER BY **DAN MORA**

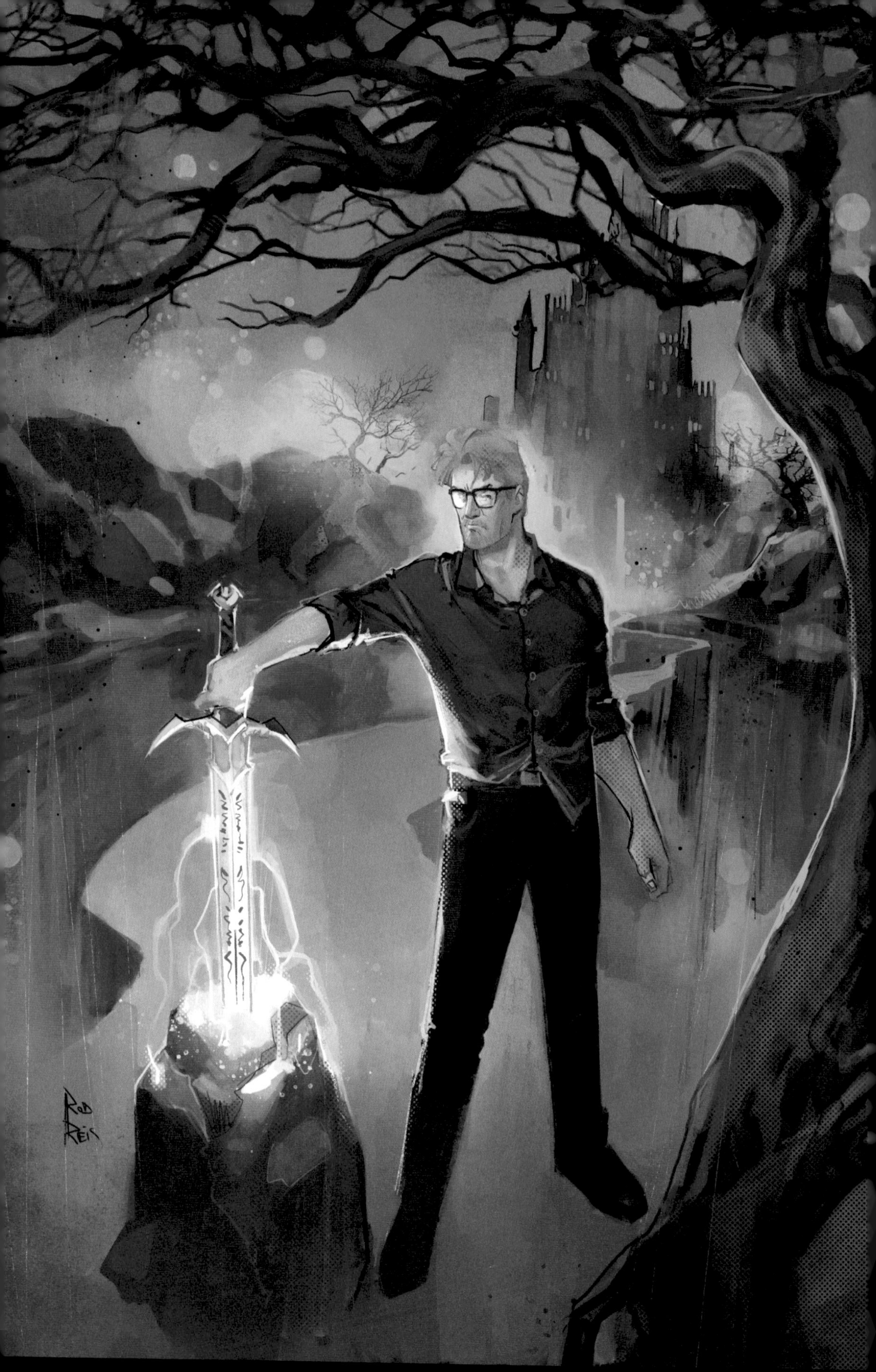
ROD REIS

ISSUE FOURTEEN VARIANT COVER BY **ROD REIS**

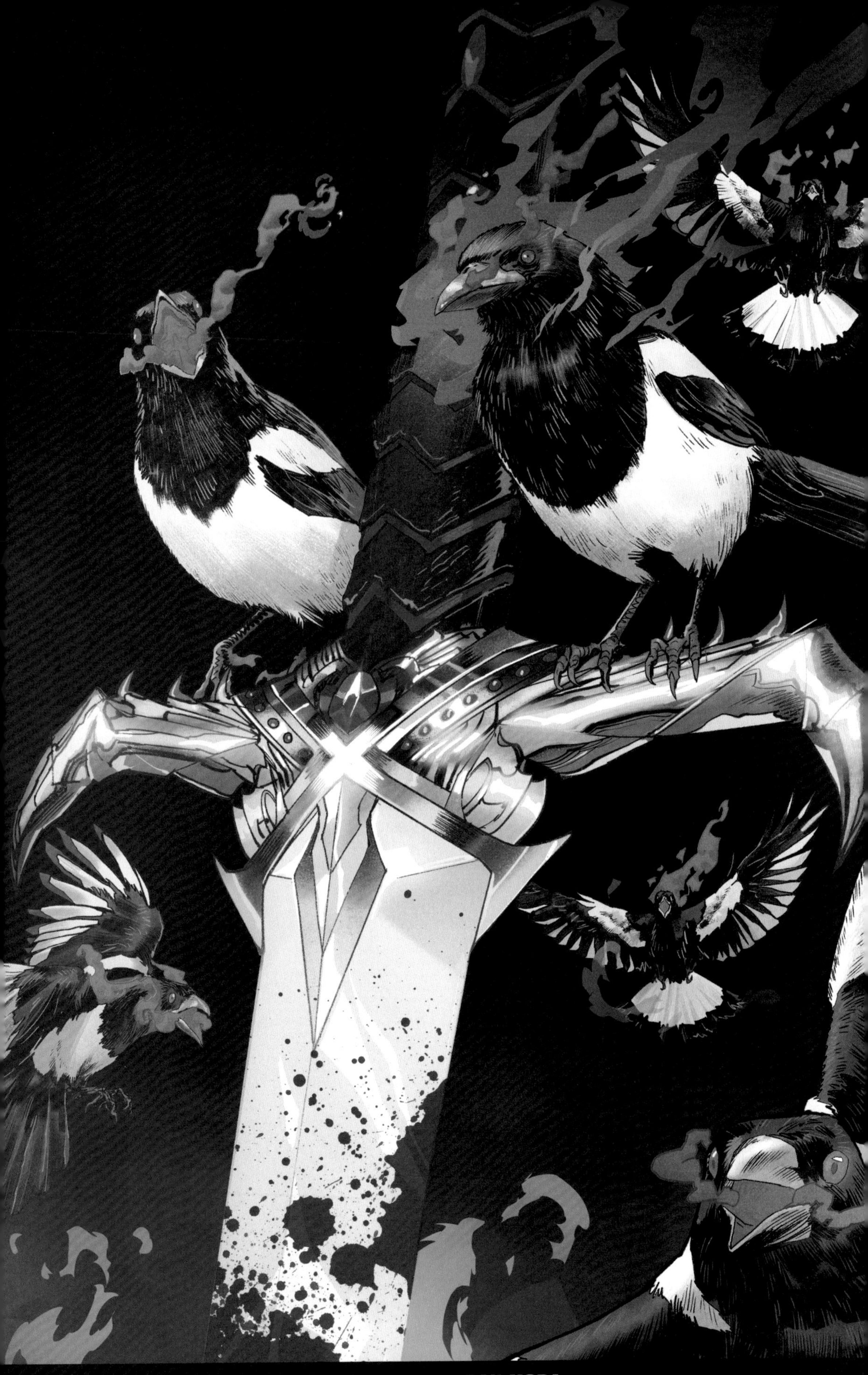

ISSUE FIFTEEN COVER BY **DAN MORA**

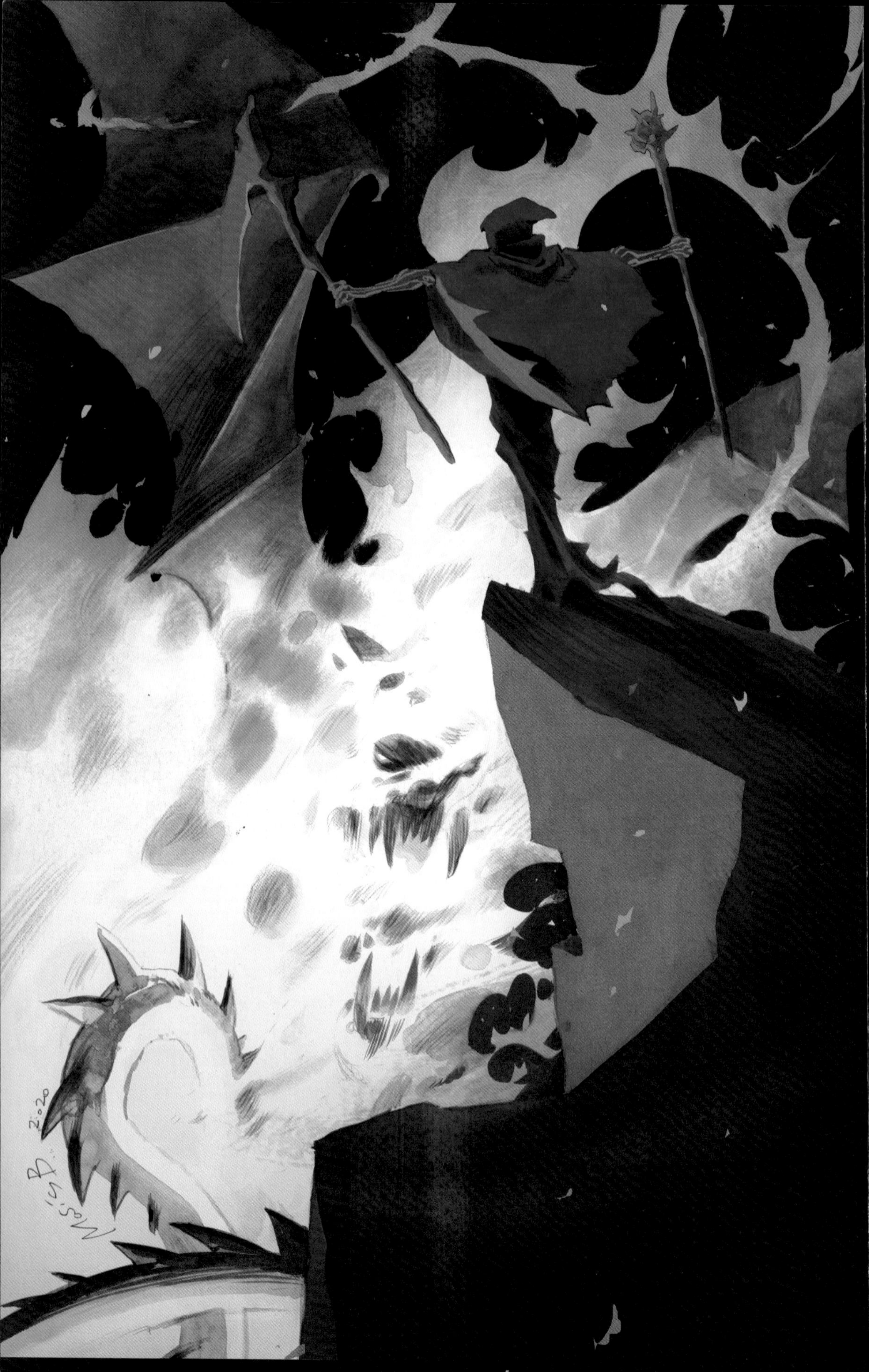

ISSUE FIFTEEN VARIANT COVER BY **MATÍAS BERGARA**

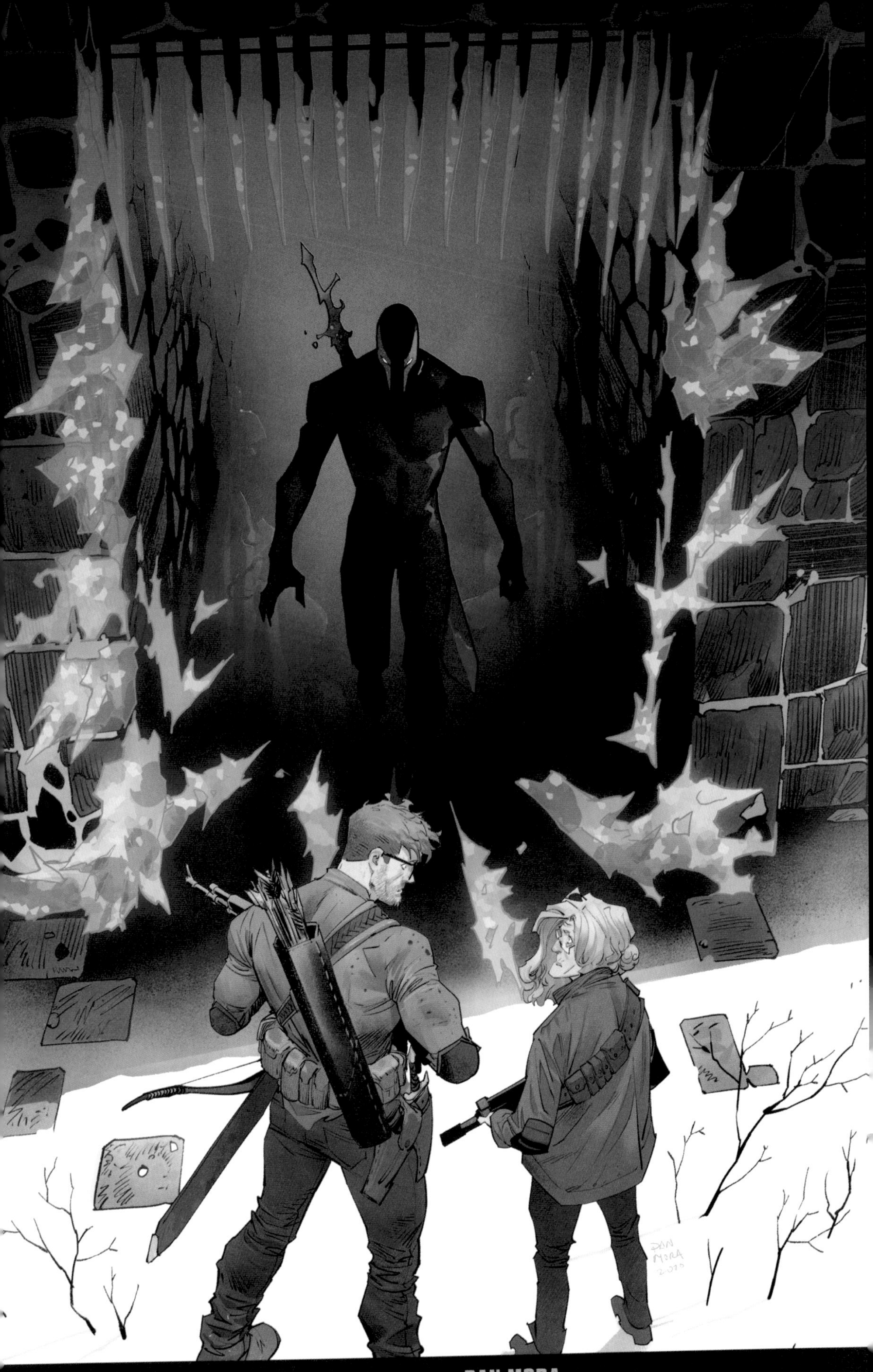

ISSUE SIXTEEN COVER BY **DAN MORA**

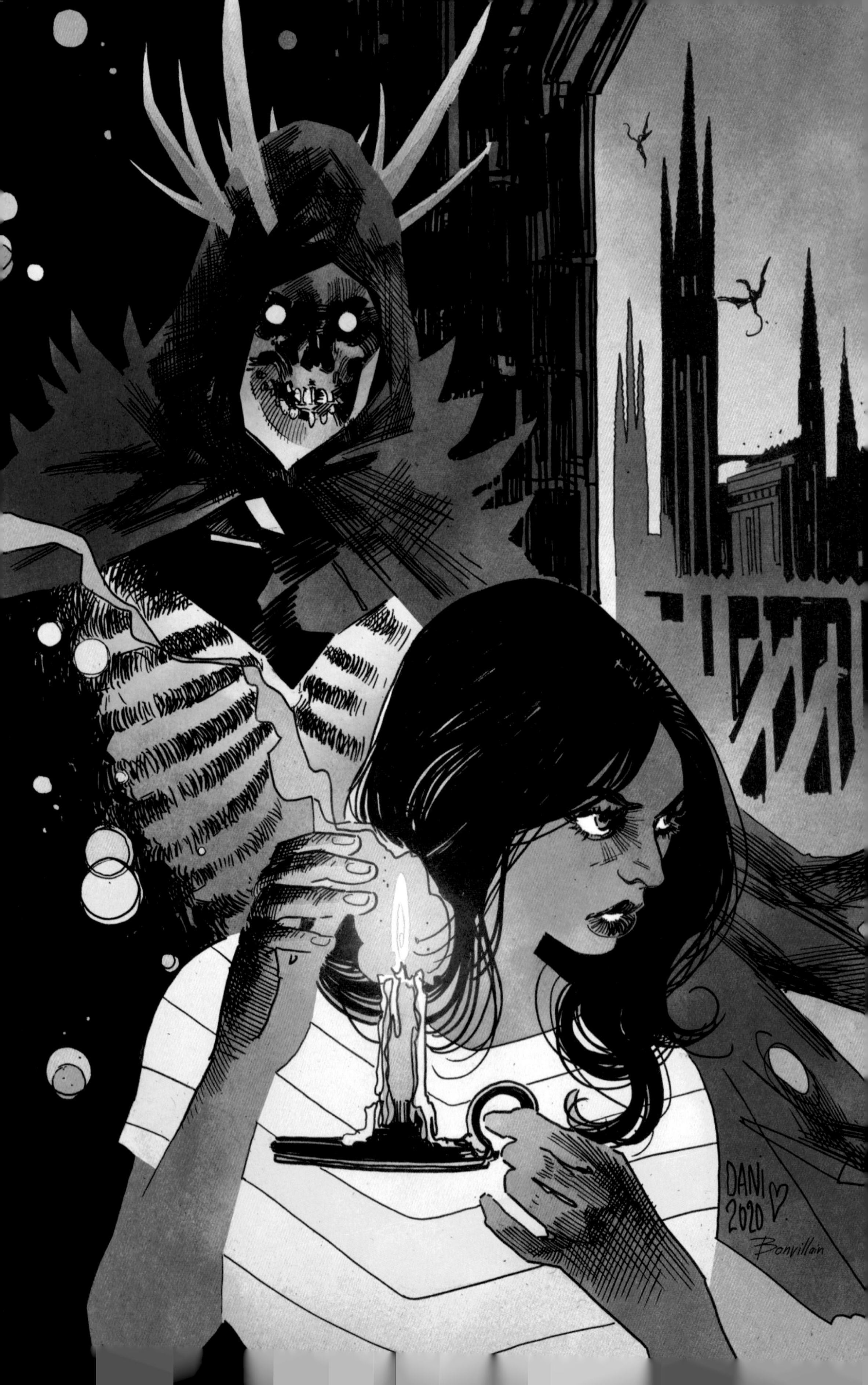
DANI
2020
Bonvillain

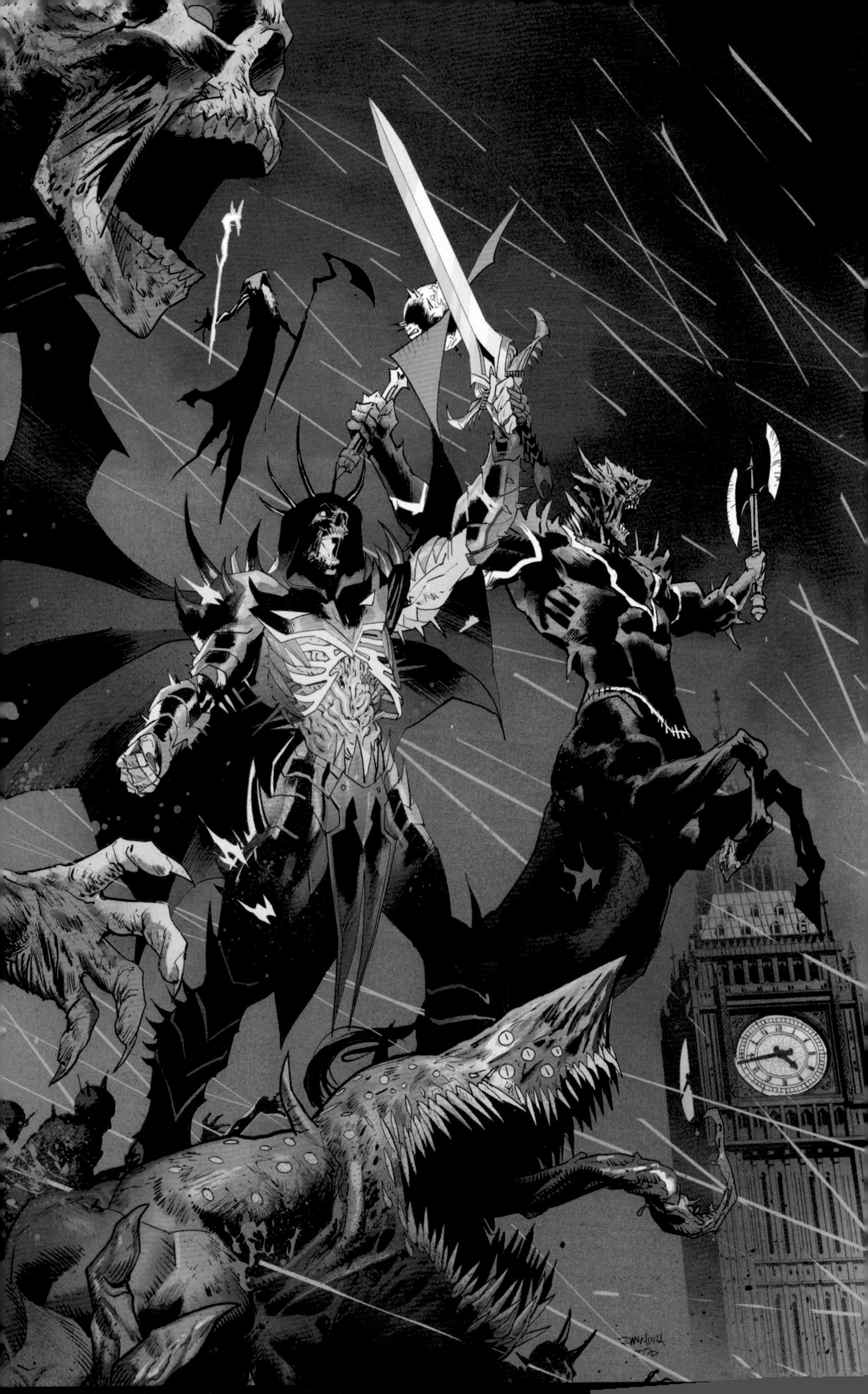

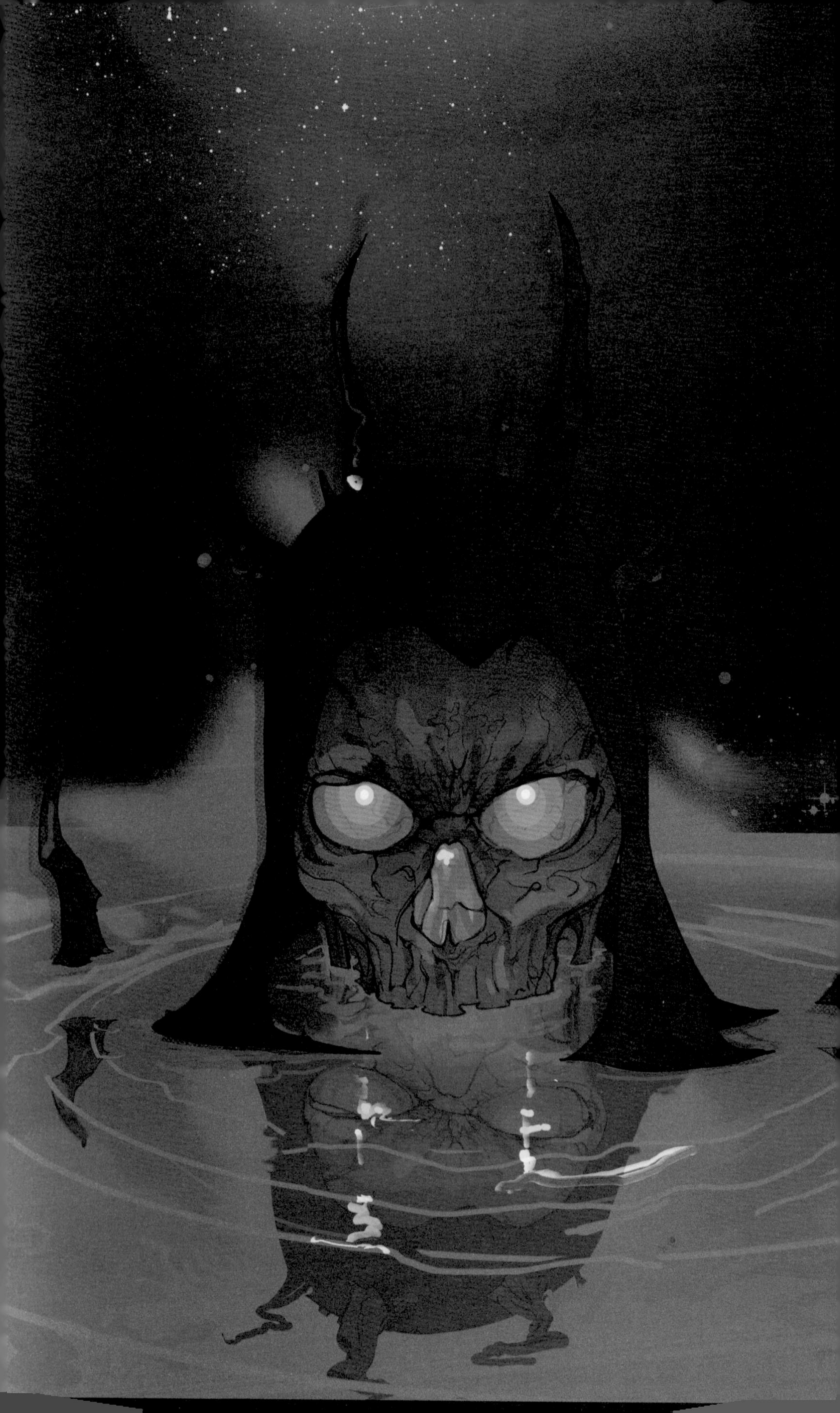

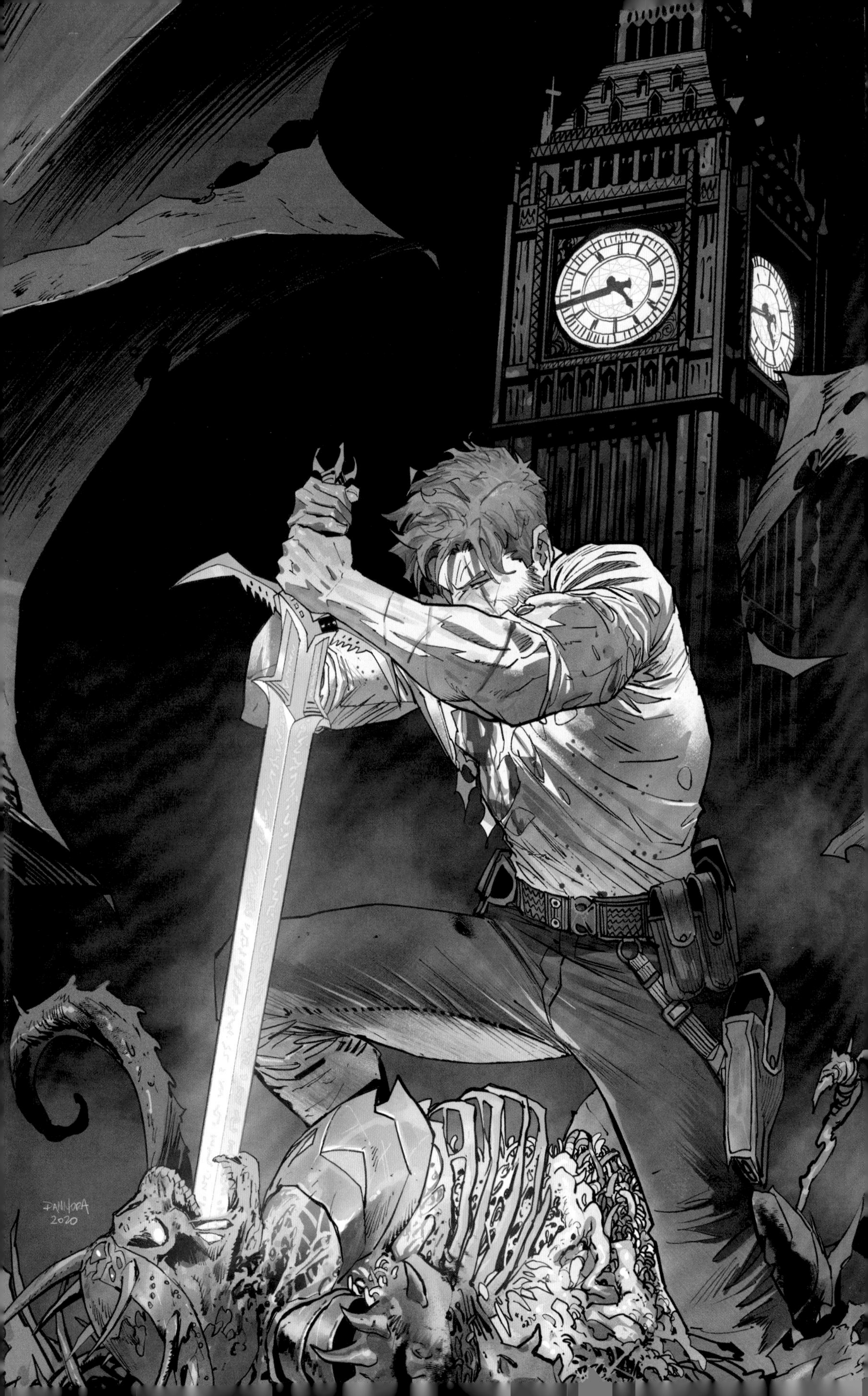

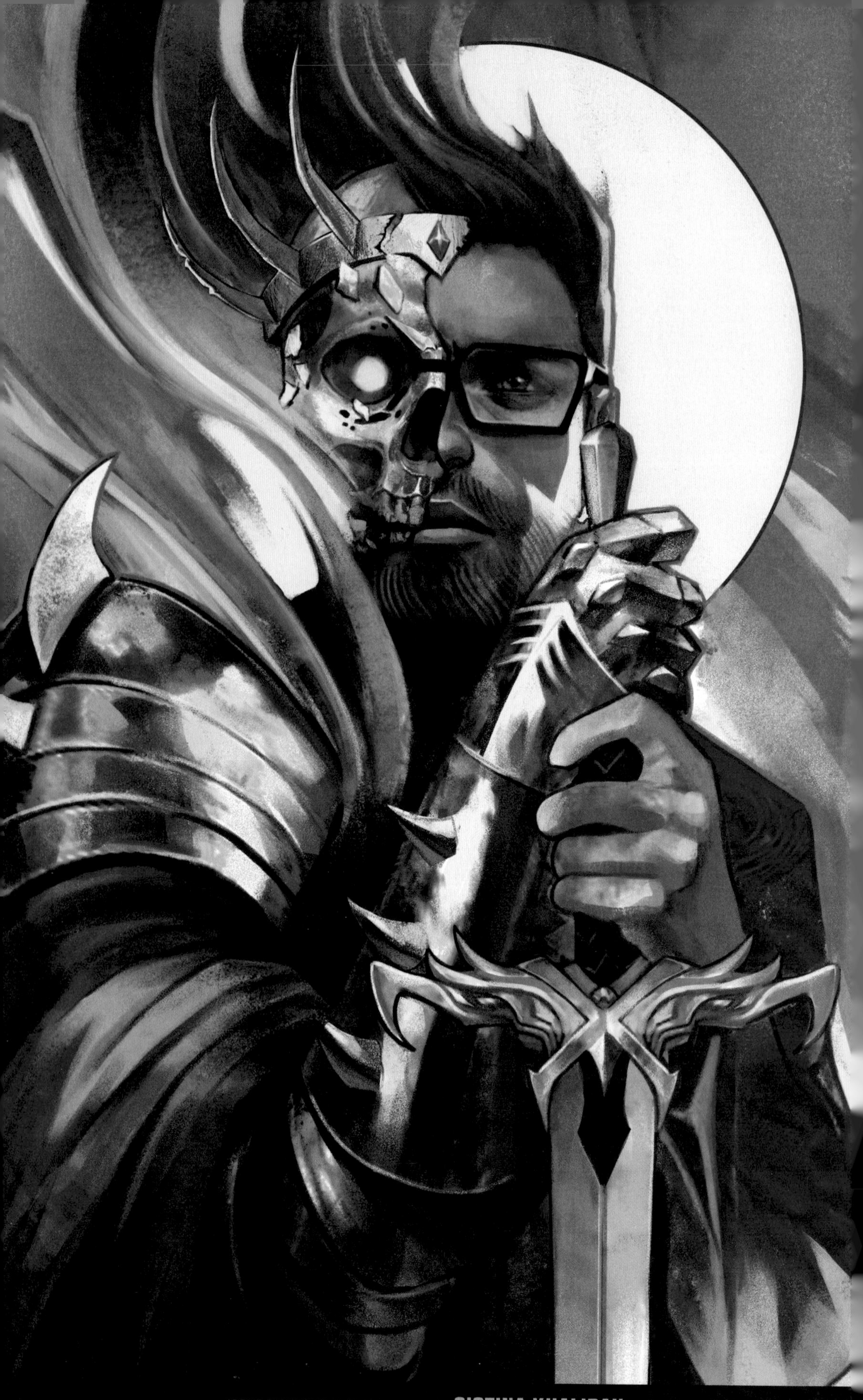

ISSUE EIGHTEEN VARIANT COVER BY QISTINA KHALIDAH